Edwin Alfred Hervey Alderson

With the Mounted Infantry and the Mashonaland Field Force, 1896

Edwin Alfred Hervey Alderson

With the Mounted Infantry and the Mashonaland Field Force, 1896

ISBN/EAN: 9783337288617

Printed in Europe, USA, Canada, Australia, Japan

Cover: Foto ©ninafisch / pixelio.de

More available books at **www.hansebooks.com**

WITH THE
MOUNTED INFANTRY

AND THE

MASHONALAND FIELD FORCE

1896

BY

BREVET-LIEUT.-COLONEL
E. A. H. ALDERSON
THE QUEEN'S OWN (ROYAL WEST KENT REGIMENT)

WITH A MAP AND NUMEROUS ILLUSTRATIONS AND DIAGRAMS

METHUEN & CO.
36 ESSEX STREET, W.C.
LONDON
1898

TO MY FATHER
WHO TAUGHT ME THAT WHICH,
DURING MY NINETEEN YEARS' SOLDIERING,
I HAVE FOUND OF MORE VALUE THAN ANYTHING
I EVER LEARNT—NAMELY, TO RIDE,
THIS BOOK IS AFFECTIONATELY
DEDICATED.

PREFACE

ON arriving home from South Africa in March last, I had no intention whatever of writing a book, and it was not till May, when writing a brief account of the operations in Mashonaland in 1896, for the Intelligence Department of the War Office, that it struck me that there were many points of general interest which had no place in an official account. This idea assumed definite form when Colonel R. S. Baden-Powell's book, *The Campaign in Matabeleland*, 1896, and Lieut.-Colonel Plumer's, *An Irregular Corps in Matabeleland*, appeared, and the thought "Why not Mashonaland too?" cropped up.

So bad example started the hare, and the hunting of it was encouraged by the following considerations:

I. Judging by the little that appeared in the papers, there was no regular correspondent, or artist, in Mashonaland, while *per contra* Matabeleland seems to have had correspondents and artists galore.

II. During the early part of the rising in Mashonaland parties of volunteers gallantly relieved the several collections of miners, farmers, and others, who, surrounded by natives, had shut themselves up in improvised laagers. Later on these same volunteers, when organized into local corps, did excellent work, and individual members of them performed acts of heroism such as always do, and always will, occur when Britons fight. The story of the above has never been told.

III. Imperial British troops had never before landed at Beira, gone up the Pungwe River, or fought in that part of Africa.

IV. In their small way the operations of the Mashonaland Field Force illustrate the following difficulties of war:

1. The embarkation, the moving by sea, and the disembarkation in a neutral port, of men, horses, guns, and stores.
2. The dealing with, the passing through the territory of, and a base in a port of, a neutral state.
3. An advance by river, rail, and road, with a line of communications over all three of

PREFACE

these, some 380 miles in length, the first part of which might be, and the last 150 miles of which was, open to attack.

4. Operations in a country, many parts of which were unknown even to the inhabitants, and of which there were no reliable maps.
5. Movements hampered by want of supply and transport, and then hurried by the necessity of concluding operations by a certain season.
6. An enemy with no capital and no main army; therefore there was no definite objective, and consequently decisive action was rendered difficult.
7. The force employed was very small in comparison with the area of the country (about 2000 men to 114,000 square miles), while it included regular troops of all arms (except cavalry, though the bulk were mounted), and irregular troops, both black and white, also of all arms.

V. The last, but not the smallest, thing which encouraged the following up of the hare, is the fact that, since arriving home, I have found that more than half the people I met imagined that Matabeleland and Mashonaland were the same thing. Knowing that one had been in Salisbury they would say—"Oh, then you must have met my cousin who is in Buluwayo," being apparently ignorant of the fact that the two towns are nearly 300 miles apart, and only joined by a waggon track!

Perhaps this is excusable when the London papers frequently reported casualties which occurred near Salisbury under the heading of Buluwayo; while one of them, when giving news of a fight in the Matopo Hills, which are some twenty miles *south* of *Buluwayo*, said, "the Matopo Hills near *Salisbury*!"

For the best of the sketches produced I am indebted to Lieut. R. W. Hare, Norfolk regiment, who served with the English company Mounted Infantry. Three of his sketches have already been published in the *Graphic*, and my thanks are due to the editor of that paper for allowing them to be reproduced. For the four photographs reproduced I have to thank the Argus Publishing Company, Umtali, and also Mr. J. M. Jensen.

Majors A. V. Jenner, D.S.O., Rifle Brigade, A. J. Godley, Royal Dublin Fusiliers, and Captain Sir Horace McMahon, D.S.O., Royal Welsh Fusiliers, all of whom served with the

Mounted Infantry, have kindly written chapters describing the operations which they personally conducted.

In conclusion, I would ask the reader to remember how difficult it is to avoid being egotistical when writing (absolutely for the first time) of events in which one personally played a part. I would also ask that my own very amateurish attempts at sketching may be leniently looked at.

E. A. H. ALDERSON

GRAND HOTEL, LOWESTOFT,
 July 1897.

CONTENTS

CHAPTER I
THE MOUNTED INFANTRY. CAPE TOWN AND WYNBERG — PAGE 1

CHAPTER II
BY SEA TO BEIRA - - - - - - - - 11

CHAPTER III
BEIRA, AND THE SITUATION THERE - - - - - 23

CHAPTER IV
THE PUNGWE RIVER, FONTESVILLA, CHIMOIO, AND UMTALI 46

CHAPTER V
MAKONI'S AND THE DEVIL'S PASS - - - - - 72

CHAPTER VI
FROM THE CHIMBI RIVER TO MARANDELLAS - - - 99

CHAPTER VII
SALISBURY, AND THE SITUATION GENERALLY - - - 116

CONTENTS

CHAPTER VIII
Exit Makoni. Supplies Short - - - - - 131

CHAPTER IX
Umtegeza's and the Gona Hills - - - - - 146

CHAPTER X
Simbanoota's, and an Abortive "Indaba" - - - 156

CHAPTER XI
Clearing the Granite Range in the Mazoë Valley 170

CHAPTER XII
The Hartley Hills - - - - - - - - 188

CHAPTER XIII
The Umvukwe Mountains and Eyre's Farm - - 212

CHAPTER XIV
The Sinoia and the Ayrshire Mine Patrol - - 220

CHAPTER XV
Fighting on the Line of Communications. Mr. Rhodes takes out a Patrol - - - - - 237

CHAPTER XVI
The "Image of War," and the Beginning of the End - - - - - - - - - - 247

CONTENTS

CHAPTER XVII
PAGE
WHOO! WHOOP! - - - - - - - - 257

APPENDIX A
MOUNTED INFANTRY FOR SOUTH AFRICA - - - - 265

APPENDIX B
LIST OF CASUALTIES (WHITE MEN) DURING THE MASHONALAND RISING, 1896 - - - - - - - 267

APPENDIX C
PART I.—PATROLS SENT OUT FROM SALISBURY BEFORE THE ARRIVAL OF THE IMPERIAL TROOPS - - - 278

PART II.—COLUMNS AND PATROLS SENT INTO MASHONALAND - - - - - - - - - - 285

PART III.—PATROLS SENT OUT AFTER THE ARRIVAL OF THE IMPERIAL TROOPS - - - - - - 288

INDEX - - - - - - - - - - 297

LIST OF FULL-PAGE ILLUSTRATIONS

	PAGE
TYPES OF THE FORCE	*Frontispiece*
THE PUNGWE RIVER AT FONTESVILLA	51
CHIMOIO	52
SCENE OF RAILWAY ACCIDENT OF JULY 8TH	54
MAKONI'S KRAAL	92
SALISBURY FROM THE KOPJE	121
MASHANGOMBI'S MAIN KRAAL	198
WESTERN PORTION OF CHENA'S KRAAL	200
THE NORFOLK AND THE HAMPSHIRE SECTIONS OF THE ENGLISH COMPANY MOUNTED INFANTRY GETTING INTO THE EAST END OF CHENA'S KRAAL	205
SKETCH MAP OF THE THEATRE OF OPERATIONS	296

CHAPTER I

THE MOUNTED INFANTRY. CAPE TOWN AND WYNBERG

IN Punchestown week, 1896, I rejoined my battalion, after having spent two very pleasant years at the Staff College.

When we returned from the second day's racing, a telegram was produced, which ordered me to hold myself in readiness to proceed to Aldershot in order to go out to South Africa with the Mounted Infantry. Having been employed with this corps on three previous campaigns, and having also been their first adjutant (when the present system of training Mounted Infantry was started at Aldershot in 1888, by Colone E. T. H. Hutton, C.B., A.D.C.), this was most delightful news. The telegram did not state in what capacity I was to go, but that made no difference; to go at all was sufficient.

Two days later (April 25th), the battalion were kind enough to dine me. Having just been away for two years, come back for a week, and now being off again for an indefinite time, it was impossible not to feel that this kindness was undeserved. To "run in off the black," at black ball pool, just before saying good bye on an occasion like this, is what many people would call a bad omen ; it happened, but, not being superstitious, it did not bother me, and certainly nothing bad came of it.

Crossing over to England the next day, and going to the War Office the following morning, I learnt that I was to command the four companies of Mounted Infantry which were being sent out to Cape Town, in case they might be wanted in Rhodesia.

Of these companies, the detail of which is given in Appendix A, the Highland company had already sailed on the 25th of April, and the others, the English, the Irish, and the Rifle companies were then assembling at Aldershot. It is probable that, when looking at the above-mentioned detail, even a non-military reader will exclaim, "How can such a scratch pack as that work?"

Well, experience has shown on many occasions that such a pack does work, and right well too. As Mounted Infantry is not a permanent corps, and does not appear in the Army List, it would perhaps be as well to briefly explain its organization.

A glance at the detail will show that each of the four companies is comprised of four detachments from certain battalions, of about thirty

ORGANIZATION

men and an officer each; these detachments are called "sections." The officer and all the non-commissioned officers and men of each detachment are specially selected by their own battalion commanding officers for Mounted Infantry work, and, in the present instance, they had all done at least one training of two months at Aldershot.

The conditions for the selection of the men are that they should be marksmen or first-class shots, of good character and physique, and not above a certain weight.

The officer should be at least a fair rider, and have some knowledge of what is required to be a "good horse-master." He must, of course, be a good soldier. The conditions for the selection of officers are not laid down, but the above qualifications are essential. The officer has to teach his men to ride, manage, and take care of horses, and how can he do so if he has not good knowledge of it himself?

The officer commanding the company is specially selected, his name being usually submitted for the approval of the authorities by the officer commanding the Mounted Infantry at Aldershot, who also submits the proposed organization of the companies.

An officer commanding a Mounted Infantry company cannot do it, or himself, justice unless he possesses the three qualifications mentioned above, as necessary for the subaltern of a detachment, in a marked degree.

The principle on which the Mounted Infantry section, company, or battalion is worked, is one of decentralization, every man, even down to one in every four in the privates, running his own show, and standing, or falling, by the results brought about by his own work.

The men in each section are told to form themselves into permanent "subsections," *i.e.* groups of four. These groups have their beds together in the barrack room, lie down side by side in the bivouac, have their horses picketed together, form up on parade together, and do their work together. Mutual confidence is thus established. The group selects its own leader, who is responsible for it in every way.

The subaltern officer, or "section leader," is solely and entirely responsible for his section, men, horses, equipment, and everything connected with them. In the same way the captain runs his company, and very little inspection, either on or off parade, is done by the commanding officer.

Thus no one feels that he is merely one in a crowd, and that what *he* does does not much matter, but each has an opportunity of showing his own *individuality*. That there is no greater incentive to work than this is certain.

Besides this, there are four other spurs at work—emulation between subsections, between sections, between companies, and *esprit-de-corps* for the Mounted Infantry as a whole.

To say what is the exact rôle of Mounted Infantry is impossible; they have done, and will do again, all sorts of work. But to say what a Mounted Infantry man is, is easy; he is simply a picked infantry soldier provided with extra means of locomotion, be it a bicycle, a *char-à-bancs*, or any sort of animal. He will probably be most efficient if you give him a pony about fourteen hands high. The first essential for a Mounted Infantry man is that he be a *thoroughly good* infantry soldier. In this he differs from a Mounted Rifleman, who need only be a good shot, and does not require the cohesion and solidity necessary to produce the discipline which enables the former to stand steady in square, or to face a severe fire when attacking a position.

Mounted Infantry are essentially an active service corps, and they do not show to advantage when marching past, or at peace manœuvres; so much is this the case that one is inclined to think that they should never attempt the former.

That Mounted Infantry aspires to, or ever can, assume the rôle of cavalry, no thinking soldier who has seen the two arms on active service would say. The former fights on foot, and is helpless if attacked on his horse; the horse of the latter is part of his fighting equipment, and his motto should almost be James Pigg's exclamation when asked to get off and pull down the fence for Pomponious Ego, "*Ar niver gets off!*"[1] The creed of the one is, "Stand steady, fire low, and no living thing can get near us"; of the other, "Swords out, knee to knee, and we can smash anything." While to ask the latter to do the work of the former is like asking a huntsman to do gamekeeper.

To again refer to the detail. The combination of the companies English, Irish, and Scotch, with Riflemen thrown in, was perfect, and I was much pleased to find that I already knew all the officers commanding companies and also many of the subalterns.

An old and valued friend of mine, poor Evans of the Derbyshire Regiment, had the English company; McMahon, Welsh Fusiliers, whom I had soldiered with before, had the Irish company; Tod, of the Seaforth Highlanders, who had just won our point-to-point race, the Highland company; and Jenner, Rifle Brigade, of Mounted Infantry in Burma fame, the Rifle company; while Godley, Dublin Fusiliers, then the Mounted Infantry adjutant at Aldershot, was to be adjutant. Sportsmen and good men to hounds every one, which is what we try to get in the Mounted Infantry.

It was good also to find that an old friend, Colour-Sergeant H. F. Nesbit, who started as orderly room clerk when I started as adjutant in 1888, and had held the position ever since,

[1] *Vide* page 370, *Handley Cross.*

was now to come with us as orderly room clerk and quartermaster sergeant.

On May 1st, the English, Irish, and Rifle companies were inspected by the Commander-in-chief at Aldershot, and on the 2nd, after being seen off at the North Camp Station by H.R.H. The Duke of Connaught, commanding the Aldershot district, they embarked at Southampton on the S.S. "Tantallon Castle" (Captain Duncan). On board we found Lieut.-Colonel R. S. Baden-Powell, 13th Hussars (now Colonel 5th Dragoon Guards), who was going out to do chief staff officer to Sir Frederick Carrington in Rhodesia, and also Lieut.-Colonel C. H. Bridge, Army Service Corps, who was on his way to Buluwayo to re-organize the supply and transport. The former, being senior to me, commanded the troops on board.

The voyage was a very pleasant, if an uneventful one; we did our best to keep the men fit by arranging for regular exercise for them, getting up athletics, tugs of war, and concerts, Baden-Powell invariably bringing down the house at the latter. At Madeira we officers all did the usual thing, *i.e.* had breakfast ashore, rode up the hill on ponies, and then tobogganed down on the cobble-stones. Near the line a saloon passenger died, while a rifleman fell out of his hammock and broke his jaw. These, and the fancy dress ball, were the only events which broke the even tenor of our days.

About four A.M. on the 19th May, we anchored in Table Bay, and went alongside the wharf about nine A.M. A little over fourteen years since I left there with my battalion in February 1882; and to again refer to omens. I can see now the rat, which, at the first turn of the screw, came up from somewhere below, got on to the outside of the ship and ran along the combing, then when it got to the stern, jumped for the wharf. Just reaching this with its fore feet, it failed to draw up its hind quarters and fell back into the dock. It was a Friday too! Fifty years ago no doubt every sailor in that ship would have refused to sail that day, and perhaps to go in her at all.

What does the individual say who will not walk underneath a ladder?

However nothing happened to us, and we had a glorious passage home. But did that rat know that that ship (the "Balmoral Castle") was shortly to be sold to the Spanish Government as a troop ship, and that she was to be burnt in the Bay of Biscay?

We disembarked that morning, were inspected on the wharf by Major-General Sir W. H. Goodenough, K.C.B., commanding the troops in South Africa, and afterwards went out to Wynberg by train. Here we were most hospitably received by the 1st Battalion Leicester Regiment, then commanded by Lieut.-Colonel C. W. Vulliamy.

There were only two or three companies of the Leicesters with their headquarters at Wynberg, and I am afraid that we, with our twenty-two officers, completely swamped the mess.

At Wynberg we found the Highland company, which had arrived at Cape Town two days before us in the "Warwick Castle." We soon learnt, much to our disgust, that there was no immediate prospect of our being wanted in Rhodesia, and further, that there were no horses being bought, or likely to be bought, for us. It *was* a damper! For a month we remained at Wynberg, having a very good time it is true ; but this was not what we had come out for, and we all felt as if we had had cold water thrown over us. We spent our time in teaching the men to work, and fight, through the bush on the Cape Town flats, having many little field days of our own. Once a week came a field day under the General, or the Chief Staff Officer, Colonel Morgan Crofton, D.S.O.

Then came the Queen's Birthday, when all the troops fired a *feu-de-joie* and then marched past on the Market Square in Cape Town. The space available would barely hold the troops, and we, who always work in single rank, had first to be in double rank, then get into single rank as we came on to the saluting base, and back again into double rank as we wheeled off it. Not a very easy manœuvre, especially with little room available, but the men did it well. It was the first time that four companies of Mounted Infantry had ever marched past together on a Queen's Birthday.

By the middle of June we had fairly settled down, had bought ponies, started polo, and been out with the Cape Hounds, which I had taken over, installing McMahon and Vernon as whips.

Our first day was rather amusing. We started, hounds, horses, and men, by train from Wynberg about eight A.M. and proceeded to Klapmuts, about thirty miles up the line. Owing to a very bad engine, we did not arrive there till eleven o'clock. A field of about thirty-five, including the General and Miss Goodenough, had trained with us. We at once proceeded to draw and very soon got on the line of something, and this, which turned out to be a hyena, we quickly ran up to, or rather he waited for us, with his back against the wire railway fence! The leading hounds hesitated before pulling him down, and, as we were supposed to be, and thought we were, running a jackal, they were whipped off.

After some more drawing, a wild cat jumped up in the middle of the pack, and escaped in a most wonderful way with its brush as big as its body! We then ran something, which proved to be a buck, quite fast for about thirty minutes, hounds being whipped off when he was viewed.

At last, about 3 P.M., we did find a jackal and ran him hard for some forty minutes; he then turned directly away from the station, and, having a train to catch, we were obliged to whip off.

CHAPTER II

BY SEA TO BEIRA

ON the 19th June the clouds, as regards some of us at any rate, rolled by, a telegram arriving to say that the British South Africa Company wished 200 Mounted Infantry to proceed to Salisbury, *via* Beira, in order to assist the local forces in suppressing the Mashona rising, which had by this time begun to assume serious proportions.

The rising had commenced on the 16th June, when the first whites were murdered at the Beatrice Mine (see map) by M'Slopa's people. This was quickly followed by other murders at Hartley, and at Norton's Farm on the Hunyani River. (A list of those murdered during the rising with places and dates is given in Appendix B, and by this list the course of the rising can be traced.)

Apparently no one in Mashonaland had even dreamt it was possible that the Mashonas might rise, every one had got so used to two or three men going to a kraal, when anything wrong had been done by the natives, and demanding to see the chief, and when that individual came forth, if it appeared good to them, breaking his own cooking pot over his head, or threatening him with, and even using the sjambok on him. That the worm might turn did not seem to have occurred to them, and the saying, " You only want a sjambok and a box of matches to take any Mashona kraal," had become proverbial. Even when the first murders were committed, they were put down to fugitive Matabele on their way to Zambesi. The result of this excessive contempt for the worm was that, when he did turn, the whites, taken entirely by surprise and totally unprepared, appear to have gone into an almost equally excessive state of alarm.

It is not the first time that we Britons have had excessive contempt for our enemy recoil on us, and demonstrates forcibly what a bad gauge we had taken of his character.

There is no doubt that at the commencement of the rising, Salisbury was in an awkward position.

It then had no police, these having been taken for the Jameson raid; the bulk of its available fighting men, and of the horses, were in Matabeleland under Lieut.-Colonel Beal, some three hundred miles away; what was worse was that arms were none too plentiful.

The town went into laager, in and around

the gaol, and this laager was made practically impregnable to any number of Mashonas. The inhabitants were told off into various local corps, the weak point in which appears to have been that they had too great a proportion of officers. Mr. Justice Vintcent, the senior official of the company then in Salisbury, was appointed Commandant General by Sir Frederick Carrington, who was then at Buluwayo. From what I have been told, the time in the laager was in many ways amusing—to look back to—though trying enough at the time. The ladies, for instance, were accommodated in the cells, three or four in each, and as there was no time to pick and choose fellow-prisoners, the result was not always happy! Some of the laager's defenders displayed lamentable ignorance of their weapons: one, when on sentry on the walls, in trying to discover the mysteries of the action of his rifle, let it off, caused a scare, and nearly shot a lady who was taking an evening walk round the laager.

This offender was promptly "run in" and brought to the orderly room the next day. Just before he came up, or just after he had been told off, the adjutant of the left, or right, wing (there were two, and it does not appear certain which it was), let off his revolver by mistake in the orderly room, the bullet ploughing into the wall not far off the commanding officer's head! This would scarcely tend to grease the wheels for the day's work? One morning, in the grey dawn, a piquet sentry saw some weird, brown-looking forms approaching his post. "Are they Mashonas?" no doubt he said to himself; "they seem to be stopping and looking, then crouching and advancing—Yes, they must be, Mashonas." Bang! goes his rifle; bang! bang! bang! go the rifles of the piquet, and in they run. Up get all the people in the laager and rush to their posts. The grey of dawn becomes the light of day, and, what do they see? a herd of tesessapi (buck about the size of a donkey), who, owing to the unwonted quiet, had come into Salisbury and were quietly gazing towards the laager.

Only a scare, the result of over-strung nerves, such as trained soldiers have had many a time in Zululand, the Soudan, and elsewhere.

I would have it understood that I am indebted to hearsay for the above, but I believe it to be true; any way, it is founded on fact. Not the least amusing part is that someone—was he a wag or was he taken in?—telegraphed to the Cape Town papers, "The Tesessapi tribe have risen and are threatening the laager."

The order for the two companies to go was received on the night of the 19th June and they were to sail on the 26th, so there was plenty of time to draw equipment, etc., etc.

The first question to be decided was, "Which two companies were to go?" Luckily I had anticipated the likelihood of being split up, and had talked the question over with the officers commanding companies while on board the "Tantallon Castle." We had arrived at the conclusion that the company commanded by the senior officer should be the first on the list for detachment, and that the company commanded by the next senior officer should be next and so on. At the time that this was settled the two junior company commanders, Jenner and McMahon, were dismal; now they were jubilant, for, as the headquarters of the corps were to go, it was a *detachment* which remained behind. This was how the Irish and the Rifle companies came to go to Mashonaland.

As bad luck for them would have it, this came particularly hard on the Highland company, who were the first to arrive in South Africa, and who had also gone out when just at the end of their training at Aldershot, and thus were the last off horses. Most of the next six days was spent at the ordnance store in Cape Town, looking after and drawing equipment and stores, and much I bothered the officer in charge, Captain H. W. Perry, to whom I am most grateful for the ready and cheerful manner in which he assisted me. Would that all officers in charge of stores were like him, especially when one is on, or preparing for, active service; for on such occasions men are sometimes met who appear to think it is their duty to keep their stores full, instead of to issue articles to people who want them.

There were also several interviews with Mr. J. A. Stevens, the secretary of the company in Cape Town, and he was most ready to give orders for us to be supplied with anything we asked for. What a blessing it is to have a man to deal with who is not afraid of taking responsibility upon himself.

The company was paying the bill, and certainly they stinted us of nothing it was in their power to provide.

Now that we were wanted, horses were necessary, and these of course had to be bought in a hurry; the result was that the numbers were difficult to make up, and that the quality was not so good as it would have been had they been bought gradually, and properly fed, during the last month, in which we had been doing comparatively nothing.

For some time prior to the purchase of the horses, forage, especially in and around Cape Town, had been very scarce and expensive, consequently the majority of the horses were in poor condition, some of them being extremely low. One hundred and forty-five horses were bought in and near Cape Town, and were put on board the Union Company's steamer "Arab (Captain Chope), which had been hastily fitted up, on the 25th June.

The next morning the following force, which

was under my command, embarked at nine o'clock, and we sailed immediately afterwards, stopping when we got out into Table Bay to take the ammunition on board:

	Officers.	Non-Commissioned Officers and Men.
Mounted Infantry, headquarters, and the Irish and Rifle companies (as per detail in Appendix A), - -	13	230
Royal Artillery (Lieut. S. C. Townsend), -	1	6
Medical Staff Corps (Sgn.-Capt. F. A. Saw, Army Medical Staff), - -	1	5

Captain J. Roach, in the employ of the British South Africa Company, who had gone into Mashonaland with the pioneers in 1891, was placed at my disposal as intelligence officer. We took with us two seven-pounder R.M.L. guns of 200 lbs., and also two .303 Maxims on low infantry carriages.

The pith of the instructions which I received from the High Commissioner were to make my "way to Salisbury with all due expedition and without digression from the direct road unless for strong military reasons."

The "Arab" had been for some time employed in carrying mules and cargo coastwise, and she was a mere shell, her bulkheads having been taken down to make room. The only cabin accommodation was on the upper deck, and that was very rough and very limited. The men were put on the fore part of the main deck, which was roughly fitted up and partitioned off from the after part, which was full of horses.

Neither officers nor men minded the discomfort which ensued, we were all only too glad to be off; but we did mind the frailness of the horse fittings and the insecure way in which they were fixed, for that might mean accidents to, and perhaps the loss of, horses, which, having no spare ones, we could not afford.

When we got out of the bay and began to round Cape Agulhas the swell, consequent on the previous day's gale, made the ship, light as she was, roll considerably, and many of the horse fittings carried away. This gave us all plenty of employment, and there was but little time to be sea-sick.

At four A.M. on the 29th we arrived in Durban Roads and, had there been steam up in the pilot's tug, we might have gone over the bar at six. As it was, the ship missed the morning tide and did not go in till four P.M. She then grounded in the harbour, and did not get alongside the wharf till nearly dark.

I went on shore with Godley early in the day in order to get telegrams, and to see the Charter Co.'s agent, Mr. Jameson, who took us to lunch at the Club.

Durban appeared to me to have much improved since I last saw it in 1882. Many new and handsome buildings had sprung up: among them a fine town hall which Mr. Jameson, who was mayor for the year, showed us with pride.

Two telegrams were waiting for me, one from the chief staff officer at Buluwayo, directing me to assume supreme command of all armed men in Mashonaland on arriving in the country, and giving me other instructions, and the other from Judge Vintcent at Salisbury, informing me that a Mr. Honey and twelve volunteers would join us at Beira.

After a visit to the ordnance store, where Captain Ledsham quickly produced the articles we wanted, we went down to the docks, only to find the "Arab" stuck fast in the harbour; while 140 odd horses were waiting on the wharf to be shipped, and the daylight was fast going. Just as it was getting dark the ship got alongside, and we at once began with the horses, and a rare game we had with some of them. The ship's side being high above the wharf, all had to be put in slings, hoisted up to the upper deck, and then lowered down on to the main deck. Some of the horses were only partially broken, and several appeared to have been scarcely handled at all, while a few had to be cast and their legs tied before they could be slung.

McMahon superintended the work, and I immensely admired the way in which he did it; every troublesome horse he either adjusted the slings on or held himself, and never one did he let go. There were several scenes of this sort: McMahon, the farrier sergeant, and perhaps four to six men, would be round a horse adjusting the slings; suddenly the horse would plunge forward dragging the whole lot with him; another plunge and two or three men drop off; with less weight to keep him down the horse goes forward in a series of bounds, perhaps nearly over the edge of the wharf into the dock, or up against the iron store shed with a tremendous bang, and anon through the doors and into the shed among the other horses waiting their turn. As this goes on the men drop off one by one, and McMahon is left hanging on by himself. No nice job this at any time, and especially in semi-darkness and in a place where there are so many things to knock against, and the dock to go into into the bargain.

As each horse was put into his place down below, the bar to keep him there was fixed up; several times we had to suspend operations till extra fittings were hastily put up by the ship's carpenters. All this delayed us, and it was 3.30 A.M. before we had got the whole of the horses on board. That there were no accidents was, I consider, entirely due to McMahon.

That evening Surgeon Colonel Maxham, Army Medical Staff, principal medical officer South Africa, and Lieutenant and Quartermaster

W. E. Barnes, Army Service Corps, joined the ship—the former having been directed to accompany us as far as Beira, in order to report on the accommodation available there for the sick and wounded, and the measures to be taken for their conveyance down the line; the latter was to take over the duties of supply and transport officer to the column. Mr. J. E. Nicholls, registrar of the High Court at Salisbury, and a lieutenant in the Rhodesia Horse, and Mr. G. Bowen, chief mining commissioner in Mashonaland, also joined us; the former subsequently acted as my senior galloper throughout the operations, and did his work in all respects like a born aide-de-camp.

We left Durban at 6.30 next morning, the 30th June. The sea being still somewhat rough, more trouble ensued with the horse fittings, many of them carrying away and a few horses getting down.

Next day one of the horses taken on board at Durban developed symptoms of farcy, of which there had been cases at Maritzburg, where the horses had been purchased. We had no veterinary surgeon with us, and, rather than run risk of infection in the crowded ship, I had the horse shot at once.

On the evening of July 2nd, we were in sight of the one solitary tree, on the low flat coast to the north of Beira, which serves as a landmark to ships. The tide not serving, we anchored near the outer buoy, some twenty miles from Beira, which is approached by a shallow tortuous channel. The next morning we upped anchor at daybreak, and dropped it again in the Pungwe River, off Beira, about ten A.M. In the river was H.M.S. "Widgeon," Lieut.-Commander (now Captain) E. Duke Hunt, who at once came to us in his galley, and he and I went ashore.

CHAPTER III

BEIRA, AND THE SITUATION THERE

ONE has often heard Aden talked of as about the most undesirable place in the world to live in, and, if we can trust the veracity of the gentleman who said that, when he visited Hades, he saw four men playing whist quite comfortably, and on asking the custodian how it was they appeared so content with their surroundings, was told, "Oh, they came from Caracas and are used to this sort of thing!" Then Caracas (capital of Venezuela) must run Aden close. But Beira might safely be backed to beat them both.

Built on sand, nothing but sand, on a sand-spit, in fact, between the sea, a muddy creek, and a mangrove swamp, Beira appears as unattractive a place to live in as it is to look at. The very streets are sand, and there is no getting away from the heat and glare of it.

If you go near the creek, the smell of the mud and the decaying vegetation make you think of fever, and drive you back to the streets, and they make you wish to be on your ship again.

In spite of the drawbacks of its situation Beira appears flourishing, has large custom houses, store sheds, etc., and the dwelling houses are some of them well built and appear comfortable.

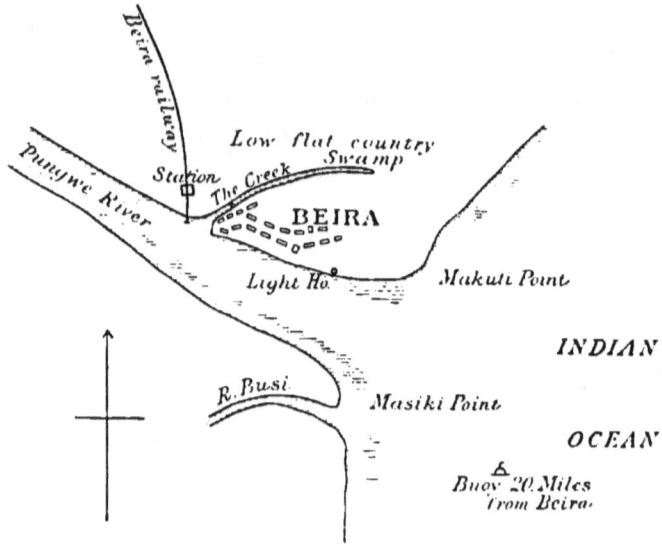

It is of course the nearest port to Mashonaland, and as that country is populated and developed, Beira is bound to become more important and thriving. What it needs is energy, and this its present inhabitants, and all connected with them, appear to lack most lamentably; indeed, we only found three people there who appeared to know what the word energy meant: these were Colonel Machado,

TROOPS WITHOUT ARMS! 25

Mr. Carnegie Ross (Her Majesty's Consul), and Mr. Harrison, who was acting as the British South Africa Company's agent for Messrs. Suter & Co.

Commander Hunt and I called on "the Governor of the territory of the Mozambique Company," this being the official title of Colonel Machado, who was most agreeable and promised to help the forward movement as far as he could. We had a somewhat amusing discussion as regards the arms. He said that his government had informed him that they had given permission for three hundred troops to pass through the country, but that nothing was said about arms, and that he wished the men to go without their arms, which could be packed in boxes and follow them. This I could not agree to, and I pointed out to him that the existing state of even Portuguese territory was sufficient excuse for the arms going with the men, and further that it might be said that men without arms could hardly be called troops. The latter argument appeared to convince the genial colonel. We then went to the consul, whom we found just recovering from an attack of fever, but very ready to assist.

Afterwards we saw the representatives of the Beira Railway Company, of the Boating Company, and various other officials. None of these appeared to have expected us, nor had they any suggestions to make in the way of helping the disembarkation and the forward movement; some of them did not appear to care so long as they personally were not bothered.

Altogether the morning spent in trudging about the blazing hot, sandy streets, was both depressing and exasperating, and Hunt and I went back to our respective ships in no good mood, having, however, gathered that the situation was as follows:

(a) The telegraph wire was cut somewhere north of Umtali (see Map), and consequently no communication was possible with Cape Town or elsewhere.

(b) The natives in Portuguese territory, and even in Beira itself, were restless and unsettled, while most of those working on the railway had deserted and gone to their kraals; should these natives rise, the Portuguese troops then in Beira were insufficient to cope with them.

(c) It was the local opinion that any sign of weakness or a single reverse would cause a rising. The effect of this would be to cut Salisbury's and our one line of supply.

(d) The one steam tug available for towing lighters up the Pungwe had a hole in her boiler, and the Beira-Fontesvilla section of the railway was still four miles short of Fontesvilla, and there were no horse trucks on it. Even supposing that this piece of line could be used, local opinion differed as to whether it was possible to get horses across the river at Fontesvilla.

(*e*) Local labour available to repair the tug, to improvise horse trucks, and to construct a landing stage and a pontoon at Fontesvilla was *nil*.

(*f*) The local officials, and the representative of the Boating Company, who was supposed to be responsible for the river transport, were supine and lethargic to the last degree.

(*g*) Added to all the above the Chartered Company's agent, and every one with local knowledge, stated that Salisbury must by this time be badly off for food. Therefore *haste* was necessary.

Not a cheerful prospect certainly, eager as we were to be on the move, and it made Hunt and myself scratch our heads and speak of Beira, and of some of the people we had seen in it, in no measured terms. Before we parted (the "Widgeon" was lying further out than the "Arab"), Hunt promised to send some of his artificers to mend the boiler of the tug, and also to call for and take me ashore early the next day.

During the afternoon the S.S. "Garth Castle" arrived in the river. On board her were the 43rd company Royal Engineers, and drafts of the Royal Artillery, York and Lancaster regiment, and also of the Medical Staff Corps, all being on their way to Mauritius.

Captain A. E. Haynes, Royal Engineers, was the senior officer, and, when the ship had touched at Durban, he had telegraphed to the High Commissioner suggesting that possibly his company might be useful in Mashonaland, and also that the ship should touch at Beira in order to ascertain.

The High Commissioner had answered to Lorenzo Marques, where the "Garth Castle" also called, approving of her going into Beira, and stating that the company might be landed, should the Portuguese Governor consider it necessary for the safety of the railway to Chimoio, and of the road to Umtali; but that the other troops on the ship were to go on to Mauritius.

Captain Haynes was also directed to report himself to, and transfer his instructions to, me on his arrival at Beira, and, on these instructions, I was to "act according to emergency, with the sanction of the Governor, in holding the line of communications to Umtali."

Directly the "Garth Castle" anchored, Captain Haynes came to the "Arab," and reported himself, giving me his telegraphic instructions to the above effect. It then of course devolved on me to act one way or the other: either to let all the troops go on to Mauritius, or to take some or all of them off the ship and join them to my force. Whichever I did *might* turn out wrong.

It was a regular case of "what should A do?" The safe course perhaps was to go to the Governor and ask him whether he wanted any assistance to make the rail and road in Portuguese territory safe, thus throwing the responsibility on him. But knowing that he had not then sufficient men to ensure safety, and also feeling that he would naturally make light of the situation as regards his own sphere; and even if the rail and road through the latter were safe, it was pretty certain that the Umtali-Salisbury road was not, I therefore thought that, though I might save myself from taking responsibility by going to him, I might not do the best for the cause, and this determined me to act as I myself thought right.

Turning the question over in one's mind, the salient points appeared to be: First and foremost, haste was necessary or Salisbury might starve, while each day's delay in the arrival of troops at Umtali would have a bad effect on Umtassa, and other chiefs near there who were still "sitting on the fence."

We could not make a move at all until the tug's boiler was mended, while to move even fairly quickly we must use the railway also. To use the latter it was necessary to improvise *covered* horse trucks, something like a big meat safe, for there was a belt of tsetse fly country between Beira and Fontesvilla. Further, as far as we could make out, by taking the mean of the local accounts, it would be necessary to improvise a pontoon and to construct a landing stage and a ramp, before horses could be got across the Pungwe at the latter place. We had not a single pioneer, and probably not a man who could drive a nail in properly, on board the "Arab"; while, as I have already said, local labour of the carpenter sort was practically *nil*. This made me decide to take the Engineers off the "Garth Castle."

Another very obvious point was the shortness of food in Salisbury, and in Mashonaland generally, and it made me argue to myself: "Suppose we go through to Salisbury with the Mounted Infantry, as we can easily do, and a rising takes place behind us, the road will be closed up again, and by taking Salisbury more mouths to feed we shall do it more harm than good." In other words, I saw then (July 3rd) that the food question would be the vital one, and after-events proved that this view was correct. The only way to ensure keeping the road open was by establishing posts on it. I could not spare any of my mounted men for this purpose, and consequently decided to take the detachment of fifty of the York and Lancaster regiment off the "Garth Castle" for it, intending with them and a portion of the Engineers, to form some four posts between Umtali and Salisbury; obvious places for three of these being near the Devil's pass, at Headlands, and at Marandellas (see Map). With the original force, on the "Arab," there were only five men of the Medical Staff Corps, and, having in view the fact that the men *ex* the "Garth Castle" would increase this force by over 100, and also that we had some three hundred and eighty miles to travel, with every prospect of fighting before reaching Salisbury, I considered it was desirable to take the ten men of this corps off the latter ship.

Regarding the Royal Artillery detachment, we had with us one officer and six non-commissioned officers and men, with two seven pounder guns, the intention being that the detachment should conduct the guns to Salisbury and then act as instructors to men of the local forces. Having been able to glean something of the nature of the country between Umtali and Salisbury, and also having gathered that it would be necessary to take Makoni's kraal before going on to the latter place, I was able to decide that it was desirable that both of the guns should have crews, and therefore took eight men of the Royal Artillery off the "Garth Castle."

This made the total of all ranks taken from that ship 111, made up as follows:

Corps.	Officers.	Non-Commissioned Officers and Men.
Royal Engineers (Capt. A. E. Haynes, Lieut. C. St. B. Sladen, Lieut. C. B. Thompson),	2	39
Royal Artillery, - -		8
York and Lancaster regiment (2nd Lieut. M. Middleton), - -	2	50
Medical Staff Corps, -		10 (includes 1 warrant officer)
Total, -	4	107

I can well imagine the reader saying about this period: "Why does he hang about so instead of getting 'forard' into Mashonaland." Well, before you can run a fox, you must find him, and all this, and a little more to come, is merely the drawing for him. Also, it may be said that the position in which I found myself was somewhat unique.

We read in military history of momentous questions having to be decided by "the man on the spot" without reference to superior authority; but, in these days of electricity, such situations do not often occur, and this is another reason why I have gone into the circumstances somewhat fully. Though the numbers were small, the question was certainly momentous for me, and I remembered that disobedience of orders, or the exceeding of instructions, could be only justified by emergency, and is often only admitted by superior authority to be justified when followed by success. In taking the men off the "Garth Castle" I was certainly exceeding my instructions, and perhaps was going near to disobeying orders. However, I thought then (and think so still) that I was doing what was right, and both Surgeon-Colonel Maxham and Hunt, who, as the two senior officers on the spot, I talked the matter over with, agreed with me.

That evening the following telegram arrived from the Commander of the Burghers at Umtali, Mr. Montague:

"July 3. At present Chief Umtassa, in whose

district we are living, is loyal, but no kaffir is to be relied upon; the adjoining chief, Makoni, is in rebellion.

"I have fortified the government buildings and a two-storied hotel here, and can hold my own if attacked. . . .

"Only two government horses fit for use, twelve private horses; the wire between here and Salisbury either cut or broken since Saturday. Whole country four miles from here up to Matabeleland in rebellion. The public here wish me to send a party to repair wire running through rebel country. I received orders from C.S.O., Buluwayo, and Judge Vintcent, Salisbury, not to weaken Umtali; have acted on these orders, and refused to send party until I heard from you on the subject."

This telegram showed clearly that the situation at Umtali was thought to be serious, and also made me think that I had been right in deciding to take the men off the "Garth Castle." I answered: "Consider your action in not weakening Umtali is wise. Am doing best to hasten my advance."

The following day, July 4th, was a busy one indeed. Hunt came for me in his galley early. What a blessing it was to have the cheery practical sailor to help one to move the lethargic people ashore into some sort of action. The tide was running out very strongly, and a stiff breeze was blowing up the river; the usual result of these conditions, high and hollow seas, ensued. Once,

c

during a squall—was it by accident, or did the sailor refrain from easing the sheet in order to frighten the soldier?—the galley lay down to it so much that the water bubbled over her gunwale, and I began to consider what articles in the boat would float, how many of her crew of three bluejackets could swim, how far we should all go towards the outer buoy before we were picked up, and last, but not least, were there any sharks on the look-out in the river? But the good little boat recovered herself well, and we got ashore with nothing worse than a slight wetting.

I was much struck by the respect and awe with which all the natives appeared to regard Hunt, as he stepped ashore, and as we walked up the town. I was told afterwards that all along the coast, and even for some distance inland, they are more afraid of a man-of-war than anything else, and that the presence of the little "Widgeon" in the river would go further than anything to prevent a native rising. Not complimentary to the soldier perhaps, but one more proof of the long arms that Great Britain possesses in her navy.

We at once went to see Colonel Machado on the subject of the extra men from the "Garth Castle" passing through Portuguese territory, to which he kindly gave his verbal consent, stating at the same time that he did not wish them to be on shore while they were waiting to advance. Hunt then said that he would take part of them on board the "Widgeon," and I decided that the remainder must go on to the already crowded "Arab" somehow.

I only had authority to detain the "Garth Castle" for forty-eight hours in any case, and every hour meant money, so it was necessary to get the men off her at once, and this was done during the afternoon.

On leaving the Governor's we went to the telegraph office, and had a conversation over the wire with Mr. Moore, the manager of the Beira railway, who was then at Fontesvilla. Here is a specimen of this conversation:

Question. Col. A. to Mr. Moore: "What is the greatest number of horses you can take by rail from Fontesvilla to Chimoio daily?"

Answer. "Thirty."

Question. "Can you send sixty horses every other day, so as to work in with the lighters?"

Answer. "Yes."

Question. "Can you take sixty men with their saddles and accoutrements complete as well as the horses?"

Answer. "No, I cannot do it the same day as the horses?"

Question. "How many men can you do the same day as the horses?"

Answer. "I think I can do the sixty with the horses, at any rate I will try my best."

And much more to the same effect regarding trains, accommodation, etc. At the conclusion of this conversation we congratulated ourselves that here was one man at any rate who would do his best for us.

We then had a conversation, again on the wire, with Mr. Montague, who was commanding at Umtali, and from whom we gathered that, though Umtali was quite safe, they did not feel strong enough to move out far, and also that the natives were in possession of the road to the north, and were holding the Devil's Pass, a very awkward place, in force. I directed Mr. Montague, at Umtali, and Mr. Fotheringham, at Chimoio, to commandeer every available waggon and span of animals for the use of the force.

This step, of which more hereafter, by no means met with the approval of the local residents and traders, nor with the loyal support of the local authorities, but it was an absolutely necessary one, as even by taking every waggon we could lay hands on, we only just got together sufficient transport for the column.

Later in the day I received the following telegram from a body, styling themselves the "Defence Committee," at Umtali:

"To Lieut.-Colonel Alderson, Beira.

"July 4th. The following letter sent Resident Magistrate, as regarding British South Africa Company, yesterday, begins: 'I am instructed by the Umtali Defence Committee to forward to you the following copy of a resolution passed at their meeting held this, Friday, afternoon, and to ask you for a written reply to the same. A

THE MAKINGS OF "RUCTIONS" 37

further meeting will be held to-morrow at ten o'clock, and I shall be glad to place your reply before the committee. Your attendance at the meeting will be esteemed a favour. *Resolution:* That in the opinion of the Defence Committee it is desirable that a force should leave Umtali for the purpose of connecting the telegraph line, and the committee request the British South Africa Company to provide all the necessary equipment, and also request the Commandant to give the necessary orders.

(Signed) SECRETARY DEFENCE COMMITTEE.'

"Meeting committee held this morning, to which Resident Magistrate sent message deferring reply till to-morrow. Meeting then resolved as follows. Begins :

"That committee instruct secretary to write Resident Magistrate and express their extreme surprise and dissatisfaction that he has omitted, according to his promise, to give them an answer to their communications of yesterday, and they wish to point out that such inaction on part of government, and disregard of the deliberately expressed opinion of the people, is calculated, in a crisis like the present, to cause serious trouble between people and government. Also that a copy of both resolutions be wired to Colonel Alderson, through the Resident Magistrate, asking for an immediate reply, and informing him that the public are clamouring for a meeting at which to hear your reply. Government representative here waiting on your committee; first place you in possession of all facts and ask your views as to sending local force to connect telegraph wires."

This telegram was somewhat involved, but it clearly showed me that there were the makings of "ructions" at Umtali, and I decided that it would not improve matters if I got myself mixed up in them from the end of a wire some 160 miles away, and therefore answered: "Not knowing local circumstances I cannot interfere between you and the Resident Magistrate. I understand that his orders are not to weaken Umtali, and this I consider wise."

In the afternoon I interviewed Mr. Wilfred Honey and his twelve volunteers; the latter wanted to know what terms they were going to serve on. This I knew nothing about, my only information regarding them being the telegram, received at Durban, from Judge Vintcent, which merely stated that he wished me to attach them to my force. Luckily I had suspected, when at Durban, that they would have no horses, saddlery, etc., and had asked Mr. Jameson, the Company's agent there, to purchase these and put them on board the "Arab," which he promptly did.

On my remarking to the men that my experience of volunteers was that they were men who did it for the love of the thing, I was met with such remarks as "Oh! not a bit of it," etc., and I then learnt from Mr. Honey, that a volunteer in Rhodesia is a man who never receives less than ten shillings a day, plus his clothes and rations, and that some of the officers draw as much as two pounds. On Mr. Honey stating that he was sure that Judge Vintcent meant these men to be on the same terms as the others, I allowed them to sign on, at the same time making a mental note that the term volunteers, applied to corps of which the very privates received half a sovereign a day, was a decided misnomer.

Mr. Honey's men, however, thoroughly earned their pay. We christened them "the Scouts," and as such they did excellent work throughout the operations.

Following on this interview came visits to Messrs. Suter & Co., and various other stores, in order to obtain the necessary supplies and equipment for the men *ex* the "Garth Castle." Those on the "Arab" were fully equipped, and we had two months' supplies for them; but the people from the former ship had no supplies and field equipment, such as waterproof sheets, etc. Very good substitutes for waterproof sheets were made by cutting some light canvas into pieces of the necessary dimensions, then soaking them in oil and drying them in the sun, while waggon sails (large stout canvas sheets, used to cover the waggons when loaded) were purchased in lieu of tents. In all this Mr. Harrison gave us the greatest assistance. All the locally obtained substitutes for the regulation equipment turned out well, but the food supplies did not. The biscuit was very hard and of inferior quality, as also was the tinned meat, and the same might be said of the tea, sugar, etc.

All were very badly packed and consequently much loss occurred in the many loadings and unloadings which they had to undergo.

In the evening Mr. Sawerthal, the Chartered Co.'s representative specially sent from Salisbury to assist and advise me in local matters, arrived at Beira. I am afraid that we did not at first "talk alike." Mr. Sawerthal had already made his own plan as to how the troops were to go up country, and this plan was that they were all to go by river to Fontesvilla, entrain there, and on arriving at rail head (Chimoio), to go on from there to Umtali as they were detrained, *i.e.* in small detachments.

This plan, which meant that nearly double the time would be taken than if the Beira-Fontesvilla section of the railway was used as well as the river, was not only contrary to sound tactics, but was also contrary to the telegraphic instructions which I had received at Durban from Sir Frederick Carrington, which were : " Assemble your command at rail head and move forward from there with all precautions." It took Mr. Sawerthal a considerable time to realize that I meant to obey these instructions, and also that anything concerning the safety or the movements of the troops with a view to military precautions was my business and not his. When once he had mastered these facts we became very good friends.

Next morning, the 5th July, we were again ashore early, and succeeded in making final arrangements for a move, both by rail and river, to commence, the latter on the following day, and the former on the 7th. The tug's boiler, thanks to the help of the artificers from the "Widgeon," was mended, and she was to

have a trial run during the morning. After an interview with Mr. Charlton, the local railway manager at Beira, and another talk over the wire with Mr. Moore at Fontesvilla, we were able to arrange for Honey's men, with all their rations and equipment and twenty-four horses, to go by train to Fontesvilla on the 7th, thence, when they had crossed the river, on to Chimoio. I promised Mr. Charlton that a party of the Engineers should be ashore early on the next morning, to fit up the frames

in the horse trucks, and to cover them with
"limbo" (limbo is a sort of thin, white, gauze-
like material, which is used for trading with the
natives), as a protection against the tsetse fly.
The sketch on the preceding page shows what
they produced.

The tug's trial trip was satisfactory, and it
was arranged that she should tow lighters up
to Fontesvilla, starting early the next morning.
The lighters were at once got alongside the
"Arab," and loaded with sixty-six horses, and the
accoutrements, etc., with two months' supplies
for some seventy men of all ranks. I decided
that this party should include two detachments
of Engineers, one to remain at Fontesvilla to
improvise a pontoon, a landing stage, etc., and
the other to go to Chimoio, to do whatever
might be necessary in the way of accommodation, watering arrangements, etc.

We had heard so many conflicting stories
about the river at Fontesvilla, the accommodation at that place, the capacity of the line, and
the halting places on it, and also about the
space available for horses and men at Chimoio,
that I decided to go with the first river party
myself to Fontesvilla, and then on by rail to
Chimoio, and to come back again as soon as
possible.

Among other things about Chimoio, we were
told that there was not sufficient space clear of
bush in which to put two hundred men and

horses, while, when we got there we found there was room for at least a whole cavalry brigade.

Again, we were told, that if we kept any number of horses there, for even two or three days, they would be eaten by lions, who walked about the streets like dogs; and my remark that possibly sentries might manage to keep them away, was received with a shrug of the shoulders, expressive of, "Poor Devil, fresh out from England; you'll see."

Surgeon-Colonel Maxham and Lieut. Hunt decided to accompany me on this expedition.

The relief to all of us of at last being able to do something was indescribable.

Perhaps it would be as well to state here exactly what the force was that we had now to disembark and get up to rail head.

A copy of the state of the force, as on July 5th, will be found on page 44.

This is the first time that the name at the top of this state, which gives the second part of the title to this narrative, has appeared. Every independent, or detached, force must have an official name, by which reference to it can be made, and by which its commander is addressed, thus: "O.C.M.F.F."

After duly considering the object for which the force had been got together, and the fact that the various local corps in Mashonaland would shortly be merged into it, we decided on the above name,

MASHONALAND FIELD FORCE

BEIRA, JULY 5th, 1896.

Detail	Field Officers	Other Officers	Total Officers	Warrant Officers	Staff Sergeants	Sergeants	Corporals	Buglers	Privates	Total W.O., N.C.O. & Men
Staff	1	3	4	—	2	4	—	—	1	7
Mounted Infantry { Rifle Co.	—	5	5	—	—	6	8	2	97	113
Mounted Infantry { Irish Co.	—	5	5	—	—	6	6	1	94	107
Royal Artillery	—	1	1	—	—	2	—	—	12	14
Royal Engineers	—	3	3	—	1	2	1	2	33	39
Detachment 2nd York and Lancaster Regiment	—	1	1	—	—	1	1	—	48	50
Medical Staff Corps	—	1	1	1	—	—	3	—	10	14
Army Service Corps	—	1	1	—	1	—	—	—	—	1
Honey's Scouts	—	1	1	—	—	1	—	—	12	13
Total,	1	21	22	1	4	22	19	5	307	358

Total Officers, - - - - 22
Total Warrant Officers, Non-Com. Officers and Men, - 358

Total, - - - - 380

Horses, - - - - 284

which was later on approved of by Major-General Sir Frederick Carrington, K.C.B., K.C.M.G., commanding the troops in Rhodesia and Bechuanaland, under whose supreme command we were.

I now handed over the command of the Mounted Infantry to Jenner, and assumed command of the Field Force myself, making the following appointments :

Captain A. J. Godley (Adjutant Mounted Infantry)—Staff Officer.

Captain J. Roach, British South Africa Company's Forces—Intelligence Officer.

Surgeon-Captain F. A. Saw, Army Medical Staff—Medical Officer.

Lieut. J. E. Nicholls, Rhodesia Horse—Galloper.

Referring to my remark to the reader on page 32, I would now say that the fox is fairly found ; how he breaks covert will be seen in the next chapter.

CHAPTER IV

THE PUNGWE RIVER, FONTESVILLA, CHIMOIO, AND UMTALI

JULY 6th, the tug was to come alongside the "Arab" to pick up the lighters at 6.30 A.M., at which time the party detailed to go was ready. Seven o'clock came, eight o'clock came, nine o'clock came, and no tug, while all this time she could be seen at anchor close to the land, with no apparent efforts at getting up steam being made. Oh, Mr. Representative of the Boating Company, who had promised that she should be alongside by 6.30, what a deal of bad language you have to answer for! At last, about 9.30, we were cheered by seeing smoke issuing from the tug's funnel. At a quarter past ten she began to move. "Hurrah, she has not broken down again," was, I think, the mental exclamation of most of us. At 10.30 she was alongside, the lighters were soon hooked on, and we were really off.

On talking to the tug's captain, by name Dickie, a very dry and amusing specimen of the sailor who has turned his hand to most things, we discovered that he never had any intention of starting before 10.30, as the tide did not suit till then, and that the Boating Company's representative had merely told us 6.30, and not troubled himself about such a minor detail as the tide!

We were all in high spirits; even to be on the move in the fresh air was good enough in itself. Crowded, as she was, with horses, above and below (we had about a hundred on the upper deck), it was very difficult to move about on the "Arab," while the horses were so closely packed, and the fittings were so primitive, that it was impossible to keep the ship properly clean, and the three days at anchor with a very hot sun had already made her smell horribly. How Bowen got through his very bad go of fever on her I do not know; the worst of it for him was that the doctors would not take the responsibility of letting him land, and he had to go back to Durban.

The Pungwe near its mouth is certainly very pretty. Perhaps two miles wide, its banks are fringed with green, and it is studded with numerous islands, covered with vegetation. As a navigable river, however, judging by what Captain Dickie told us, it does not seem that it is to be depended on: it is shallow, and its channel changes with almost every tide, while after each rainy season it probably is entirely different. Apart from its prettiness, one felt a certain indescribable sense of sport being in the air. Was it because the little that we had read about the river was in books on big game shooting, or was it that one knew it to be one of the few remaining wild and little used rivers, and that it led one through a country which had not been shot out by so-called "sportsmen"?

Whatever the reason, we were all on the *qui vive*, and those who had brought their sporting rifles got them out, and were very soon popping away at the numerous crocodiles who were basking in the sun on the strip of mud below the banks, and most of which took no notice of our noisy tug. Several were hit, but all, except one, dived into the water; this exception jumped at least five feet into the air, and when he fell remained still.

It is perhaps permissible to shoot a crocodile at any time, whether you can pick him up or not; but I did not like the shooting at the droves of hippopotami we saw later on, because, had one been hit, we could not have waited for him to float so that we might "gather" him. However, we passed both these droves some distance off, and as they only had the tops of their heads above water, the odds were much in their favour, and I am glad to say that none were hit. Every now and then we saw on the banks marks of where the hippo had gone into or got out of the water, and these alone were interesting to most of us, who had before this only read of them. It was too late, and too early, in the day to see much game; it was probably all lying up in the reeds or bushes, but occasionally we saw a few buck on the banks, or a few water-fowl on the river.

Hunt and I spent the afternoon on the bridge with Captain Dickie, and we were much struck with his knowledge of the river, and with the way in which he seemed almost able to *see* the bottom, and to tell by instinct where the channel had changed since he last went up. The "Kimberley," our tug, really drew much too much water (I think about five feet was her draught) to be suitable for the river, and several times we ran aground, had to back off, and find a better place.

About 4.30 P.M., when we were some two and a half miles from Fontesvilla, we came to a place that beat both Captain Dickie and the language which he used at the river and at his crew. I certainly never heard a man who had a better flow of the most expressive nautical oaths. But it was all no good, and after vainly trying to find a channel through the mud bank, we, as a last resource, went full speed at it, got well on to the top, and there stuck.

Captain Dickie, like a sensible man, at once dropped into his usual self-contained manner, and quietly said that we must spend the night where we were.

We certainly did not appreciate this. A white mist was just beginning to rise from the river and its banks, along which we saw a number of the locally called "fever trees," which, being of a lighter green than the surrounding vegetation, were easily distinguishable from it. Further, it was now slack water, and we should soon be left with the evil smelling mud all round us.

However, there was nothing to be done but make the best of it, and really, I believe, there was not much danger of the men getting fever at that time of year.

After watering and feeding the horses, the men had a meal, followed by a dose of quinine and a small tot of rum, as fever preventives, and then we all turned in, every man getting under cover of some sort, so that he should not sleep in the mist.

Captain Dickie hoped to get off with the morning tide, about four; but this we failed to do, and, as I wished to get to Chimoio and back as soon as possible, I, with Surgeon-Colonel Maxham and Hunt, left the "Kimberley" in the dingy about five. We reached Fontesvilla about 7.30, had breakfast at the shanty dignified by the name of "Railway Hotel," and, thanks to the kindness of Mr. Moore, left again about 9.30 in a special train, which consisted of one carriage and an engine.

The railway is a tiny one, the gauge being only two feet and the carriages overhanging the wheels about the same distance on each side.

THE PUNGWE RIVER AT FONTESVILLA
THE "KIMBERLEY" IN MID-STREAM

Before leaving we had a look round, and decided where the men and horses should go when they arrived. For the former we found a tin goods' shed capable of holding about two hundred men, and for the latter there was sufficient space in the station yard.

Fontesvilla is certainly about the most feverish looking spot that can be imagined, and from all accounts, and judging by the two nearly full cemeteries, it is as bad as it looks.

Nearly all of the few houses are built on piles, as it is often flooded during the rainy season, and we were told that when burials take place the coffins have to be weighted to make them sink, as the graves fill with water as soon as they are dug.

Truly a man should be well paid to work in such a place! and I hope that the railway people, who form the bulk of the small population, are. So bad is the climate, that in the rainy season the railway has a double staff of engine-drivers, guards, etc., and a man is only kept at work for short periods, and then sent away to recruit. How many lives the railway cost to build has, I believe, never been published.

For the first twenty miles or so, the line goes as straight as an arrow from Fontesvilla, through a perfectly flat and most gamey-looking country —long grass, with here and there patches of thick scrub, or of trees about twenty feet high of various sorts, including borassus palms. I do not think I ever enjoyed a railway journey more; here we were, spinning along, not too fast, in a perfectly new, and to us, most novel country, seeing every now and then herds of game of all kinds: zebra, buffalo, and innumerable sorts of buck. None of these seemed to mind the train in the least, and many stood within easy shot and looked at it. We much regretted to hear that they were at times shot at from trains, a most unsportsman-like practice; for, if killed, they were not picked up, and if wounded, they either must die a lingering death or be caught by the first lion that came across them.

At Forty Mile Station (all the stations are named according to their distance from Fontesvilla) we began to enter the forest country, which extends from there up to and some distance beyond Chimoio. The trees are mostly small and badly grown but very thick, and below them is a dense and in places impenetrable scrub. It would perhaps be as well to give here a rough table of distances. Here it is:

<blockquote>
Beira to Fontesvilla,   40 miles by river.
Fontesvilla to Chimoio, 118 miles by rail.
Chimoio to Umtali,   73 miles by road.
Umtali to Salisbury,   155 miles by road.
</blockquote>

Beira to Salisbury, 386 miles by river, rail, and road.

We arrived at Eighty Mile Station, near which is the railway hospital, about seven P.M. Here

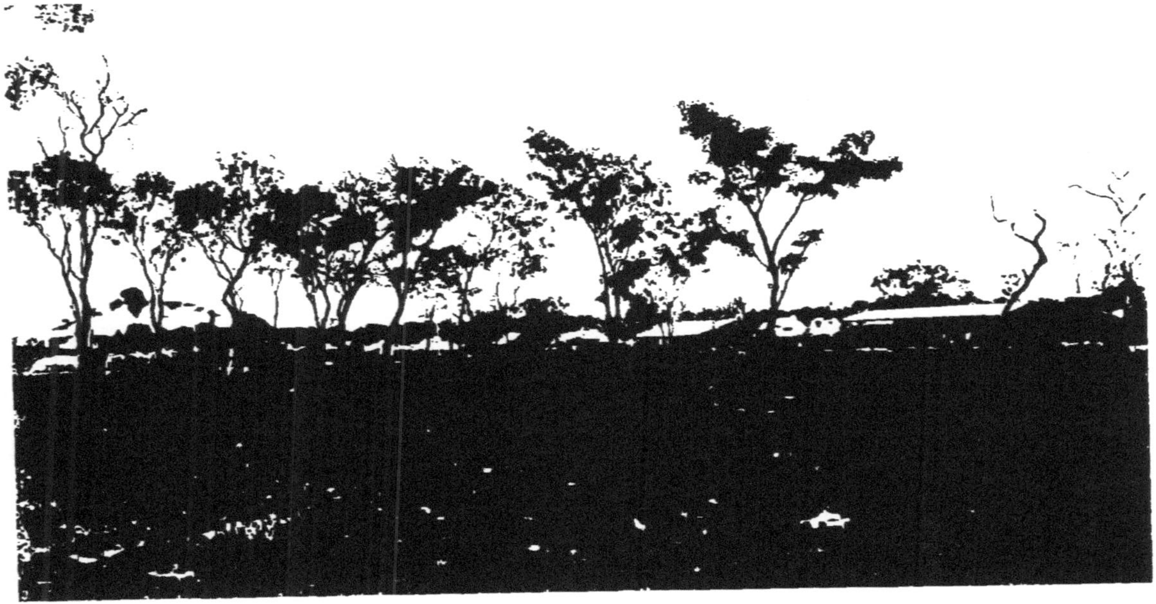

CHIMOIO

we met Mr. Hylands, the chief engineer of the railway, who kindly asked us to dinner and gave us an excellent one, the foundation being buck and guinea fowl, both of which were shot in the neighbourhood by his native hunter.

About eight P.M. we went on, after arranging with the proprietor of the so-called hotel, to supply each batch of troops as they passed through, with coffee and bread and cheese. We reached Chimoio at midnight, and thankfully turned into our beds in the shanty hotel. Personally I did not get much sleep, as my room was practically part of the bar; the wall, which was supposed to partition it off, not reaching the ceiling, I could hear every sound in the latter, in which three men kept playing some sort of card game for drinks, using much bad language, till about three A.M. Two of them apparently wanted to go away long before this, but the third, who appeared a strong-minded individual, *would* have "just one more game."

Our train was to start back at seven A.M., and at six we were up and out looking round Chimoio; very dirty and uncomfortable looking we found it, but there was plenty of space for both men and horses. Having, with the help of Surgeon-Col. Maxham, who was horrified at the dirtiness all around, selected the cleanest place for a camp, I got Mr. Fotheringham, who was collecting transport for us on behalf of the Company, to promise to have some tents improvised out of waggon sails, so that the first detachment of troops arriving would have some sort of cover to go under at once.

On the way back we again stopped at Eighty Mile, and had breakfast there. At Sixty-two Mile we were to cross the three first up-coming troop trains. When we arrived there about two P.M., one of these was in, and reported the others to be close behind it. We waited an hour, and then in came a native runner with the news that the second train, which consisted of five horse and one baggage truck, had upset, about the 57th or 58th mile peg, and that all the horses not hurt were loose in the bush! to which my thoughts added, "among the tsetse flies and the lions!"

We decided to at once take our engine with an empty truck, and as many break-down tools and native navvies as we could lay hands on, and start for the scene. About the 56th mile peg, just as we were rounding a sharp curve at a fair pace, we heard a whistle, and at the same time saw an engine coming *up*, on the other end of the curve, and not a hundred yards from us! Both drivers shut off steam, put on the break, and then jumped, and so did we, the P.M.O., the O.C.H.M.S. "Widgeon," the O.C.M.F.F., the niggers, and all. Crash! we went, down a rather steep embankment all among the bushes and the boulders, and *bang!* went the two engines together, breaking up, and entangling their cow

A RAILWAY ACCIDENT

catchers, but luckily doing no other damage and both remaining on the line. Had they been disabled, or upset, the delay might have been serious for the horses, as we were within the fly belt, or rather, in the country where the buffalo were (the tsetse fly follows the buffalo, and is said to breed in their droppings). No one was hurt beyond a barked shin, or a few scratches, but I think that the niggers, with their bare feet, came off the worst, and I saw several of them limping afterwards. *How* the beggars did chatter about it!

It took us some time to disentangle the engines, so tightly had they gripped each other with their cow catchers. When this was done, the up-coming engine backed, and we went on, to the scene of the accident. There we found a pretty mess: the whole of the second troop train, except the engine, had, in rounding a curve, gone over a three-foot embankment, the result being that the trucks were turned almost upside down, all their upper works were smashed, two horses killed outright, two so badly hurt that they had to be shot, and four had galloped off into the forest. I began to see some of our men dismounted already! Luckily no men, there had been about five with the horses, were hurt.

Godley, who was in charge of the three trains, had already sent off parties after the loose horses, and had begun to pick up the pieces and clear the line.

Truly the excitement attendant on the breaking of covert was beginning early!

The turned-out horses were led along the line up to Sixty-two, where they remained for the night in charge of St. Aubyn's section. We afterwards heard that St. Aubyn, who was by no means pleased at having his men and horses turned out of the train, was much incensed at a native who, with the best intentions, but with total ignorance of where a horse could and could not go, showed him a short cut by which to take his horses to water, but which went over such difficult ground that, dark as it was, it took them far longer than if they had gone along the line.

When the line had been cleared the third train steamed up to Sixty-two, and we of course had to go back there in order to let it pass us.

One result of all the pother was that we did not reach Fontesvilla till 2 A.M. the next morning, and then I know that I, for one, was far too tired to care a rap about the rats who steeplechased over my bed in the Railway Hotel at intervals during the few remaining hours of darkness.

Before starting for Beira the following morning, July 9th, we had another look round Fontesvilla, and found that the Engineers, under Sladen, had two days before improvised a pontoon, by lashing two small lighters together and building a platform on them, and had also made a landing stage, and a ramp. By means of these the horses of the scouts had been easily got across the river, ten or twelve at a time. This was good business, and we saw that, bar further accidents on the railway, it should not now be many days before we had all the men and horses off the ship.

As a precaution against more accidents, I requested Mr. Moore to reduce the speed of the troop trains. This meant that sixty horses and men could leave Fontesvilla every third day, instead of every second day; but the extra day did not, I considered, matter, when put against the chance of losing more horses, and perhaps men, and of breaking up more of the limited rolling stock.

Half way to Beira, which we reached at four P.M., the Consul met us with some very acceptable food and drink.

On getting on board the "Arab" we found that Jenner had been hard at work during the three days we had been away. In addition to Honey's men with twenty-four horses, he had got off by train Stephen's section of the Rifle company, men, horses, and all supplies and stores, complete; had loaded two lighters with eighty horses and baggage ready to start up river when the "Kimberley" returned, and had sent other horses and baggage ashore to be in readiness to leave by train.

The "Kimberley" turned up that evening, and some seventy men of all ranks, and two lighters with stores, as well as the two lighters previously loaded by Jenner, were at once sent off with her. The spring tides were gaining strength, and Captain Dickie said that he did not anticipate any more sticking.

On the 10th most of Pilson's section were sent off by rail, and on the 11th the "Kimberley" returned and took another four lighters up, while King-Harman's section went by rail. On the 12th the disembarkation was completed, the detachment York and Lancaster regiment landing and going by rail.

The fact that it took us six days to get the 380 men and the 284 horses away from Beira, shows how limited was the towing capacity of the tug, and the carrying capacity of both the lighters and of the railway. Had we not been able to use the Fontesvilla-Beira section of the latter, it would have taken nearly as long again; that we were able to use it was almost entirely due to the Engineers. I went as far as Fontesvilla with the detachment York and Lancaster, Hunt kindly taking me ashore in his steam cutter. During the few days I had known him we had overcome many difficulties together, and I was *really* sorry to say farewell. I was also sorry to see the last of Captain Chope and his officers (though not of his ship!), who had done their utmost for us in every way.

At Fontesvilla we found that Haynes had now got everything very ship-shape: he had fixed up

AN UNEXPECTED REINFORCEMENT 59

watering troughs for horses, washing and drinking places, and latrines for the men, and was hard at work repairing the trucks broken in the accident of the 8th.

On the 13th I went on from Fontesvilla to Chimoio, this time taking my own horses. These were (1) "Grimstone," a very well bred horse, about 15 hands, and a winner both on the flat and over a country, bought at Cape Town; (2) "Charlie" (afterwards re-named "Makoni"), a very useful chestnut pony, about 14 hands, also bought at the Cape; (3) a good-looking pony bought at Wynberg for, and which belonged to, the British South Africa Company.

On the 14th, the first party, about 100 of all ranks, under Jenner, marched from Chimoio for Umtali.

On the 15th we heard of the arrival at Fontesvilla of a detachment of 4 officers and 150 men West Riding regiment, 1 officer and 6 men Medical Staff Corps, and 2 men Army Service Corps.

The officers were: Captain F. H. A. Swanson, Captain W. W. Wood, Lieutenant P. Coode, West Riding regiment; Captain W. L. Pease, K.O.L. Infantry (attached West Riding); Surgeon-Captain C. H. Hale, Army Medical Staff.

Had I known before that these men were being sent, I should certainly not have taken the detachment York and Lancaster regiment off the "Garth Castle," though I should still have taken the men of the Medical Staff Corps, and a portion both of the Engineers and of the Royal Artillery.

From the 14th until the 20th, men, horses, or stores were arriving at Chimoio daily. On the 17th the Royal Engineers and the Royal Artillery, under Haynes, marched for Umtali, two sections Mounted Infantry, under French, following them on the 18th, while McMahon with the Irish company Mounted Infantry, and all the remaining details of the troops *ex* the "Arab" and the "Garth Castle," left Chimoio on the 20th. So short was the ox and mule transport that we had to give Haynes, whose party were all on foot, seven donkey waggons which had been commandeered; with these it took him from 2.30 P.M. till 12 midnight to get to the first water, a distance of only three miles! He rode back himself and told me this, and by great good luck I had just heard of four more empty donkey waggons that were about due from Umtali, and so told him to take these when he met them, and lighten his loads.

While waiting, both at Fontesvilla and at Chimoio, the Mounted Infantry officers had done a good deal of horse-breaking, and there was plenty of material to practise on, for there were several horses which did not appear to have been backed. One three-year-old (nice age for active service!) in particular gave McMahon plenty of amusement, throwing itself down with him several times. That every horse marched out of Chimoio carrying a man is greatly to the credit of these officers, as is also the fact that the shipping of the horses at Cape Town and Durban, the unshipping into lighters at Beira, the loading up and the unloading from the trains, and the crossing of them over the river at Fontesvilla, was all done without a single accident.

On page 36 I speak of the difficulty we had in getting sufficient transport, and of the want of cordiality on the part of local authorities and others in doing their best to obtain it. This was particularly the case at Chimoio. We soon, however, found out the reason, and this was that local traders, etc., wished to send private goods up to Salisbury behind us in safety, and sell them there at famine prices. We actually found several waggons being loaded with private stuff, *principally liquor*, when it was well known that food was urgently needed up country. I had all the liquor loaded taken off, and food stuffs, either for the column or for Salisbury, put on in its place.

The legality of this commandeering of waggons, though they were owned by Rhodesians, in *Portuguese territory*, appears doubtful, and I was several times threatened with the law; but being bound to have the waggons, merely replied, "We will have the waggons first and the law afterwards." Thus we got the waggons, and up to the present have heard no more about the law. In spite, however, of all the commandeering we could do, it was necessary for the Mounted Infantry to carry all their greatly reduced kit, except their blankets and water-proof sheets, on their horses until the waggons became lighter through the using up of rations and mealies. We had also to reduce the officers to one valise each.

I left Chimoio with Godley, Barnes, and Mr. Sawerthal, soon after the Irish company, on the 20th, intending to ride to Umtali, seventy-three miles, in two days. Sawerthal had not tried, or had not been able, to raise a horse, and started with us on a very small donkey, which we told him would break down with him, but which he stoutly maintained would do the journey easily.

After riding about an hour we overtook the Irish company, and found that all the horses had settled down, and were going well. When we overtook their advanced guard we found them in a considerable state of excitement, because the scouts had sent in word that there were two lions in the bush just ahead. We did our best to spot these lions, but failed, though we saw a couple of baboons, and I strongly suspect that these were the Irishmen's lions. After going about ten miles Sawerthal's donkey began to cry "enough," and I told him to wait for the Irish company to come up with him, and then ask McMahon for a horse.

At Bendulas, twenty-two miles from Chimoio, we passed Haynes' column, all well and cheerful, but the donkeys were going *very* slow. We reached the Revue River, thirty-four miles, in the evening, and put up at Hawes' store.

Here we found French and Stephens, with the two Mounted Infantry sections which had marched from Chimoio on the 18th. They appeared very comfortable, and French had the horses picketed in a very ship-shape manner. Later on Sawerthal joined us. Next morning, the 21st, we were off early. About eight A.M. we

LOOKING NORTH-WEST FROM LESLIE'S STORE.

reached Massikessi, or Macequece, which is the principal Portuguese town, or rather cluster of buildings, in the western part of their territory. We called on the commandante, who was most polite. With him we found the Portuguese Chief Staff Officer, who had come up "to see us off the premises," *i.e.* over the border, which was a few miles further on.

About four P.M. we passed Botley's store, and a little further on crossed a small stream, and were in Mashonaland. The Chief Staff Officer then bid us a courteous farewell, wishing us good luck.

After passing Leslie's store, we began to get into very broken and hilly country, the nature of which is shown in the sketch on page 63.

Here the road winds about among high, rocky, and thickly wooded hills, crossing numerous dongas and spruits. This would be a very awkward place in which to be attacked by an enterprising enemy. Sunset saw us on the top of Christmas Pass, on the Penalonga Range, where we got a distant view of Umtali.

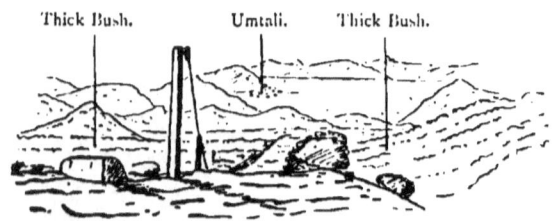

LOOKING NORTH-WEST FROM THE TOP OF CHRISTMAS PASS.

After making a short halt at the store at the foot of the pass, we arrived at Umtali about eight P.M. The horses had done the two long days well, and the only person who suffered was Stow, my civilian servant, who had never ridden before—he *was* stiff!

We found Jenner and his men comfortably established in the police barracks, which consisted of a cluster of mud huts, about a mile from the town. Next morning I went into Umtali and saw Mr. Montague, the Mining Commissioner, who was commandant of the Burgher force which had been raised to defend the town. I also saw the acting Resident Magistrate, Mr. G. Fermaner, and other officials. From their accounts it appeared that the Burghers were discontented and would not serve much longer. The only thing to do seemed to be to disband them, and to raise a corps of volunteers (paid ten shillings per day mind!) in their places. So Mr. Fermaner issued a proclamation disbanding the Burghers, and calling a public meeting for that afternoon.

This meeting I had to go and address, and had to explain to those present the situation, the formation of, and the conditions of service in, the proposed volunteer force, and finally to suggest that, though they would, I supposed, wish to select their own commander, they should not forget that Major Hamilton Browne, who had had much experience of irregular corps, was there.

"Maori" Browne,[1] as he is commonly known, whom I had not met before, but some of whose people I knew well, was shortly afterwards elected commandant of the corps, which was called the "Umtali Rifles," and ran up to about a hundred and twenty strong, all ranks "signing on" to serve the British South Africa Company for three months, in any part of Rhodesia.

[1] "Maori's" experience of the world in general, and of irregular corps in particular, was undoubtedly great. For twelve years he had fought the Maoris in New Zealand (thence his nick-name), had hunted bushrangers in Australia, been a Papal Zouave, fought the Sioux under Colonel Dodge in America, and had fought in the Galeka, the Zulu, the Dinizulu, and the first Matabele war.

I certainly had not imagined when leaving Cape Town, that my work in Mashonaland would include the raising of irregular corps and also public speaking. Of the former I had had no previous experience, and of the latter my experience was limited to addressing the farmers at the Shorncliffe, and the Staff College, Drag Hunt dinners.

As some of the "Maori's" corps were to be mounted, the next step was to commandeer all the horses in Umtali. In this again I was not well supported by the local authorities: it was allowed to slip out the day before action was to be taken, that the horses would be commandeered, the result being that several of the best were sent away, while of those which were collected, some were returned on very meagre evidence that they were necessary for the carrying out of the owners' professions or businesses.

"Maori" very soon had his corps in hand, and, when I inspected them a few days later, I found a very serviceable looking lot of men. This corps did excellent work while we were in the country, and I see by the papers that they are still doing so, and also that "Maori" still commands them.

On the 23rd July a telegram from the High Commissioner, which had come *via* Delagoa Bay and hence by sea to the Consul at Beira, informed me that the detachment York and Lancaster regiment were to be withdrawn from the force, and were to return to Beira for re-embarkation. At the same time the Consul telegraphed that the Governor objected to their returning into Portuguese territory. There was thus nothing to do but order the detachment to remain at Umtali until the latter changed his mind.

For the next three days we were all, especially our supply and transport officer, Barnes, Army Service Corps, hard at work hiring, and commandeering, waggons and spans, and then detailing them to corps. Barnes seemed to "catch on" with the local waggon owners, and in several instances came to terms with them when the company's agent had failed to do so.

Some spans of oxen were hidden in the bush, but "Maori" Browne ferreted them out. At last, on the 26th, Barnes was able to report that we had just enough waggons to move us and our two months' supplies.

I wanted to march the next day, but the first fifty men of the detachment West Riding, for which I had telegraphed to come on as quickly as possible, in order that they might take the place of the detachment York and Lancaster regiment, could not arrive at Umtali before the 27th, therefore we had to wait.

Some people think Umtali pretty. It did not, however, strike us as being so, but perhaps we saw it under disadvantageous circumstances. We were impatient to be on the march, and no one seemed eager to help us, while the place appeared to be under the influence of a glut of whisky.

The sketch below shows Umtali's position, which is, tactically, about as bad as it could be. Surrounded by high and wooded hills, which are close enough on three sides to command it with rifle fire, and on one, so close that an attacker could collect under cover for a rush, it would be a

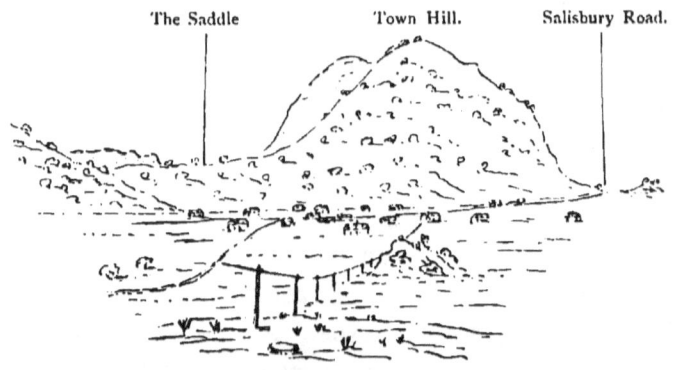

UMTALI, LOOKING WEST FROM THE HILLS ON THE EAST.

bad place to defend with an enemy who had any enterprise. I had then no knowledge of the fighting qualities of the Mashonas, but, as the inhabitants seemed in fear of an attack, I sincerely hoped that they were very much worse fighters than the Dervishes, who were the last natives I had had experience of.

The civil hospital at Umtali was full, and as we then had some sick, and should perhaps have some wounded to send back later on, I decided to establish a base hospital there. Dr. Englebach,

TO DEFEND UMTALI 69

who was in the service of the Chartered Company, was then at Umtali, and I placed the hospital in his charge, leaving three men of the Medical Staff Corps as attendants. We were also able to secure the service of Dr. Lovell and of Mr. Hamilton, who both accompanied the column as assistant medical officers.

For the defence of Umtali we left the fifty men of the York and Lancaster regiment, under 2nd Lieut. Middleton, fifty men of the Umtali Rifles, and fifteen men, under Lieut. Fichardt, who had been specially enlisted to work the seven-pounder gun in the court-house laager, and who were called the Umtali Artillery.

The York and Lancaster men were placed in a small fort, which we had constructed, as far away from the hills as possible, and near to the water. The Umtali Volunteers were to laager near the saddle between the hill at the west and that at the east end of the town, over which appeared the most likely way for an attack to come, if it came at all?

The Resident Magistrate was requested to appoint a laager commandant for the court-house, or town laager, and to instruct him to tell off the necessary number of the inhabitants (they were all to go there in case of alarm) for its defence, and when, on the afternoon of the 27th July, Captain Pease, King's Own Yorkshire Light Infantry, who was attached to the detachment West Riding, arrived in command of the fifty of that regiment which I had telegraphed for, I appointed him commandant of Umtali, which then became No. 1 post of the line of communications.

With the arrival of the above detachment the force with which we intended to march on the 28th was complete.

It would be well here to say something about our transport. We had, as already stated, collected with great difficulty forty-five waggons, about one-third being ox, and two-thirds mule; each of these waggons had a team of ten to fourteen animals.

An ox waggon is usually thought to be capable of carrying about 8000 lbs., but our oxen were nearly all infected with the rinderpest, and consequently weak, and they were not expected to do more than this one trip to Salisbury, while, as a matter of fact, all died before reaching there.

The mule waggon can carry about 5000 lbs. Mules travel faster than oxen, in fact too fast for men on foot to keep up with them comfortably, but they are not nearly so sure, especially when the roads are wet, and when they get into difficulties, for instance, when the waggon is stuck in a "drift" (*i.e.* a ford over a river), they often refuse to try any more if they fail to drag it out at the first two or three efforts, while oxen will go on doing their best.

Again, mules require food (mealies) to be

AN AMATEUR ESCORT

carried for them, while oxen will do well on the grass they eat during halts.

In our case, however, it was no question of choice of oxen or mules, it was simply a case of taking *every span of both which we could lay hands on*. Mr. H. C. Deary, a member of the well-known (in Mashonaland) firm of Deary & Co., had a private ox waggon at Umtali, and he, with some ten other business men of Salisbury, asked permission to accompany us. To this I consented, provided they did their share of the work as regards laager guards, etc. Under these conditions they marched with us, and right well they kept to them. I told them off as permanent escort to Townsend's guns, beside which they always marched.

CHAPTER V

MAKONI'S AND THE DEVIL'S PASS

THE Mashonaland Field Force Order No. 9 of the 27th July, was as follows:

Advance and Order of March.

9. The force will be in readiness to march at 10 A.M. to-morrow. The march will be in the following order:

Honey's Scouts. Two sections of the Rifle company Mounted Infantry.

The advanced guard, strength as per margin, under Captain Jenner, D.S.O. Mounted Infantry.

The remainder of the Rifle company Mounted Infantry, with one machine gun.

The main body of the Royal Engineers.

The detachment Royal Artillery, with the two seven-pounder guns, and Mr. Deary's party as escort.

Twenty-three waggons (in the order to be detailed by the transport officer).

The detachment West Riding regiment.

The unmounted portion of the Umtali Rifles.

Twenty-two waggons.

A party of the Royal Engineers under an officer, with tools likely to be useful in repairing broken-down waggons. The

ORDERS

strength of this party to be detailed by the officer commanding Royal Engineers.

Two sections of the Irish company Mounted Infantry with one machine gun.

Two sections of the Irish company Mounted Infantry. The mounted portion of the Umtali Rifles. The rear guard, strength as per margin, under Captain Sir H. McMahon, Bart., Mounted Infantry.

The officer commanding the Rifle company Mounted Infantry will detail the right flank guard, and the officer commanding the Irish company Mounted Infantry, the left flank guard. The strength of these guards will be notified later.

During the first portion of the march laager will be formed, and units shown their places in it.

Where the road permits, the waggons will march in two or more lines, and the troops will conform to their movements.

The mid-day outspan will probably be at the five-mile spruit, and the night one at the Odzi River.

The above order brought the force into the formation shown in the diagram on the next page. The distances between the various bodies necessarily differed according to the ground. Honey's scouts were generally from two to four miles ahead of the advanced guard.

I have gone into this, the order of our first march, fully, because it shows the principle on which we always marched.

The first thing to be guarded against was surprise.

With the formation shown on the next page, surprise was theoretically impossible ; but as theory does not allow for many things, such as peculiarities of ground, of weather, for bad scouting, and, above all, for the vagaries of natives, each party was told that when passing through country in which it could not see and keep touch with the flank guards, it was held responsible for

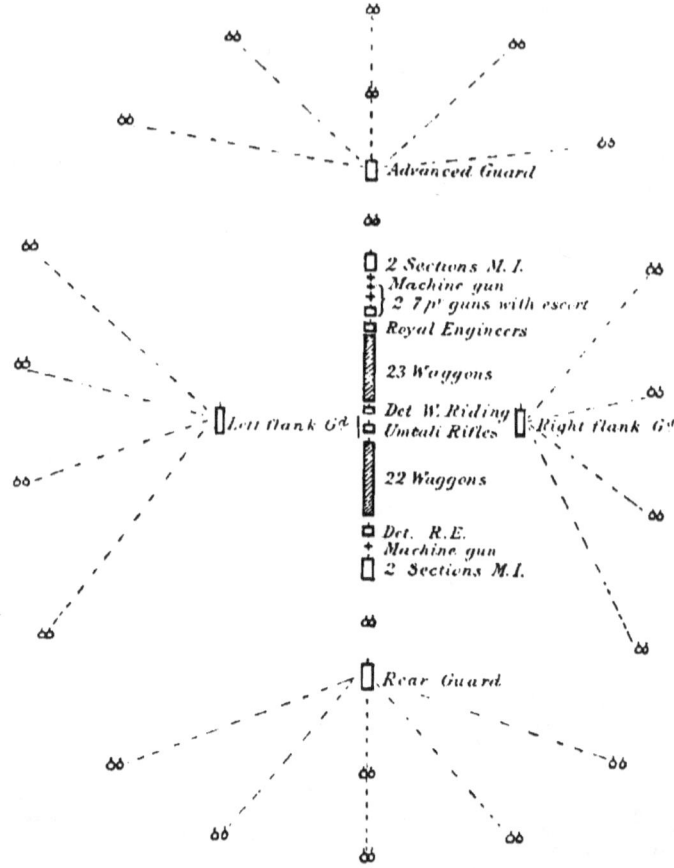

the safety of its own immediate flanks; this rendered surprise, the one thing to be feared from natives, practically impossible.

When in single line and well closed up the

forty-five waggons covered a length of a mile and a half to two miles; and when the inevitable gaps between waggons occurred this was often drawn out to four to five miles. Thus the column was too long for the number of men available to defend it, and therefore very vulnerable to any enterprising and mobile enemy. In deciding how best to defend it, it was necessary to remember that it was no use to scatter the men in a thin line all along it, and thus make them weak everywhere. It then had to be thought, what were the likely points to be attacked. These seemed to be the head and the tail, and perhaps the middle, and these considerations guided me in placing the men as shown in the diagram. Should head or tail be attacked, the middle could reinforce either; should the latter be struck at, both of the former could detach men to its assistance, while any intermediate point could be quickly got at by two out of the three bodies of men.

I had purposely named a late hour for the start, knowing the difficulties attendant on getting such a scratch pack as we had of both men and transport on the move for the first time, and even as it was, it was nearer twelve than ten before the column was clear of Umtali.

The road, or, to speak correctly, waggon track, for it is nothing more, was at that time of year fairly good, though perfectly innocent of macadam and of repairs. It is hard or soft according to the soil it passes over, and when it wears out in one place, waggons, if the nature of the country permits, go a little wide of the old track to the right or left. It thus happens that in some places there are no end of different tracks, and he who does not know the road can only speculate as to which one will be the best. It might be mentioned here, that the only maps we had of the country were on a scale of forty miles to an inch and were very inaccurate.

We outspanned as intended at the five-mile spruit for the mid-day halt, and formed laager for the first time. We had arranged with Mr. Human, our chief waggon conductor, to form a square laager, and this formation we adhered to during the march. But we afterwards found that a diamond-shaped one was by far the most easily and quickly made, and also the most convenient for a force composed as we were.

We reached the Odzi River, on the other side of which we were to outspan for the night, about dusk, but the "drift,"[1] though then shallow, caused so much sticking of our heavily loaded waggons, that it was nine P.M. before we were laagered on the far side. A fine opportunity it would have been for Makoni, or any one else, to attack us in the dark with half our waggons on one side and half on the other; there were, in fact, all the makings of a disaster.

[1] Ford over the river.

That night and thereafter we adopted an outpost system, somewhat as follows.

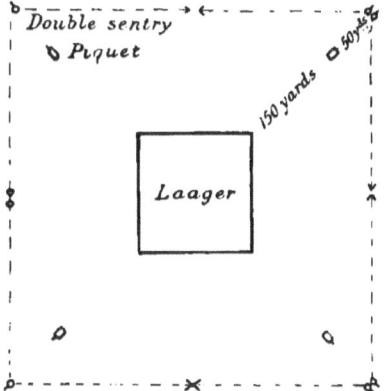

Each guard or piquet consisted of six men and a non-commissioned officer, and found one double sentry; the piquet was 150 to 200 yards from the laager, and the double sentry 40 to 50 yards from the piquet, according to the nature of the ground.

The sentries patrolled alternately right and left, and met the sentries of the other piquets; there was thus a continuous patrol round the laager.

In our square laager of many waggons the men slept inside, and mules and oxen were tied to the dissel-booms (poles) of the waggons.

Each waggon always went to the same place in the laager, and so did all units.

The machine guns and the seven-pounders were placed at alternate corners.

We occasionally put the piquets opposite to

the faces instead of to the corners of the laager, so as to reduce the chances of their being "sneaked" by the enemy, though I doubt *now* if the Mashonas ever even thought of this. Still in war, even with an unenterprising enemy, it does not do to give chances, any more than it does to do so at cricket with feeble bowling, and in my small experience I have seen several good men bowled over simply because their commanders did *not* "play the game."

The next day, July 29th, the "rouse" went at four A.M. and we were off by six.

Having obtained reliable information that Makoni was holding the Devil's Pass, a very bad place on the main road some twenty miles from the Odzi, and having gathered from "Maori" Browne, Mr. Ross, native commissioner of the district, and others with local knowledge, that it would not be advisable to attempt to force this pass with our present big convoy, I decided to move by the road known as O'Reilly's road, which branched off from the main road a few miles beyond the Odzi, turned the pass on the south side, and struck into the main road again near the Nyamatswitswi River, nearly due south of, and about eight miles from, Makoni's.[1]

During the march three lions were seen by the scouts. Evening saw us outspanned at the Rusapi River.

[1] See Sketch on page 86.

THE FIRST SHOTS

The following day we were again off at six A.M., but so bad was the road, and so difficult the drifts, that by eight we had only made two miles. During this afternoon we got in touch with the enemy, and the first shots were fired, much to everyone's delight, for we were somewhat apprehensive of a " walk over." The enemy appeared to be some two to three hundred strong, and were probably 'the right-hand party of the force holding the Devil's Pass.

Honey and his men came in for a good deal of desultory firing, but had no casualties, though Mr. Ross, native commissioner, who was with them, was twice nearly cut off, and only escaped through the cleverness of his pony, who galloped down some very awkward places like a goat.

We laagered that night at the Umfusi River, taking the precaution of burning the long grass all round the laager. To do this safely it is necessary to turn out most of the men, with boughs of trees in their hands; the grass is then lighted on the lee side of the laager and allowed to burn in a strip round it, being kept under control by the men, who beat out the fire where necessary. When the ring round the laager is complete the grass is lighted outside it, and allowed to burn as it likes.

It was the general opinion that we should be fired into during the night, but we were left in peace.

On the 31st we were off at daybreak and

reached the Inyampombere River, where we outspanned, in the evening, having seen nothing of the enemy. "Maori" Browne was very anxious to go off that morning and try to find the party who had fired at us the day before; but I did not wish to use up men and horses in useless skirmishes, and also thought that the party holding the Devil's Pass would be sure to retire when we got on the main road in their rear.

Near our outspan was Meziti's kraal, and there we found a considerable number of bags of mealies which belonged to a Mr. Clayton, and which Meziti, who had remained loyal, had faithfully taken care of. The scouts had unfortunately fired at Meziti's men by mistake, and the latter had all taken to the rocks, where they sat in clusters watching us, and looking like so many ravens.

Mr. Taberer, chief native commissioner (an old Oxford and Essex county cricketer), went to explain matters, but they would not come down. It was near here that Makoni and Umtassa had, what they called, a desperate pitched battle a few years ago, the casualties being two wounded on one side and one on the other!

During the next day (1st August) three very bad drifts delayed us and tired the animals so much that we were obliged to halt at one P.M. at Nyarota, near which we burnt some deserted kraals, and several men made themselves ill from eating too many monkey nuts.

A CONFERENCE

On the 2nd August we struck the main road again near the Nyamatswitswi River about eleven A.M., and laagered near the four or five huts locally known as the "new police huts." On the way we passed under, and tapped, the Umtali-Salisbury telegraph wire, but got no results.

During the afternoon I had a conference with Messrs. Taberer and Ross, and others with local knowledge, and afterwards decided to make a night march on Makoni and attack him at daybreak the following morning. Mr. Ross, who had been to Makoni's kraal before, undertook with the help of his two native boys to act as guide.

Nothing was given out about the night march, as, for all we knew, there might be some among the Native Contingent, or the native drivers, who would go off and warn Makoni. All necessary preparations, such as the improvision of scaling ladders, etc., by the Engineers, were done as quietly as possible. The only order issued was as follows:

"The two companies Mounted Infantry with one maxim, two officers and twenty non-commissioned officers and men Royal Engineers, all the detachment Royal Artillery, with the two seven-pounder guns, Mr. Honey's scouts, forty of the Umtali Rifles, all the Native Contingent, and a proportion of the Medical Staff Corps, will parade at 1.45 A.M. to-morrow. All will be dismounted except the scouts. The Mounted Infantry will carry 140 rounds of ammunition per rifle, the remainder 100 rounds.

"The day's rations will be carried in haversacks, and water bottles will be filled with cold tea. Reveille to-morrow will be at 5.30 A.M. Breakfasts at six A.M."

There is an air of "business" in the above order to a soldier, in the same way that there is to an old hunter when his master appears in the morning wearing a pink coat. The last paragraph, which orders reveille at 5.30 A.M. and breakfasts at six, when parade is at 1.45 A.M. may appear odd; but it was put in for the force remaining to guard the laager (which consisted of the detachment West Riding regiment, the balance of the Engineers, and of the Umtali Rifles), and also partly as a blind, the bugle-calls being duly sounded at the hours named, so that any lurking Mashona might think that things in the laager were going on just as usual.

No bugle-calls were sounded at or before 1.45 A.M., and the men composing the force which was to make the march to Makoni's got up, and fell in, as silently as possible.

Night marching, even at peace manœuvres, is always anxious work, and one sees men get quite excited over it in the Long Valley, when success or failure to be up to time, or to hit the right point, means so little. It can therefore easily be imagined how the anxiety increases in ratio in an unknown and rough country, and when failure may mean the escape of the enemy, or perhaps the loss of many lives.

The units composing the force were ordered to rendezvous some little distance from the laager, and as quietly as they could. There they were formed up as closely as possible, and I explained to them what the object of the parade was, and how it was proposed to carry it out, it being most important that every single man should know this. I concluded with the remark that this being Bank holiday (it was the first Monday in August) I was going to give them the best day out they ever had in their lives! When men are engaged in a serious undertaking, like a night march, and are going, as most of them were, to be under fire for the first time in their lives, it is good to give them something else to think about; and it is good also for the Commander to try and give them the impression that he does not think the enterprise on which they are about to start is a difficult one. I hoped that the reference to Bank holiday might tend to do this.

It was a little after two A.M. when we commenced the march in the order shown in the diagram on page 84.

Mr. Ross's opinion was that we should be discovered on nearing the kraal, and that the enemy would then come out and attack us, and, as neither he, nor any one else, could give me any idea of what their tactics would be, I considered that it was advisable that we should be able to form square quickly in case of a

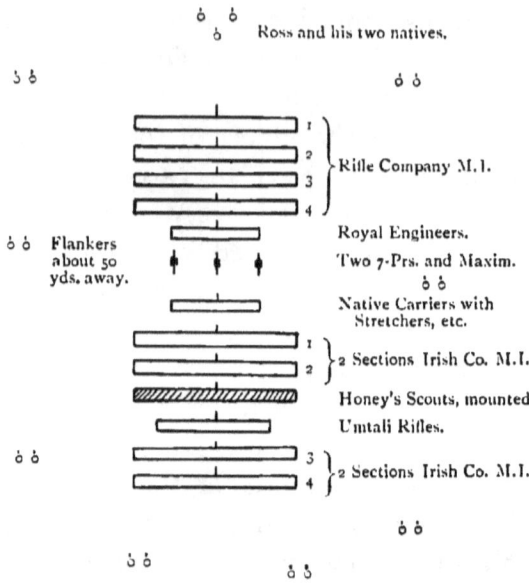

sudden rush in the dark. The march formation shown above lent itself readily to this, and square could be formed very quickly, as shown on page 85.

To those who knew the "miserable" Mashona of barely a month previous to that date, to think of forming square may appear absurd, but, as I have already said, I had seen before *non* "playing of the game" result in needless loss of men, and, moreover, the very men who had previously been used to talking of taking Mashona kraals with a

THE RESULT OF A DETOUR 85

"sjambok and a box of matches," now impressed upon me the necessity of caution.

Makoni had placed a piquet on the top of a rock underneath which the direct track from near our laager to his kraal ran; this necessitated us making a considerable detour, which entailed the passing over of a good deal of rough ground, and

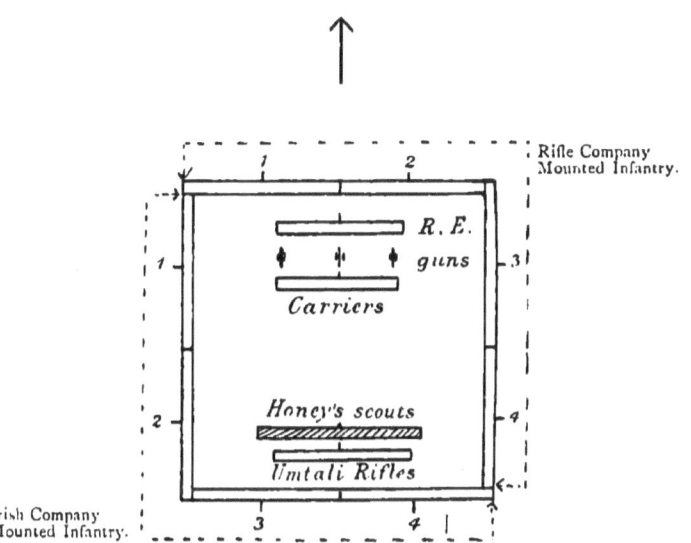

of many mealie and rice gardens; over these the guns had some difficulty in keeping up. The sketch map on the next page shows the direction of our march from Umtali to the Nyamatswitswi, and also of that from the laager to Makoni's.

The night was fine, with sufficient moon to enable us to pick our way, but not enough to

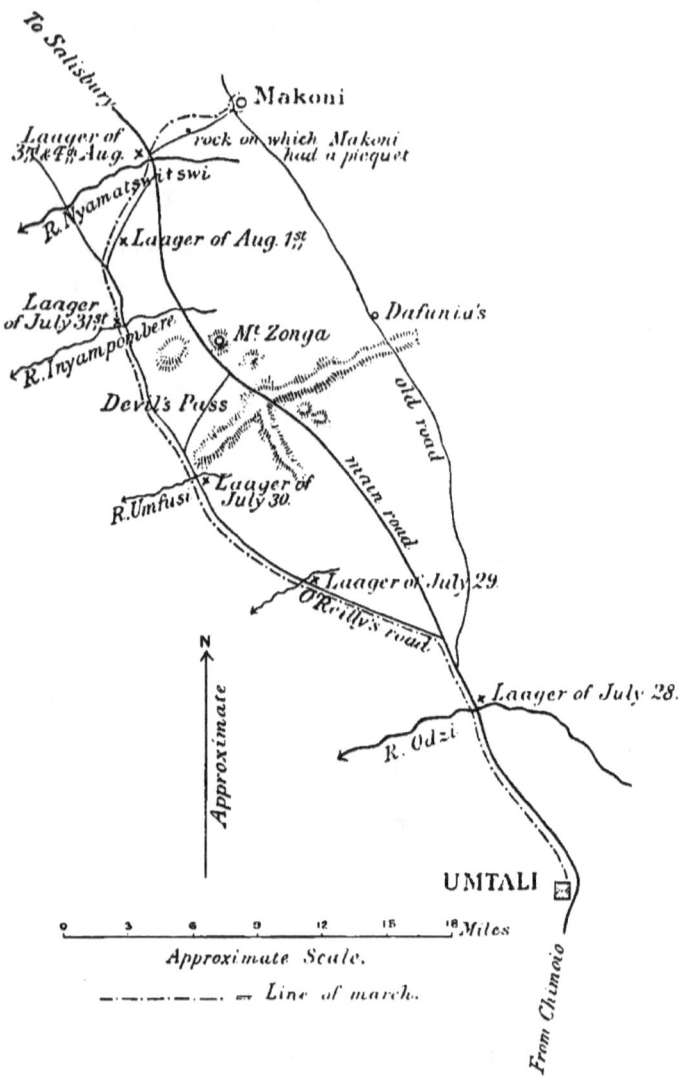

show us to the enemy any distance off. What wind there was luckily blew *from* Makoni's.

The first hour or so passed uneventfully, with only occasional halts to let the force close up. But presently we got among the mealie gardens, and had to cross a small stream or two, and it was then that I saw that we had made a mistake in only having two mules, instead of four, in each seven-pounder and machine gun, as halts to let these come up became very frequent, and I began to be afraid that daylight would be on us before we reached the kraal.

About 5.15 A.M., when the sticking of the guns was at its worst, Mr. Ross told me that he was afraid that he had miscalculated the distance, and that we were still two miles instead of one away from the kraal, and that we could not be there before daylight. This meant no surprise, the loss of the great moral effect which it has, and either the escape of the enemy and his cattle, or greater loss to us in taking the kraal. Our thoughts (Jenner's, Godley's, and mine) were not cheerful, but we kept our own counsel, and pushed on, hoping for the best.

A few minutes afterwards Mr. Ross again came back and said it was all right, he had recognized his surroundings, and we were at the point marked X on the plan shown on page 88.

It was at this point that I had decided, judging from Mr. Ross's description of the kraal and the lie of the ground round it, to divide the force into two parties, sending Jenner with the Rifle company Mounted Infantry, the Umtali Rifles, and a machine gun to the south side, and going myself with the Irish company Mounted Infantry, the Engineers, and the seven-pounders, to the north-west side. Jenner had a shorter distance to go, but he was not to come into action until he heard the seven-pounders open fire. This would ensure the attacks being simultaneous.

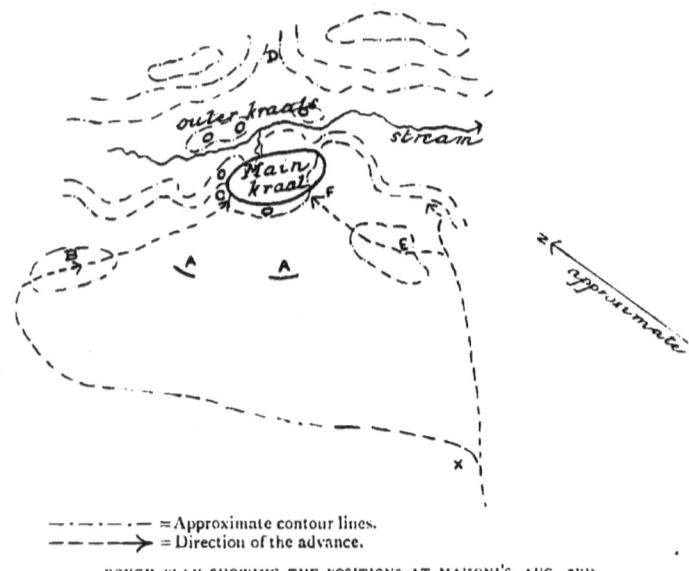

—·—·— = Approximate contour lines.
———▶ = Direction of the advance.

ROUGH PLAN SHOWING THE POSITIONS AT MAKONI'S, AUG. 3RD.

After leaving Jenner, we (*i.e.* my portion of the force) moved cautiously along the west side of the kraal, within perhaps half a mile of it, following the line indicated on the plan.

While doing this we distinctly heard sounds of singing, the remains apparently of the big beer

AN INTERRUPTED FEAST 89

drink, which, as we afterwards heard, had taken place the night before. To this singing, and also to the fact that we were down wind of them, may be due the fact that the Mashonas on duty in the shelter-trenches, along *A, A*, did not hear us moving round them. Perhaps, however, they also had had their share of beer, and were asleep. At 5.50, just as the grey of dawn was turning into the light of day, we arrived at the point marked *B* in the plan. This was the point from which Mr. Ross had told me that we could to some extent command the kraal, and we found that his information was correct.

It *was* an exciting moment. There, some 800 yards from, and slightly below us, lay the kraal, just beginning to show its ragged outline through the mists of dawn. Several fires were burning in it, and round these, judging by the sound of the singing, were grouped the last revellers of the night before. What a feast they had! Oceans of kaffir beer, and unlimited beef of stolen cattle, to make them strong and brave to fight the hated white man, who would not, as Makoni thought and told them, be there before noon the next day.

But it is getting light. "Bring up the guns!" Up they come. "Action front" (in a whisper). "Mr. Townsend, lay No. 1 on the centre of that big white rock in the middle of the kraal, and No. 2 on the huts to the left of it." "No. 1, fire!" "Bang!" goes No. 1 ; "screech, screech," goes its shell; then "boom"; we hear it burst, and we see it star, exactly where intended (see freehand sketch at page 92). A second after, "bang" goes No. 2, and its shell bursts in and sets fire to the huts at which it was aimed. "Well done, indeed, the gunners."

"My w-a-y!" "My w-a-y!" (this, of which more anon, is what the Mashona expression indicative of extreme surprise sounds like) scream the revellers; then "Tom-tom, tom-tom, tom, tom-a-tom tom," go the war drums; out go the fires; in run the careless and sleepy outlying piquets, and in a minute the whole kraal is like a stirred up ants' nest. Another minute, and "bang," "bang" go the rifles, and "ping," "ping" come the bullets at us from its outer walls.

The surprise is very complete. "Well done, Mr. Ross, to have guided us so well."

It may be asked, why did not we rush the place at once instead of stirring them up first? Had I to attack it again, knowing it as well as I do now, I would do this. At the time there were no means of knowing what either the outer or the inner defences were like, and I did not think it desirable to run the risk of having men jammed up against an unclimbable wall, or an impassable chasm, in the dark, especially as we had no idea how many of the enemy were in the place. (We afterwards heard that Makoni had about 1200 men there.)

A few more rounds from the guns, and then we

COOL GUNNERS

begin, with the Irish company and the Engineers, to work up to the corner marked *C* on the plan.

It is soon evident that some at least of the enemy can shoot fairly straight. The guns came in for a good deal of their attention, and are repeatedly hit; in spite of this Townsend and his small detachment continued to work them coolly and effectively. Presently the Royal Irish section of the Irish company Mounted Infantry get a man bowled over; this causes most of the men to make better use of the thickly strewn boulders as cover than they had done before. It also causes the Native Contingent, some of whom are with us, to be considerably exercised in their minds. With some of them this takes the form of firing off their rifles anyhow and anywhere; but, as they are behind us, this has to be at once suppressed; others literally flatten themselves behind the nearest rock. One I saw doing this behind a case of shells! which he and others had been carrying. One and all begin to jabber, the burden of it being apparently what they will do to the Mashona when they catch him. This, though not as bad as the rifle firing over our heads, is a nuisance, and it also is suppressed.

We gradually work closer to the corner that we mean to get in at. In doing this the Royal Irish section, under French, have to cross a considerable piece of open ground, in moving from cover to cover, and very gallantly they follow him over it under a brisk fire, luckily only getting one man hit.

About this time we hear Jenner's Maxim at it on the other side, and we see a good many natives crossing the valley below the kraal and moving up the gorge shown in the freehand sketch, and marked D on the plan on page 88. Are they running away, or are they contemplating a counter-attack on our left flank? We cannot tell, but "let them have it" to hasten their movements in any case.

About 7.30 we got as close to our corner as the cover would allow us, and there remained some 200 yards of open ground between us and the wall, which was still obstinately held. I had by this time seen that the wall could be scaled, and that there was apparently no great obstacle inside it, so decided to make a simultaneous rush on it, and sent Godley round to tell Jenner to advance over the slope marked E on the plan. Presently we saw the heads of his men appear, and then, with two sections in the first line and two in support down, they charged with fixed bayonets at the wall about F. Such a pretty sight it was, quite a picture charge in fact. When they got about the same distance from the wall as we were, I gave the order to advance, and at it we went also, getting in at our corner C about the same time as Jenner's men got over the wall at F (see plan).

This was too much for the Mashonas, and,

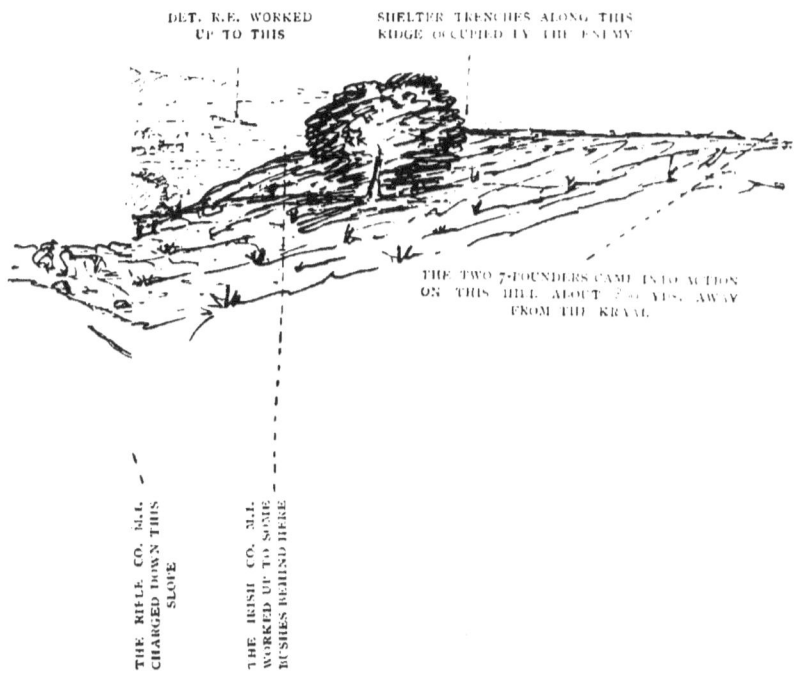

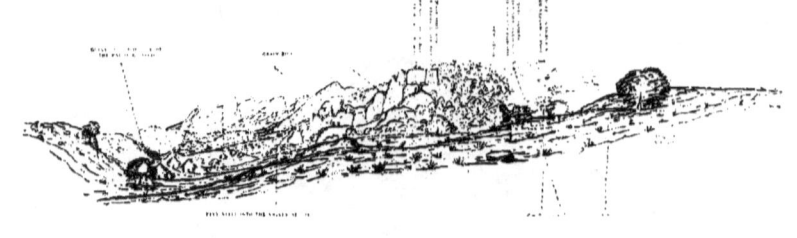

WANTED A FERRET! 93

firing a few hurried shots, the majority bolted for the caves, only one man remaining to be bayoneted. Yet it was hotter work inside than out, and it was in clearing the inner walls and the huts that poor Haynes of the Engineers and Private Vickers of the Rifle company were killed and other men hit. A few minutes of desultory, short range, sort of Jack-in-the-box firing, and the kraal was ours, every live Mashona having gone to ground. This was about 8.30 A.M.

The question now was, how to get them out? Many men volunteered to go into the caves, but I did not consider that I was justified in incurring the loss which must ensue if I let them do so. A white man going from the light of day into the darkness of a cave, about which he knows nothing, is almost entirely at the mercy of the savage, who is as much at home in it as a rabbit in his burrow.

We could not dig them, because it was all solid granite. We were in fact like people out rabbiting without a ferret, and without a spade, when every rabbit has a gun, which he lets off every now and then from some fresh, unexpected, and unseen bolt hole!

Blockade them in and starve them out? Yes, we could do that, though we could not cut off their water, of which a stream issued from what appeared to be one of the main entrances to the caves. But starving meant time, and this was the one thing we dare not spend, because we had no news from Salisbury, and to spend some days at Makoni's might mean starving the inhabitants of the former as well as those of the latter.

Dynamite? Yes, we might *frighten* them with that, but the place was so big, and so rabbit warreney like, that we could not do much damage in the time we could spare. Moreover this seemed an unsoldier-like way, though perhaps the only one, of solving the problem; and at that time, when I had as yet had no experience of the treachery of the Mashona, the idea of using it was repugnant to me.

So, having no time to wait, there was nothing else for it, and, about 2 P.M., we evacuated the kraal, after setting it on fire in several places. When it was completely burnt out, we started on our march back to the laager on the Nyamatswitswi.

Except that we had not captured or killed Makoni, and had failed to bolt his men from the caves, this, the first fight of the Mashonaland Field Force, was very satisfactory. We had walked into and destroyed the kraal of the biggest Chief in Mashonaland, inflicted on him a loss of some two hundred men, including his principal witch doctor and ten of his counsellors, made him go to ground like a rabbit, and, greatest blow of all, had captured 355 head of his cattle, and 210 goats and sheep, while barely 50 head had got away. The surprise had prevented the enemy from driving his cattle into the hills,

AN IRREPARABLE LOSS

and they had been "rounded up" during the fighting, by Honey's men, an American named Fielder being responsible for the largest share. Our casualties were as follows:

Killed.—Captain A. E. Haynes, Royal Engineers; No. 5231, Private W. Wickham, Royal Irish regiment; No. 8075, Private S. Vickers, 3rd Battalion King's Royal Rifles, both serving with the Mounted Infantry.

Severely Wounded.—No. 4231, Private W. Mackey, Royal Irish regiment; No. 7825, Private R. Broad, 2nd Battalion Rifle Brigade, both serving with the Mounted Infantry; Trooper D. Young, Umtali Rifles.

Slightly Wounded.—No. 7256, Private H. Lock, 3rd Battalion King's Royal Rifles, serving with the Mounted Infantry.

Poor little Haynes was, as I have already said, killed inside the kraal (about where shown in the freehand sketch), after having gallantly led his men over the wall. In him we had suffered an irreparable loss. With his bright keenness, his fertile brain, and ready resource, he had already made himself invaluable. Apart from his professional value to me, I never met a man whom I grew to like so much in so short a time. Both the privates we had had killed were good useful men, whose loss we could ill afford.

I am afraid that the wounded had a very bad time of it going back over the rough track in the improvised ambulance, which we had sent to the laager for.

We arrived back at the laager just before dusk, and found that the men left there had made good progress with the building of the fort which was to be established there, and which poor Haynes had designed the previous day. This fort was naturally christened "Fort Haynes."

As we had four wounded, and three seriously sick, men, it was now necessary to establish a hospital as well as a fort. For that purpose we used the empty police huts, and made the men as comfortable as was possible under the circumstances. I placed Dr. Lovell in charge of this hospital, leaving some Army Hospital Corps men with him, and I consider that it is much to his credit that both sick and wounded (the latter included an amputation) made good and rapid recoveries.

The following morning, August 4th, I went off soon after daybreak with a Mounted Infantry company, the Scouts, and a few Engineers, the latter in an empty mule waggon, to reconnoitre the Devil's Pass, and to mend the telegraph wire.

We found that the Pass had been evacuated by the enemy, apparently on the day in which we turned it on the south. Judging by numbers of the schances (small stone walls) and scherms (bush shelters) erected there, it had been held by some 500 men.

Below the Pass we found the wire cut in two places; the poles, which were all very rotten, had been knocked down, and the wire then hacked in two by battle-axes.

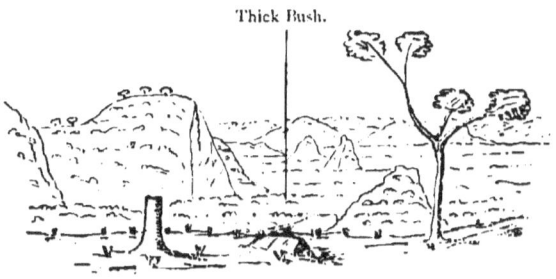

LOOKING SOUTH-SOUTH-EAST FROM THE DEVIL'S PASS.

The Engineers joined the wire and put up the poles; we then tapped it and got communication with Umtali, whose inhabitants were delighted to hear of Makoni's defeat.

LOOKING NORTH FROM THE TOP OF THE DEVIL'S PASS.

I telegraphed down to Umtali reports of the action, to be sent on, on the first opportunity, to the High Commissioner and to the Chief Staff Officer at Buluwayo. While I received a message from the latter (which had been waiting at

G

Umtali) that it was important to get supplies up to Salisbury as soon as possible.

On the way back we burnt several kraals, including the one shown below. This is very typical of the bulk of the Mashona kraals.

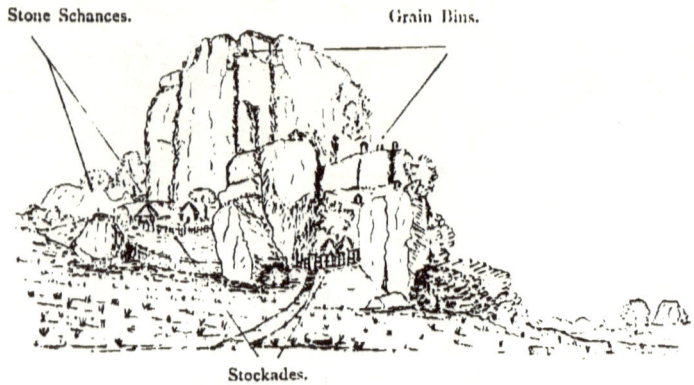

KRAAL, NEAR THE DEVIL'S PASS, BURNT AUGUST 4TH.

We did not get back to the laager till 9.30 P.M. During the day poor Haynes and the two men of the Mounted Infantry, killed, had been buried in a well-chosen site under two spreading trees, about a quarter of a mile from Fort Haynes. We found that the friendly Chief Dafunya had visited the laager while we were away; he informed Godley that Makoni had thought that our avoidance of the Devil's Pass meant that we were afraid to attack him.

CHAPTER VI

FROM THE CHIMBI RIVER TO MARANDELLAS

ON the 5th we made a short march to the Chimbi River, leaving the fifty men of the West Riding regiment, and ten of the Umtali Rifles, the whole under Lieut. P. Coode, West Riding regiment, as a garrison for the fort, which formed No. 2 post on the line of communications.

At the Chimbi we found Chipunza, a friendly chief (at any rate now!), who stated that he had been a prisoner at Makoni's during our attack, and that so demoralized were Makoni's men, that they had allowed him to walk out and away the next day.

Chipunza put their loss at 200 killed and many wounded, and said that many ran into the caves with "small holes in them," and afterwards died, alluding no doubt to the Lee-Metford bullet wounds. He also stated that Makoni had not spoken since the fight.

If the British South Africa Company have got nothing else in Mashonaland, they certainly have a country which in many places is most beautiful. The Chimbi, where the main road crosses it, is one of these places. Here is a grand rippling stream, varying in width from ten to fifty yards, now running shallow over a smooth rocky bed, now with still deep pools, and anon tumbling down several feet over a rocky fall. Such trouty-looking places it has too. Where the road crosses the stream, there is, in the dry season, a natural bridge of rock, the water disappearing on one side of the road and coming out again on the other in a low fall,—a grand place the latter is to bathe under.

On the banks all round are trees of various sorts and shades of green, with here and there open blades of grass. Take away the Mashona, the locust, the rinderpest, the horse sickness, and the fever, which might come in the rainy season (and no doubt the railway will take away many of them), and you have an ideal place in which to build a house.

The next day, after trekking some ten miles, which brought us nearly to Lone Kop, we met Major Watts' column, which had been sent from Buluwayo, *via* Charter and Marandellas, to assist in forming posts on the Umtali-Salisbury road, while Watts himself was to command the line of communications. This column consisted of 100 men detached from the Matabeleland Relief Force. (This force, raised, organized, and commanded by Lieut.-Colonel Plumer, did excellent work in Matabeleland.) Our meeting was rather funny: Watts had been attacked when among the kopjes on the Charter side of Marandellas, had had several men and horses wounded, and had been stopped for some time, and so was of course very much on the lookout for further attacks. It so happened that our scouts when first sighted were engaged in filling their nose bags with grain from a deserted kraal, just on what was the sky line to Watts' scouts. The latter thought they were the enemy, and reported to this effect to Watts. He, naturally, at once halted his waggons, put his men in battle array, and then advanced cautiously with a reconnoitring party, and was coming up the hill with his men extended behind him, as I cantered over the top to meet him, our scouts having sent back word to me that the column was in sight.

It must have been a pleasant surprise to Watts' small and tired column to find, that instead of exchanging shots with the enemy in a nasty defile, they had to exchange news and congratulations with our column. We had several things to talk about and arrange, so I asked Watts to turn back and laager near us at Headlands that night, which he did.

I found that he had left thirty men at Marandellas; these I thought it would be better to increase to fifty, so asked him to detach twenty more to go on to Marandellas with us, and to take the remaining fifty of his men down to Umtali, so that they might be available to escort the next convoy of supplies up country.

Watts' men were very badly off for boots, clothes, etc., and much needed a refit all round. Among them Godley spotted his young brother, whom he knew had gone to Matabeleland, but had not the least idea that he was with Watts. When he had been washed and clothed in some of his brother's little spare kit, we transferred

HEADLANDS STORE AND TELEGRAPH OFFICE, LOOKING SOUTH.

Trooper Richard Godley from the Matabeleland Relief Force to the Umtali Rifles, in which he was subsequently made a lieutenant, and he acted as one of my gallopers until he took over the charge of the food-issuing stores at Salisbury a few weeks later. He is now Quarter-master of the British South Africa Company's Mashonaland Police.

In the evening we reached Headlands, near which I intended to leave "Maori" Browne and most of the Umtali Rifles, to form No. 3 post on the line of communications.

We laagered in the open some distance away from the store and its surrounding rocks.

Such a mess the Mashonas had made of this store, and the telegraph office; everything smashed in both, battery all to pieces, jars broken, furniture like match-wood, mustard, pepper, salt, flour, etc., and broken bottles strewn all over the place. Here and there articles of clothing—male, female, and children's; the pictures on the walls with assegai holes in them. In fact, every devilish bit of damage possible had been done, and we noted with sorrow that there were no *full* bottles of any sort left! Among the debris I picked up part of a letter, written in a very big, round, childish hand, evidently to a relation who had shortly before gone to England. This might have been pathetic had not the people at the store been able to get away in time.

This Headlands was the place that Mr. Taberer, chief native commissioner in Mashonaland, had been so blamed by a certain section of people in Umtali for retiring from some weeks before. Personally I think he was quite right to abandon the place. He had women and children with him, had very little food, and Umtali could not promise him support if he stayed there. Besides, the store is commanded on three sides by rocks close to it.

There are always people in every community who talk loudly of what they would have done, and what other people should have done, under certain circumstances, after the event, but who forget entirely that the people on the spot had to act at once, knowing perhaps only half of what they now know. These talkers are generally bad actors when it comes to their turn.

Mashonaland has its share of the tribe, and as members of it I placed those who abused Mr. Taberer for abandoning Headlands.

One solitary native was seen perched on the top of the rock behind the store, looking like a sentinel rook, and Honey's men did their best to circumvent and catch him, but he made himself scarce before they got half round him. Watts and some of his officers took pot luck with us that night, and we heard all about their march from Buluwayo. They had been pretty hotly attacked on the Charter side of Marandellas, and for a time apparently, had been practically "stuck up." They had had three men wounded, and three horses killed. As Watts was to assume command of the line of communications, we decided that Umtali would be the best place for his head-quarters, at any rate for the present.

Next morning, August 7th, McMahon, with two sections of his company, started at daybreak to burn a kraal belonging to one Nedwidji, a few miles distant, while we established "Maori" Browne in his laager among a clump of trees about three-quarters of a mile from the store. About mid-day McMahon returned with two loads of oat hay (in South Africa there is no hay proper, and as a substitute oats are cut green and

CHITSA'S KRAAL

stacked). We then resumed our march towards Salisbury, and Watts his towards Umtali. That night we halted at a somewhat dreary-looking spot called Black Vley.

During the next morning's march I took two sections of the Rifle company Mounted Infantry and one of the seven-pounder guns, to visit Chitsa's kraal, which lay about two miles to the south of the road.

In the distance this kraal looked very much like the mediæval castle, thus:

CHITSA'S IN THE DISTANCE.

On nearing it we saw the usual Mashona look-outs perched on the top, and treated them to a few shells. One section then worked round to the right of the ridge *A* to get at the back of the kraal, and the other went straight up at *B*.

On arriving at the top of the ridge the castle resolved itself into what is shown on page 106. And very formidable it looked. The ground went down almost sheer into the plain on three sides, while on the fourth was the narrow approach shown in the sketch.

However, the riflemen were not to be denied, and were very soon creeping along the slippery sloping rock at *C*. This brought them to the entrance, which was so strongly barricaded with logs of wood that they were some time getting in. There was practically no opposition, a few shots only being fired from the caves.

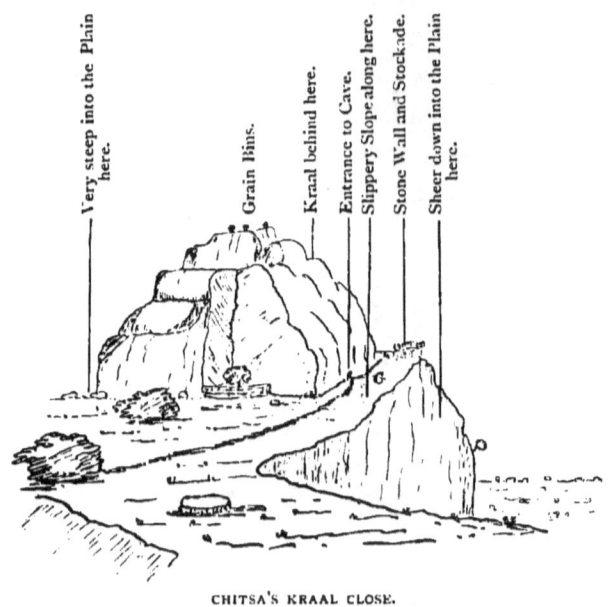

CHITSA'S KRAAL CLOSE.

I sat down on the rock in front and made the sketch while the kraal was being burnt. We (Godley, Nicholls, and myself) then cantered on and caught up the column at the Machecci River, where they had outspanned.

Here the Engineers mended the telegraph wire, tapped it, and we at last got communication with Salisbury, and learnt that, though food supplies were none too plentiful, they were in no danger of starving. A pity we did not know this before we left Makoni's?

That afternoon we met a small column under Captain Nesbitt, V.C., of the Mashonaland Mounted Police, coming down from Salisbury with a view to mend the telegraph wire. As we had already done this, I directed Captain Nesbitt to turn about and get back to Salisbury as quickly as possible, sending with him the bulk of the cattle captured at Makoni's, and some waggon loads of flour.

That night we were at Botha's farm, and again in very pretty country. Close to the road on the north side are high, rocky, well-wooded kopjes; on the south, the park-like land falls gently to the stream, then rises again, and on its skyline, two to three miles away, are high fantastic-looking granite kopjes.

Many doves and pigeons flutter about and coo in the trees. In fact, the country, like that near the Chimbi, verges on the ideal; but again the Mashona spoils it for the white man—the peaceable white man I mean—in the same way as I am afraid we spoil it for the doves, many of which found their way into our cooking pot that night. For it was from these same pretty-looking kopjes that Watts had been heavily fired at only a few days ago, and, on looking closely at them, one saw the schances erected for this purpose among the rocks. It was indeed a case of "only man is vile."

Much to our disgust, however, the blackbirds, of which we were in quest rather than the grey doves, had all flown.

On August 9th we reached Marandellas at sunset. During the march I climbed to the top of an outcrop of smooth grey rock, some ten miles from Marandellas, and got an excellent view of the country right up to that place. This is what I saw.

LOOKING NORTH-WEST FROM THE TOP OF A ROCK ABOUT TEN MILES EAST OF MARANDELLAS.

At Marandellas we again communicated with Salisbury, and learnt that as there was no grain in store there, Judge Vintcent would be glad if we visited Gatzi's, Mangwendi's, and other kraals near Marandellas, and collected as much grain as possible before going on.

In accordance with these wishes I marched for Gatzi's the next day (August 10), with the bulk of the Mounted Infantry, some of the Royal Engineers, the two seven-pounders, and part of the Native Contingent, taking eight empty mule waggons, which we hoped to fill with grain.

GATZI'S KRAAL

Barnes asked to be allowed to accompany us, and, as the collection of grain came within his province, I, after some hesitation, consented to his doing so. On several occasions I have seen men, who have accompanied troops, when it was not part of their duty to do so, as volunteers in fact, come to grief, and this made me hesitate before giving my consent to Barnes' coming, but the grain question turned the scale in his favour. What little things guide our destinies!

Marching at seven A.M. we reached Gatzi's about eleven. After reconnoitring, without seeing a sign of the enemy, I decided to attack it on two sides, keeping the reserve opposite to the third.

The kraal was more in the open, and appeared less capable of being defended than any we had yet seen, and events proved that this was also the opinion of Gatzi and Co.

McMahon with the Irish company Mounted Infantry took the south side, Jenner with the Rifle company the north, while I with the remainder of the force took the east.

Some of the Native Contingent, with McMahon, got close on to the wall before being seen; the enemy then commenced a conversation with them, saying that they didn't want to fight, and had done no harm, etc. (Makoni's defeat was already bearing fruit.) I am inclined to think that these natives would have come out and "indabaed," (*i.e.* talked), had not the Irish company suddenly appeared behind the Native Contingent. This made them go to ground like rabbits, exclaiming that "The white man must want to kill them all or he would not have come in such numbers." Still no shots were fired, and we walked into and quietly occupied the kraal.

One native, who had been working in a mealie garden near by, was captured, and we made use of him as a "go-between" with those who had gone under ground. Finding what seemed to be one of the main entrances to the caves, we tied this gentleman's hands behind his back, put a rope round his waist, and lowered him down to talk with Gatzi, keeping a sharp look-out that none of the inmates of the cave ran up to him with a knife to cut the rope.

A queer scene it was. There were some half a dozen officers, and a few men, grouped round the mouth of the cave, taking very good care however to keep out of the line of fire from it. Two non-commissioned officers holding a rope and *feeling* (as though sea fishing with a hand-line), as it were, the movements of the native at the end of it, who could just be discerned in the gloom of the cave. Two men with rifles at the ready, as if they were snipe shooting, in case there should be any attempt at rescue. Down into the cave the prisoner was shouting "Gatz-i-weer," and telling that gentleman that if he came out he would not be hurt, and that we wanted to

THE FAMILY GUN

talk to him, etc. From what seemed to be a long way down in the cave came the faint sounds of an answer, which was, according to our prisoner, to the effect that "Gatz-i-weer" was afraid we should kill him if he came out. We were just beginning to get tired of this conversation, when "boom" we heard a "family gun" go, lower down in the kraal.

When once you have heard it, there is no mistaking the sound of the "family gun," which is sometimes an old-fashioned large bore elephant gun, but generally an old tower musket, sometimes with a flint lock. I picked up one at Makoni's marked "42nd Regiment" as well as "Tower"; perhaps this was at Waterloo? Out of these the Mashonas fire anything they can lay their hands on—pot legs, bits of iron, telegraph wire, nails, bits of brass taps, etc. off machinery (one of these went fairly close to McMahon on one occasion), stones, stoppers and necks of glass bottles, and home-made bullets of all sorts. (A man of the local forces, who was hit some weeks later, had the stopper of a Worcester sauce bottle cut out of his cheek!)

As a rule a "family gun" is fired at close range; sometimes it is shoved out through an unnoticed crack in the rock, and almost touches those it is fired at. Thus its "boom" often meant a man hit, and this fact made one quite dread the sound, though our men would only say, "Hurrah! there goes a family gun."

In the present instance, however, we did not pay much attention, because we were at the time actually parleying with the enemy; it was therefore all the greater shock, when Taberer came up a few minutes afterwards, and said, "Barnes has been shot dead."

It seems that poor Barnes had been walking round the kraal, on the look-out for grain, and whilst doing so had incautiously looked into the mouth of a cave, with the result that he was shot in the chest and died in a few minutes.

After this act of treachery it is small wonder that the men longed to "get at" the Mashona. But this was just the one thing we did not seem able to do. Solid rock makes a man pretty safe, and underneath this the Mashonas were. Having told "Gatz-i-weer" through our prisoner, that we should make it very unpleasant for him if he did not come out, we tried burning some sulphur, which we lowered in a bag into the mouth of the cave. But, although the smoke came out of various holes all round the kraal, the Mashonas stopped in, and in we left them, after thoroughly demolishing and burning the kraal.

I am afraid that this time they had the best of it; we had one wretched prisoner, and had burnt their kraal, while they had killed a valuable and hard-working officer.

That night we laagered just outside the kraal, and next morning, after having relighted any undestroyed portions of it, we moved on to Mangwendi's. We arrived there about midday, and found it a most formidable looking place, three sides of it being quite inaccessible.

I sent the Native Contingent to reconnoitre the fourth side, or back, and they returned with the news that the kraal was occupied.

MANGWENDI'S KRAAL.

We then shelled it, and after this the Irish company Mounted Infantry went over the ridge *A* to attack the back, while we continued to show a force in front. As local report said that this kraal had no caves, we thought we were bound to give the Mashonas a lesson this time. But we reckoned without our host, for the Irish company walked in, and found no one there, except a dog or two, and a few pigs! while among the inanimate articles found was a large Portuguese flag. It seems that the Native Contingent had borne poor Barnes' death in mind, and had not gone very near to the place when reconnoitring it; and seeing the gate shut,

H

and hearing a dog bark inside, had come to the conclusion that it was strongly held.

The worst part of it was that nearly all the grain in this, and the numerous other kraals which we took and burnt on the way back to Marandellas, had been taken away and hidden. Very tired and sad, we reached Marandellas about 9.30 P.M.

Both men and animals having had two very hard days' work, August 12th was made an off day. Men rested, and had an "altogether" wash, for the second time only since leaving Umtali; while animals grazed.

We buried poor Barnes in the morning, and in the afternoon took stock of our food and grain; the latter we found only amounted to seven days' supply, and the animals were put on half rations at once. It was this day that I had another lesson as to the necessity of always "playing the game." We were on the end of a high plateau, the highest ground in Mashonaland in fact, and in front of and below us we could see the Salisbury road winding its way across the veldt; between us and this plain ran two streams. We should, on an ordinary day, have had vedettes on the plain across these streams; in fact, I had given orders for them to be placed there. It was however represented to me that the horses badly required rest and grazing, and I reluctantly consented to have dismounted men on the plateau, instead of mounted ones in the plain.

In the afternoon, while the men were bathing and washing in the stream, a party of Mashonas crossed this plain; had we had our vedettes there they would have been seen, and we should have got notice at once, and probably been able to capture them. As it was, by the time we got the news in the laager the Mashonas had disappeared and it was too late. Had they had any enterprise, they would have had a fine chance of cutting off some of the half a dozen officers who were bathing some way down the stream. One of these, French I think, fired off the contents of his revolver while standing, *in puris naturalibus*, in the water, with a view to keeping the Mashonas away while he dressed, much as a boy scares rooks!

CHAPTER VII

SALISBURY, AND THE SITUATION GENERALLY

AS Judge Vintcent expressed a wish, in a telegram, for me to get to Salisbury as soon as possible, I decided to start the next day (August 13th), taking Godley, Nicholls, Roach, and an escort of two Mounted Infantry sections under St. Aubyn and King-Harman with me; as transport we took four mule waggons and the coach, with the mails in it.

I handed over the command of the column to Jenner, giving him instructions to destroy all the kraals round Marandellas, collect as much grain and oat hay as possible, and then come on to Salisbury.

We marched early, outspanned at Turk's, and then trekked on to Graham and White's. When nearing the latter, St. Aubyn spotted, what we made out to be cattle, being driven along on the horizon. I sent him after them with part of his section, but much to our disappointment, as we thought we had got a prize, they turned out to be the oxen belonging to Lieut.-Colonel

Beal's convoy, which was coming down from Salisbury to Umtali to load with food stuffs, and which had just outspanned. Beal himself was going down to take over the control of all the supply and transport arrangements for the company.

With this convoy was Judge Vintcent, who had come down for a change and to meet us. I was very pleased to meet him, and we had a long talk over things in general.

The next day both parties were off early, we up, and Beal down. The Judge transferred his kit to our waggons, and turned back with us.

We all found it a great treat to be travelling with only four waggons instead of forty-five; nothing to think about, no anxiety about breakdowns and sticks, and no bother about forming laager. During the afternoon, Roach, whom I had sent with a small party to ride along the telegraph line, was fired at by the inhabitants of some kraals about two miles off the road. These we decided to visit the next morning, and accordingly started for them at daybreak with St. Aubyn's section, King-Harman going on with the waggons.

It was quite a treat to see the Judge. He was like a schoolboy out hunting in the holidays at the idea of having a go at the Mashonas. Unfortunately we drew every covert, or rather kraal, blank, though I have no doubt that the owners were watching us from somewhere in the bush, and I hope they liked the bonfires their huts made. In one kraal we found a good deal of loot—wearing apparel, white shirts, gold studs, and also some empty gun cases. We made all this into a bundle and put it on to a spare horse; pretty awkward it was to fix on, and had I not known how to make a diamond hitch, I don't think we should have got it to keep on at all.

I saw this diamond hitch described in *The Field* some two years ago, and, thinking it might some day come in useful on service, I cut the description out, and subsequently learnt to make the hitch, tying trusses of straw on to my hunter. It is an excellent way of fixing any shaped bundle on to a pack, or other saddle, and well worth any soldier taking the trouble to learn. Little did I think, when learning it at Camberley, that I should within eighteen months be using it in Mashonaland.

After burning the kraals, we, under the Judge's guidance, struck across country for Balleyhooley (detaching Roach and St. Aubyn with some men to ride along the telegraph wire). On arriving at the store we found King-Harman already outspanned.

Balleyhooley, which is a sort of Saturday to Monday resort, a Brighton in fact, to Salisbury, is another of Mashonaland's pretty places: it was however very nearly the scene of a double murder. Mr. and Mrs. Orton were living there

THE FIRST VIEW OF SALISBURY

when the rising broke out. One afternoon, when he was on the farm, and she in the store, the Mashonas came down. Both the Ortons appear to have jumped on horses independently and ridden for Salisbury, and both were heavily fired at as they rode, Mr. Orton getting a bullet into the stock of his gun. He reached Salisbury first and reported his wife murdered; she arrived soon after and said that he had been killed.

SALISBURY FROM THE TOP OF BEESA'S.

Mr. Orton was a chemist, and there were evidences of his profession, in the shape of medicated cotton wool, etc., strewn all over the place. He also had a fine collection of guns and rifles, which the Mashonas got.

I was told that the Ortons' claim for compensation amounted to £5,000.

That evening we were at Beesa's kraal some four miles from Salisbury, where we outspanned, and, on climbing to the top of the rock on which the kraal is built, we got the view of the town shown above. From there it did not look unlike Aldershot.

Nicholls rode on into Salisbury, and came back with some champagne in his saddle-bags, so we went in for mutual health drinking. Roach and St. Aubyn turned up late, having lost their way, or rather Roach, who was supposed to be guide, lost it for them; he was nevertheless full of "buck," and claimed to have fixed bayonets, and charged a kraal with seven men during the afternoon. I don't know whether it was that we had had none for some time, or whether the journey to Salisbury had not agreed with that champagne. Anyhow the wine didn't at all agree with us, and we were all decidedly off colour the next morning. This being the case, it was good luck that there was no need to be up so early as usual, and we rode leisurely into Salisbury about eleven. Captain Hon. C. White (late 7th Royal Fusiliers), who had come from Buluwayo to the relief of Salisbury with a detachment of the Buluwayo Field Force, rode out to meet us. Godley and I went into Beal's house, which we found very comfortable. St. Aubyn and King-Harman went with their men to the nursery farm, some two miles out to the north of Salisbury, where there was grazing of sorts to be got.

The following day I took over the command at Salisbury from Commandant General Vintcent, and made the acquaintance of the various local authorities, while Godley and Nicholls fixed up an office in "Leander Buildings" (called so after

MR. JUSTICE VINTCENT'S HOUSE.

ALL THIS PART OF THE TOWN IS CALLED "THE KOPJE."

MR. PAULING'S HOUSE, USED BOTH BY LORD GREY AND MR. RHODES.

THE POST OFFICE.

ALL THIS PART OF THE TOWN IS CALLED "THE CAUSEWAY."

THE CATHEDRAL.

THE GOVERNMENT OFFICES.

THE MARKET HALL.

GAOL, ROUND WHICH THE LAAGER WAS FORMED.

VIEW OF SALISBURY, FROM THE KOPJE.

THE SITUATION AT SALISBURY

Dr. Jameson, whose Christian names are Starr Leander; that there are also "Starr Buildings" in Salisbury goes without saying).

Lieut. (local captain) P. A. Turner, West Riding regiment, who was doing staff officer to the Judge, was put in orders as assistant staff officer to the Mashonaland Field Force, and joined Godley in this office.

We found telegraphic messages, from the General, Lord Grey, and also Colonel Machado, congratulating us on the fight at Makoni's, waiting for us at the post office.

I will not describe Salisbury, but will let the picture facing this page do so for me.

The reader having arrived at the capital, I would ask him or her,—I beg pardon, ladies first!—her or him, to glance at the situation there, and in Mashonaland generally, at this time (August 17th).

As regards Salisbury, the situation, from a military point of view, was better than we expected to find. The town had gone out of laager, and even the outlying houses, some of them a mile and a half from the laager, were being reoccupied; that the Mashonas had not touched one of these says little for their pluck or enterprise, but no doubt they feared a trap.

With the return of Lieut-Colonel Beal's column from Matabeleland, on July 17th, Salisbury had got back its fighting men and its horses. As well as these it had the 60 odd Matabelelanders under

White, making a total of some 230 white men and 150 natives, exclusive of what was then called the Salisbury Garrison, and of the male inhabitants, all of whom bore arms when in the laager.

Since the commencement of the rising on June 16th, and prior to our arrival, August 16th, the parties, or, as they are locally called, "patrols," enumerated in Part I. of Appendix C, had been sent out from Salisbury. This list is well worth looking at, and it would help the reader to grasp the situation at this time if he would look at it now.

It would be tedious to go into the details of all the "patrols" in the list, but the particulars of some are interesting, and in some cases the way in which overwhelming numbers of Mashonas were beaten off can scarcely fail to make the reader proud of being a Briton.

No. 5, on the list above referred to, should I think be taken first, because its commander, Captain R. Nesbitt, Mashonaland Mounted Police, has since been awarded the Victoria Cross for his gallant fight. This patrol left Salisbury on June 19th, with the object of relieving the people in laager at the Alice Mine in the Mazoë valley; its strength was only thirteen, all being volunteers.

A patrol (No. 3) under Mr. Judson, director of telegraphs, had gone to Mazoë some days previously to endeavour to relieve the people there, but had been obliged to join them in the laager. At the entrance to the Mazoë valley Captain Nesbitt met a native runner, bearing a note from Mr. Judson to Judge Vintcent. This note stated that at least a hundred men and a Maxim gun were required to relieve the laager. Captain Nesbitt read the note to his thirteen men, and then asked them to go on to Mazoë with him. This they did, having to fight their way through the valley.

Once in the laager the question was, how to get the three women and the miners out, and back to Salisbury. I have been told that it was very sensibly suggested that it should be attempted at night; but this was unfortunately overruled, and, on the morning of the 20th June, they started, the women being placed in an armour-plated cart. The party had to fight its way all through the valley, the Mashonas creeping up in the long grass and firing at close quarters. In this running fight three men were killed and five wounded, while eight horses were killed and seven wounded.

It says a great deal for the pluck of the little party that they got through the great numbers of the enemy at all.

I am told that Messrs. R. A. Harbord (a scion of the family of which Lord Suffield is the head) and Honey particularly distinguished themselves, and that once, when on advance guard, they were cut off from the party, and might have gone safely on into Salisbury (as one man did), but instead of doing so they turned back to its assistance.

The 4th patrol in the list, that under Captain P. A. Turner, West Riding regiment, is also a noticeable one. Captain Turner was in charge of the forty volunteers from Natal which were on their way to Buluwayo, moving *via* Beira and Charter.

This "Natal Troop," as it was called, left Charter for Buluwayo about the time the rising in Mashonaland broke out. Judge Vintcent then sent a message to request Captain Turner to proceed to punish M'Slopa's natives, who had murdered the people at the Beatrice Mine (see Map).

Captain Turner took and burnt M'Slopa's kraal, and went some eight miles beyond it, towards Hartley. He was then almost surrounded by large numbers of natives, while in a difficult part of the road, and was obliged to retire; one of his waggons sticking in a drift, most of its contents had to be thrown off, under a heavy fire and abandoned. Captain Turner then succeeded in withdrawing his party and took it to Salisbury. His losses were: one white man and two Native Contingent killed, three whites wounded, seven horses and one mule killed, and five horses wounded—quite enough for the size of the party?

No. 17—Mr. A. F. H. Duncan's (Surveyor

JUST IN TIME

General to the Chartered Co., and late Royal Navy) patrol to Abercorn—a difficult and most necessary one, very well carried out—should also be noticed.

Mr. Duncan was on his way back from Buluwayo, where he had been acting administrator. When he arrived at Charter he heard of the state of affairs in Mashonaland, and, with two men as escort, he rode through in the night to Salisbury, (65 miles).

The next day (July 11th) he started with the patrol for the Abercorn mine, over fifty miles to the north. The patrol had two skirmishes on the way there, and found that the Mashonas had made various obstacles on the road, such as cutting down trees, digging away the drifts, and in one instance cutting a deep and broad trench in the road, and covering it up with branches and earth.

This was so well made that it had evidently been engineered by natives who had worked in the mines. There were also at several places empty "bully beef" tins, etc., tied on strings and placed across the road, evidently to give notice of the presence of any one using the road at night. All these obstacles were no doubt intended to prevent the escape of the miners laagered at Abercorn. Happily Mr. Duncan was just in time to save these, six in number; but they were in a bad way, and one subsequently died from exhaustion. They had had nothing to drink for some days but gin and lime juice, the Mashonas holding the nearest water.

No. 19 patrol, under Captain Hon. C. White, succeeded in relieving ten white men who were laagered at Hartley, and in inflicting considerable loss on the enemy; but they were pretty severely handled, as will be seen by their list of casualties, and could not reach Mashangombi's.

Patrols No. 26 and 28 were still out when we arrived at Salisbury. The former, under Major Hoste, Rhodesia Horse, was establishing a Fort in the Mazoë Valley near the Alice Mine; and the latter, under Captain Moberley (of what was then called the Salisbury Field Force, and late Royal Artillery), was escorting supplies to Charter.

Part II. of Appendix C shows the columns sent *into* Mashonaland to assist in the suppression of the rising, and also the patrols and actions of these columns when on their way to Salisbury. As will be seen, its only contents are the movements of Beal's and White's columns, when on their way to Salisbury from Buluwayo; and the movements of my column on its way from Umtali to Salisbury. These have already been dealt with. The end of this list brings the reader up to date with the military movements which had taken place prior to our arrival in Salisbury.

From the foregoing it will be seen that, though no serious defeat had been inflicted on the enemy, the Salisburians had by no means been sitting still.

THE STRENGTH OF THE FORCE

Looking further afield, Charter and Enkeldorn were still in laager, but, from all accounts, well able to hold their own. Victoria, in the south, was not in laager, and the district in its neighbourhood was quiet. The armed men in the country at this time and their stations are shown in the state on page 128.

This state, although it is that of a time when the force was at its highest strength (the re-embarkation of the Engineers, of the detachment York and Lancaster regiment, the departure of White's men for Buluwayo, and other causes, shortly after reduced the force in the country below two thousand men), may be taken as a fair sample of the strength and distribution of the armed men, white and black, throughout the operations. It will be noticed that the force is much scattered, and when this, and the fact that Mashonaland has an area of 114,000 square miles, is taken into consideration, the reader will not be surprised to hear that it was never possible to concentrate more than five hundred whites for offensive operations, and very seldom were as many available.

Shortness of supplies and of transport were, however, greater obstacles to the quick suppressing of the rising than was the smallness and the scattered condition of the force. There were no mealies in Salisbury, and no slaughter cattle; while food stuffs generally, and especially flour and biscuit, were becoming short throughout the

DISTRIBUTION OF THE FORCES IN MASHONALAND.
AUGUST 20, 1896.

Station.	Detail.	Officers.	N.C.O.'s and Men.	Natives.	Horses.
Salisbury.	Staff,	4	2	—	2
	Mounted Infantry,	2	50	—	56
	Medical Staff Corps,	—	2	—	—
	Captain Hon. C. White's Column of the Buluwayo Field Force,	3	63	—	54
	Rhodesia Horse,	9	122	38	102
	Salisbury Garrison,	11	92	60	35
	Salisbury Artillery,	2	13	—	15
	Natal Troop,	2	44	—	37
Victoria.	Victoria Rifles,	11	134	142	—
Enkeldorn.	Enkeldorn Garrison,	3	64	80	—
Charter.	Charter Garrison,	2	40	94	6
	Salisbury Artillery,	1	10	—	2
	Salisbury Garrison,	3	56	85	3
Chishawasha.	Salisbury Garrison,	—	17	15	4
Mazoë Fort.	Salisbury Garrison,	1	29	25	—
On the march from Marandellas to Salisbury.	Salisbury Artillery,	—	4	—	—
	Mounted Infantry,	8	164	33	195
	Royal Artillery,	1	14	—	—
	Royal Engineers,	2	39	—	—
	Medical Staff Corps,	1	11	—	—
	Army Service Corps,	—	1	—	—
	Honey's Scouts,	1	15	—	16
	Umtali Rifles,	2	6	8	6
Marandellas.	Matabeleland Relief Force,	1	50	—	2
Headlands.	Umtali Rifles,	5	49	40	10
Fort Haynes.	Mounted Infantry,	—	2	—	—
	Det. 2/West Riding Regt.,	3	98	—	4
	Medical Staff Corps,	—	4	—	—
	Umtali Rifles,	2	10	3	5
On the march from Salisbury to Umtali.	Volunteers under Colonel Beal,	4	40	—	4
Umtali.	Det. 2/West Riding Regt.,	1	52	—	—
	Medical Staff Corps,	—	3	—	—
	Umtali Artillery,	1	12	—	—
	Umtali Rifles,	5	50	40	10
	Matabeleland Relief Force,	4	46	—	4
Macequece.	Mounted Infantry,	—	1	—	—
On the march from Umtali to Chimoio.	Det. 2/York and Lancaster Regiment,	1	50	—	—
Chimoio.	Army Service Corps,	—	2	—	—
	Total,	96	1461	663	572

```
Total officers,        96
  ,,  N.C.O.'s and men, 1461
  ,,  natives,          663
         Grand total,   2220     Horses (public only),  572
```

country. The rinderpest had killed all the oxen, and the mule transport, then in the country, was not sufficient to ensure the proper supply of the troops and of the population.

Having mastered what had already been done, it now remains to see what there was still to do, and how best to do it. Looking at the map in conjunction with Appendix C, Parts I. and II., it will be seen that little had been done to the north, west, and south of Salisbury, beyond the relieving of small parties of miners, prospectors, and farmers, who had shut themselves up in laagers. The most numerous and the most defiant natives were those in the Hartley district, whose paramount chief was Mashangombi (pronounced " Ma-chi-an-gombi "). These natives had, as has already been said, made it very hot for the two patrols, Captain Turner's and Captain Hon. C. White's, which had been there. It was supposed that Mashangombi, with whom were reported to be many fugitive Matabele, had been the prime mover in the Mashona rising. It was therefore most important that he should be visited as soon as possible.

Away to the north-west of Hartley was Lomagundi's country, in which the murders at Eyre's Farm and the Ayrshire Mine had been committed.

Thirty miles south of Charter was a gentleman named Umtegeza, who was reported to have said that he was only waiting for the whites to attack him, and was not a bit afraid (this individual waited a bit too long, as far as his own interests were concerned).

In the Mazoë Valley, a very fertile district, in more ways than one, to the west of Salisbury, were numbers of truculent natives under Chidamba, Amanda, and various other chiefs. It was in a large granite range in this district that the celebrated witch doctress Nyanda lived and held her court.

Along the banks of the Hunyani and the Ruya rivers, to the south-east of Salisbury, numerous small chiefs, all of whom were hostile, had their kraals.

At Chishawasha, some twenty miles north-east of Salisbury, the Jesuit Fathers, assisted by a small guard, were laagered in their mission station, the principal chiefs near them being Chiquaqua and Kunzi, both of whom were hostile and bumptious.

There was thus plenty of work to do; the men to do it with would shortly be in Salisbury, and I proposed to visit the Hartley Hills directly Jenner with the bulk of the column arrived from Marandellas, and in the meantime to send small patrols to clear the near districts, and to relieve the present pressing need by the collection of grain. How, and why, the first intention was a long time in being carried out will be seen in the next chapter.

CHAPTER VIII

EXIT MAKONI. SUPPLIES SHORT

ON the 18th August the news was received that Makoni had sent in to the officer commanding Fort Haynes, saying he would surrender if his life would be spared, this being the only condition he asked. The next day there was a meeting of the Council in Salisbury, which I was asked to attend. Those present were Judge Vintcent, Sir Thomas Scanlan, and Mr. A. F. H. Duncan. Makoni's surrender was discussed, and it was unanimously resolved to accept it on the one condition he asked. This decision was at once telegraphed to Lord Grey at Buluwayo. On the 20th the Council again met, and had a conversation on the subject over the wire with Lord Grey and Sir Frederick Carrington. It then transpired that the High Commissioner would give Makoni the condition he asked provided that, "on his being brought before a court of justice and fairly tried he was not proved to have been directly connected with any murders." This clause would, the Council considered, prevent Makoni's surrender, and so it did, as he either was afraid of standing a trial, or did not understand the conditions, and was suspicious; anyhow he did not come in. Perhaps the wily chief was merely negotiating in order to gain time in which to get his men, who had scattered after the fight on the 3rd, together again?

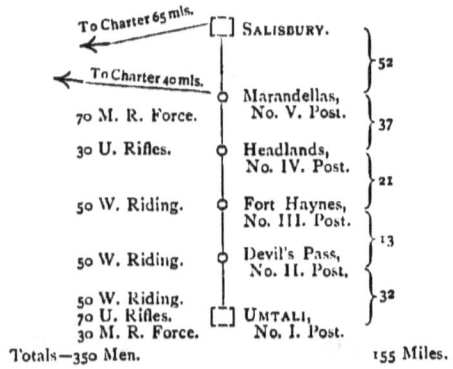

DIAGRAM SHOWING THE POSTS ON THE LINE OF COMMUNICATIONS.

NOTE.—The number of men at each post varied according as they were required for escorts to convoys moving up or down country.

When the negotiations with Makoni commenced I telegraphed to Major Watts, who was at Umtali, asking him to concentrate a portion of the line of communication troops at Fort Haynes (the diagram above shows the posts on the line and also the troops stationed at them), and to go there himself, in order to be present at the laying down of arms, or to immediately proceed against the chief should he fail to surrender.

Although only just recovering from an attack of fever, Watts promptly carried out these instructions, and by the 26th had some 230 men concentrated at Fort Haynes.

On the 27th Makoni sent in a message to Native Commissioner Ross to say that he would come in and give himself up the next day. He did not do so, but, as Ross suggested his being given another day, Watts deferred attacking him until the 30th. He marched from Fort Haynes at 1.30 A.M. on that day, taking the same route as my column had taken on the 3rd. His march, the occupation of the kraal, the blockading of the caves, and the subsequent capture of Makoni are graphically described by him in Colonel Plumer's book, *With an Irregular Corps in Matabeleland* (Watts belonged to Plumer's corps, and some of the men of it were with him at Makoni's), and I do not therefore propose to go into details.

He occupied the kraal at daylight without opposition, but was fired at from the caves; these he then blockaded most effectively until the 3rd September, when Makoni was either caught on coming to the mouth of a cave, or gave himself up. I have heard two accounts of the circumstances from the few who actually saw Makoni brought out of the caves.

Having got Makoni, the next thing was what

to do with him? Watts intended to send him to Umtali under strong escort, but on Ross representing strongly that this would entail the risk of a rescue, he decided to try him by a Field General Court Martial for "armed rebellion." The Court, composed of both imperial and local officers, found Makoni guilty, and sentenced him to death. Watts then telegraphed to the High Commissioner to confirm the sentence. There being no telegraph office at Fort Haynes this message had to be sent by native runners to Umtali, and an answer would necessarily be some days in coming.

The night after the Court had sat, Makoni's son and two of his principal Indunas (chiefs), who were also prisoners, escaped; this, coupled with the representations of Ross, made Watts decide to confirm the sentence himself, and Makoni was shot in his kraal on the morning of the 4th.

This prompt method of dealing with a rebel was hailed with delight by the inhabitants all over Mashonaland, and in one way at any rate it did good, by causing Umtassa, and other local chiefs, who were still "sitting on the fence," to come in and offer to provide carriers, etc. In another way, by making other chiefs who were thinking of coming in afraid to do so, it may have done harm.

Makoni was, for a Mashona, in many ways a fine fellow. His argument was, "It is all very well to call me a rebel, but the country belonged to me and my forefathers long before you came here." He, I am told by an eye-witness, died most bravely. Just before the order was given to the firing party to fire, he said to one of his Indunas, who was standing by, "When I am dead you will see that I am properly buried"; the man, from fright, or some other cause, did not answer. Makoni then said, "Ah! when I was your chief you jumped at my smallest word, now you will not answer; may the curse of the gods rest on you for ever if you do not see me properly buried,"—or words to that effect.

While these events had been taking place on the line of communications, we at Salisbury had not been idle.

Part III., Appendix C, shows the patrols sent out after our arrival at Salisbury, and of these Nos. 1 to 10 went during this time. Of this ten, some two or three deserve notice. No. 2 was led into a nasty defile by its guides and was then suddenly attacked. It was however extracted with ability by its commander, Lieut. St. Aubyn, Mounted Infantry. Nos. 4 and 5 were intended to be a double-barrel patrol, one starting south from Salisbury, and the other south-east, their orders being to strike the Hunyani River and work along it, one up and the other down till they met. Owing however to the horses of White's men (who were employed in this patrol on their way back to Buluwayo) knocking up. St. Aubyn's, or the right barrel, missed fire, in spite of the determined attempt he made to go on with his own Mounted Infantry section only. In those two patrols four men were wounded.

It will be noticed that the left barrel (No. 3 patrol) was under Captain Nesbitt, a local officer, and that it contained some imperial troops. This was the first of several occasions on which a local officer commanded a mixed patrol. I did not consider it fair that those who had already done hard and excellent work should be entirely deprived of the chance of commanding patrols; and it would have led to friction to put local captains under imperial subalterns. I was told afterwards that this view was appreciated, and certainly I had no cause to regret having taken it, the several commands so entrusted being carried out with ability and tact.

No. 5 patrol, under Capt. Sir H. W. McMahon, Mounted Infantry, collected a good quantity of grain and burnt many kraals. At Kaheia's kraal they had an "indaba" with the enemy, each behind his own covering rock, and Kaheia sent McMahon a shilling as a peace offering; but obstinately refused to come out and talk.

It was during this patrol that Sergeant W. B. Colling, of the Salisbury Rifles, was wounded in one arm and in the other hand:

the latter had to be amputated, and I am afraid that the former will be permanently disabled. I often saw this man in the hospital afterwards, and he was invariably most cheerful and plucky.

The 7th patrol on the list is *Major* (at my request he had been granted local rank) Jenner's to Umtegeza's, of which more anon. The 10th is of course Watts' to Makoni's, which has just been described.

On the 19th (August), Major Hoste's patrol (No. 26, Part I., Appendix C), referred to on page 126, returned to Salisbury, having had four days, fighting in the Mazoë district, where they burnt some twenty kraals and established a fort. They had two white men wounded, one of these being, much to everyone's sorrow, Captain F. K. Montgomery, Rhodesia Horse. This officer, who had already greatly distinguished himself by his pluck and dash, received a very nasty wound in the head from a shot fired from a cave which he was close to. The day before he had had his hat knocked off by a bullet under similar circumstances, and when he received this wound, the only remark he made, was, "What a d——d big head I must have." It was with difficulty, and with considerable danger to themselves, that Major Hoste and others got Captain Montgomery out of the line of fire of the cave from which he was hit.

It was about this time (20th to 25th August) that Mr. H. Wilson Fox, then public prosecutor (now I believe Attorney General for Rhodesia), took over, at the request of Judge Vintcent, charge of the supply and transport arrangements on behalf of the British South Africa Company, and a precious good job it was for every one, especially for the local troops and the population, that he did so. This gentleman speedily discovered that the food supply of Salisbury was in a worse state than was expected, and that the flour and biscuit would be finished by the 29th, and one of his first acts was to write me a letter asking if we could hand over, for the use of the town, a certain amount of the flour and biscuit which formed part of the sixty days' rations we had brought up. We could not give him all he asked for, but were bound to help, and so gave him half of our supply. This reduced the imperial troops to ten days' rations, and thus, though the loan was subsequently repaid, made it impossible for any lengthy patrols, like that to Hartley for instance, to be undertaken for the present. The first up-coming convoy of food stuffs was not expected to arrive before the 7th September, about which time it did reach Salisbury; we were then pretty short, and its contents did not go far. Other convoys followed at intervals, but all through September we lived from hand to mouth, and it was not until the first week in October that the receipts had gained sufficiently on the issues to enable Mr. Fox to give me the three weeks' rations (I did not consider it advisable to start with less than this, and would rather have had a month's supply) for the 400 odd men, with which I was all the time anxious to start for Hartley.

Mr. Fox and I had many pleasant talks over this unpleasant subject, shortness of food.

Grain for the animals there was none, beyond the small amount (the natives had either hidden or used it nearly all) which patrols occasionally brought in. What made this worse was the fact that, it being nearly the end of the dry season, the grass was all withered and burnt up. The way the horses and mules worked under these conditions was wonderful.

Not only had immediate wants in the food way to be supplied, but it was necessary to get up to Salisbury, and also into the outlying stations, a sufficient stock to tide over the rainy season ; during which it is not usually possible to "ride transport," especially with mules, and there were no oxen left, except a few weak "salted" (*i.e.* have had, and recovered from, the rinderpest) spans.

Mr. Fox worked out the amount required to be six hundred tons, and he promptly set to work to get it, and the transport to distribute it, into the country. Some rain might be expected in November, and to be safe all the stuff should be on the high veldt, *i.e.* west of the Devil's Pass, by the middle of December. To do this both energy and money were required, and they were supplied without stint, the former by Mr. Fox, and the latter by the company, and to his judicious application of both must be attributed the fact that the work was done and the people fed.

One cannot help thinking that, in many ways, the people in the British South Africa Company's territory are lucky. If short of food they were fed, if their farms or stores were raided by Mashonas, their claims for compensation (sometimes largely in excess of what they ever possessed!) were paid with very little questioning. If out of work and they soldiered, they were called *volunteers*, paid ten shillings per day, and clothed, and fed!

On the 25th August the imperial column arrived at Salisbury from Marandellas, and they joined St. Aubyn and King-Harman at the Nursery Farm.

Jenner's report was interesting. Since we left him, on the 13th, he had visited all the kraals and farms within reach of Marandellas, burning the former, and collecting oat hay at the latter. At White's Farm, on the Charter road, a letter was found, written by White just after the native attack on the 20th June. This letter stated that Lieut. Bremner (20th Hussars) was dead, and that the writer was badly wounded, and about to die from loss of blood. A body, believed to be poor Bremner's, was found and buried by Watts' party, when they passed the farm on their way from Charter some days before Jenner was there.

On the 17th, Jenner took Ushewekunsi's kraal without loss, but after its capture Mr. J. B. S. Jolliffe, a transport rider, was unluckily shot dead from a neighbouring kopje. He had accompanied the guns without Jenner's knowledge. Another instance of a good man losing his life through going to a fight on his own account!

The column reached Law's store on the main road, on the 21st, and found its ashes still warm. This store had been all right when we passed it on the 14th.

On the 22nd the column took a swing off the road into Chiquaqua's country, where they found all the accessible kraals deserted, and got but little grain.

Now that the imperial troops had arrived in Salisbury, Major Hoste, and many other officers of the local forces, who had originally joined Beal's column to go to the relief of Buluwayo, wished to return to their several businesses. It thus became necessary to re-organize these forces. As can be imagined, and as was only natural, with a force got together hastily, and in which men who had a few weeks before all been equal, and were now of necessity placed one above the other, the question of command was a difficult one.

Judge Vintcent kindly gave me a free hand, and after consulting with Major Hoste, Major Tennant, and other local officers, I decided to divide the existing local forces into four distinct and independent units, and to omit the name volunteer, but to retain that of Rhodesia Horse. These units were:

1. The Artillery Troop Rhodesia Horse, under Major Tennant,	some 50 strong,
2. The Mounted Troop Rhodesia Horse, under Captain Daly,	,, 70 ,,
3. The Dismounted Troop Rhodesia Horse, under Captain Newman,	,, 50 ,,
4. The Salisbury Rifles, under Captain Nesbitt,	,, 115 ,,
	285

What had been called the Salisbury Artillery was merged into the Artillery Troop, Rhodesia Horse, while the corps now called the Salisbury Rifles was the old Salisbury Garrison under a new name, which the men preferred, and it was time it had one; for, as its members only "signed on" to garrison Salisbury, some of them had refused to go outside the town!

Nearly all the old officers and men, who had not businesses to attend to, joined one or other of the above corps. The conditions were that they were to serve the British South Africa Company, in any part of Rhodesia, for a period of three months (this was in most cases afterwards extended to 31st March, 1897).

The pay was to be the same as before, *i.e.* the privates received 10/- per day, and other ranks in proportion, while all were clothed and rationed.

THE ZINJANJAS

Each of these four units soon acquired, to a certain extent, *esprit de corps*, and all did excellent work. The division lessened the risk of friction, increased the efficiency, and gave four officers chances of commanding instead of one. In addition to the above was the Natal Troop, already mentioned on page 124. This troop was now under Captain Taylor.

Towards the end of August reports were received from Charter and Victoria, that the Zinjanja natives, who had remained friendly, were willing to co-operate with the whites against Umtegeza. Colonel Paget, with some of the 7th Hussars, was at this time in the vicinity of Victoria, and, being unable on account of shortness of rations, to move any of the Mashonaland Force so far from Salisbury, I, in reporting by wire to Sir Frederick Carrington about the Zinjanjas, suggested that perhaps Colonel Paget's force might co-operate with them and the Charter Garrison against Umtegeza. However, by the time this suggestion reached Sir Frederick, Colonel Paget had moved away from Victoria, and the General then telegraphed to me to arrange the attack at once.

Under our hand-to-mouth circumstances this at first appeared rather a stumper. Salisbury to Charter is 65 miles, and portions of the road are heavy; with our grass-fed mules it would take six days to get there. Umtegeza's is thirty miles beyond Charter, say nine days from Salisbury.

We could not afford to give the 150 men I proposed to send more than ten to twelve days' rations, thus their supplies would be nearly finished by the time they arrived on their battleground. Charter had just telegraphed to say that it only had five days' supplies, so that, even if it went on half rations, it would be more likely to ask for than to give help.

On receiving the General's order I went to talk over ways and means with Fox, and finally decided on the following:

Jenner, with the Rifle company Mounted Infantry, Honey's Scouts, and one seven-pounder, to start for Charter, *via* Marandellas, on September 1st, with just sufficient rations to take him to the latter place; there he would meet one of Fox's up-coming food convoys, draw three weeks' rations from it for the whole of his force, and some for Charter, and then take the Marandellas-Charter road (40 miles). To provide for Charter's immediate wants I sent the Natal Troop, which was to form part of Jenner's force, direct to Charter with what food Fox could spare. This arrangement would cause the attack on Umtegeza to come off a good deal sooner than if we waited for the food to arrive in Salisbury and then sent the troops off.

When he had finished Umtegeza's Jenner was to return to Charter, and move from there on Hartley to co-operate with my column from Salisbury.

This we hoped would be about the 25th of September, but the food question again turned up and put it off ten days.

Jenner's movements from the day he left Salisbury (1st September) to the day (10th October) that we effected a junction with him at Mashangombi's, are told in his own words in the next chapter. I will only say that he, as usual, carried out his instructions most successfully.

CHAPTER IX

UMTEGEZA'S AND THE GONA HILLS

By Brevet-Major A. V. Jenner, D.S.O.

AT the end of August the civil and military authorities displayed considerable anxiety to have a gentleman of the name of Umtegeza captured, or otherwise rendered incapable of doing mischief in the Charter district.

We gathered from those who had been entertained there that Chateau Umte was situated in a charming rural neighbourhood, with south-west aspect and lovely mountain views. It stood high, being about 7000 feet above sea level, and consisted of substantial stone-built residential rocks, containing bed and sitting-rooms and the usual offices; undulating, picturesque pleasure-grounds of inexpensive upkeep, with excellent shooting and fishing in the vicinity—280 miles from a railway station, 24 from a post-office, and 72 from a church.

Our future host did not, as a rule, send to meet his visitors, though he had a reputation for "doing" them well when they got there.

We started on our little shooting trip appropriately enough on the 1st September. There was not enough food in Salisbury to ration the column, so, instead of going direct to Umtegeza's we had to go round by Marandellas, where we hoped to meet a convoy with the necessary supplies.

The column at first consisted of one seven-pounder gun and detachment Royal Artillery; the Rifle company Mounted Infantry; Honey's Scouts.

The Natal Troop went direct to Charter to await our arrival there, and we were afterwards joined by about two thousand friendlies from districts near Victoria.

We marched to Marandellas along the telegraph line, this being some distance from the main road (about ten miles away from it at the furthest point), our object being to collect what grain we could for our half-starved horses and mules.

The ammunition for the seven-pounder was at a very low ebb, in fact, we had so few shells that we could not think of using any till we reached Umtegeza's. We collected what grain we could near the route. A village situated between the telegraph line and the main road gave considerable resistance before it was burned and depleted of grain. It was here that Frost, a rifleman belonging to the 3rd battalion 60th, and serving with the Mounted Infantry, received the wound from which I regret to say he subsequently died.

On arrival at Marandellas we found that the expected convoy had not arrived; but we had not long to wait, and then began a great off-loading and sorting and rearranging and re-loading of stores.

There was a good deal of difficulty about the mules too, but we managed to make a start the next morning and very glad we were.

The road between Marandellas and Charter was not quite so well watered in some parts as most of the roads, and the grass was very extensively burnt; we then had finished all our "collected" grain, and the horses and mules were very weak in consequence.

When we arrived at Charter we found the Natal Troop, but nothing much else.

Charter had the appearance of a gipsy encampment, just before being told to move on by the local police. This surprised us a good deal as Charter is at the junction of several important highways, and, from every point of view, the land round there ought to be well worth investing in for farm purposes.

It possessed a telegraph office, in which I passed many hours in mutual recrimination (by telegraph) with the civil officer at Salisbury, whose duty it was to see that every available and other waggon was free to carry supplies to Salisbury.

The inadequacy of the transport was a constant trouble. The oxen had nearly all died from rinderpest and there were not enough mules for the job. This led to endless difficulty and most seriously hampered all operations.

Instead of being able to have quick moving parties always travelling from five to ten miles away from and parallel to the waggons, the horses were scarcely able to crawl along the very shortest marches.

There was plenty of grain at various points on the railway, but there were not enough mules to bring it up. The grass was burnt, as it always is at that time of year; consequently the horses and mules would have frequently died if they had not been constantly "saved."

The arrangements were completed by midday on Sunday 13th, and we made a start to the south that afternoon.

Mr. Taylor, the Native Commissioner of the district, accompanied the column, and his services were most valuable. He had not been in the district long, but the information he had obtained was extremely accurate, and he devoted himself to helping us in every way. He had considerable influence over the natives that he was in touch with, and this doubtless accounted to a great extent for his information being so correct.

We bivouacked on the night of the 14th at "Shaw's," and left the road there at five A.M. on the 15th and made for Umtegeza's.

It was a little difficult to find, as we got into a hilly country, and our guide had not actually been to the kraal, though he knew its whereabouts pretty accurately. It turned out to be, like all the kraals that were held, a very strong natural position honeycombed with caves.

There was a river running through the valley, between the hill on which the kraal was and the hill over which we approached; and there was a great array of caves down to the water's edge.

The question was, How to extract Umtegeza?

There was as usual plenty of firing on both sides, and then it was decided to inform the gentleman that we had taken our little trip entirely on his behalf and request him to walk out.

Mr. Taylor had, with great foresight, brought a most intelligent native with him—a relation of Umtegeza's—and to this man was entrusted the duty of conveying our invitation for "Umte's" personal attendance.

So the "cease fire" was sounded, and the two sides conformed as if they had been trained by a steady course of Aldershot field days.

The "niggers" emerged from their holes and sat about on the rocks, in more or less elegant attitudes, and Umte sent to say that he regretted his inability to accept our kind invitation, but he feared that it might seriously affect his health, in fact, shorten his life, if he complied.

He sent us out a present of cattle and gave our messenger a handsome tip of two sovereigns.

We replied with a promise that he should not be killed, and he then came out and gave himself up.

His young men did not follow the excellent example of their chief, so they were told that we should proceed to business, burn their kraal, and kill a good many more of them. The "commence fire" sounded, they went back into their holes, and the field day went on. The result was that the kraal was absolutely destroyed, and every particle of grain from it and the surrounding kraals was carried away or spoilt. A good few prisoners were taken, and those that were not killed or taken prisoner cleared away in the night. These last were of course the largest number, as was always the case unless the kraal itself should be of a sort easily sat round.

The friendlies were of great service, especially in discovering and carrying off or destroying the grain. They knew exactly where to look, and their large numbers saved an infinity of labour. Old Umte was most good-natured, and very anxious to dispense with his guard of honour; but we would not hear of that, as we should have been so sorry had his visit been brought to an abrupt conclusion.

He accompanied us throughout the trip and was sometimes most entertaining. He broke into song one night quite late. I don't exactly know what the song was, but fancy it must have been a Mashona rendering of the "Lost Chord"—at any rate he never completed it. Eventually he went into Salisbury and was handed over to the civil authorities.

After leaving Umtegeza's kraal we made a tour through his district, visiting the likeliest places, viz., Zabi, Gona, and Mzimilima's.

At Zabi the friendlies had a fight "on their own" whilst we were reconnoitring the hills. They were most successful, and captured fifty head of cattle. The natives deserted the place that night.

Gona was on a range of steep hills which extended for several miles, and we stayed there for a few days, fighting each day until we finally cleared them out, and destroyed their villages and carried off the grain.

From there we marched to Mzimilima's, another very strong place, but by this time the natives in the district had tired of the game and they left this last stronghold before we *arrived*.

We got a fair bag of grain and cattle there, which was some compensation for a very long and very hot day's ride.

We then returned to Charter, reaching there on the 25th September. Our casualties on this expedition were one rifleman and five friendlies killed; Captain Taylor, commanding the Natal Troop, one man of Natal Troop, and three friendlies wounded. Arrived at Charter we at

THE BEATRICE MINE RE-VISITED

once set about making arrangements for co-operating with Colonel Alderson's column against the rebels in the Hartley Hills, and we left Charter on the 6th October to join hands with him. The friendlies had left us a short time before, and there was some difficulty in getting any one who knew the country to act as guide.

We travelled through a very nice country, some of it swarming with game; but our guide lost his bearings somewhat, and one evening it took us a very long time to find water.

The next morning we came on the road near the Beatrice Mine, which was a good deal north of the line we had intended to take; but as there were said to be kraals on this road, and not on the other, it was perhaps just as well, as it was useful and interesting to find out if the natives were living in them.

The Beatrice Mine did not appear to have been visited by the natives for a long time, probably not since they murdered the whites who were living there about the middle of June. It had open country all round it, and had they not been killed in the most treacherous manner, they would probably have been able to hold out until relieved from Salisbury.

We outspanned rather late for the midday halt, at the Beatrice Mine, and went on about eight miles further that evening.

The following day, the 9th October, we started early and in about three miles came to M'Slopa's kraal. This was being strongly rebuilt and fortified, but was not held. It took us some little time to collect the grain and destroy the new huts, and as much of the fortifications as possible. We went on again about two o'clock and found another deserted kraal on the road, and our advanced guard reached the drift on the Umfuli River about half-past four in the afternoon. The drift was commanded by several hills, on three of which there were kraals.

The moment the Scouts drew near the river, they were fired at from the high ground, so we dismounted, and leaving the horses in the open country with a small guard, we crossed the river and took the high ground nearest to us on that side. We then had a good deal of running about, as there were a succession of good positions for the enemy on the various bush-covered hills round the drift.

The river has two beds here which join near the drift, and in crossing these to attack the positions, we discovered them to be marvellously rough walking.

The natives who had retired before us into the kraals, began to stream out on our approach, and run off towards Mashangombi's; I suppose they did not consider the caves here held enough of them, and the accurate volleys must have been discomposing. A few good shots remained behind till the last moment in both kraals. It was getting late and there would not have been time to assault each kraal in succession, so we split up and went for them separately, and completely cleared them out.

It was in assaulting one of these kraals that Eustace, of the 4th battalion 60th Rifles, serving with the Rifle company Mounted Infantry, to our very great regret, received a severe wound in the foot.

We bivouacked that night close by, burnt the remaining kraal the next morning (October 10th), and went thoroughly over the hills, but there were no natives left anywhere there. We then brought the waggons across the drift, marched through about two miles of high rocky hills, and joined Colonel Alderson's column at Mashangombi's kraal, shortly before eleven o'clock.

CHAPTER X

SIMBANOOTA'S, AND AN ABORTIVE "INDABA"

ON September 8th, a mixed patrol (No. 13, Part III., Appendix C), under Major Tennant, Artillery Troop, Rhodesia Horse, started for Simbanoota's kraal, on the Ruya River. On the 9th, this officer sent in to say that the greater part of the tinned meat issued to him was bad. A fresh supply had to be sent out, and this of course accentuated the food question. A good deal of the tinned meat we were now using had, I believe, been in Salisbury several years, some people said since the pioneers came up in '91; others since the first Matabele war in '93; anyhow, none of it was very good. Major Tennant found Simbanoota's rather a hard nut to crack, and, although he took part of it on the 10th, he sent in that evening to ask for reinforcements and I then sent him out 25 men of the Mounted Troop, Rhodesia Horse, and the same number of the Salisbury Rifles. On the 12th, I started at daybreak with Nicholls and F. Wilson Fox (brother to H. Wilson Fox). I had made the latter my 2nd galloper, *vice* young Godley, who had gone to the supply department in Salisbury, to visit the patrol and have a look at Simbanoota's. On the way we met the ambulance bringing in Corporal Creswick, Rhodesia Horse, who had been wounded by a slug in the stomach while breaking through a stockade.

On the same day, Lieut. P. Coode, West Riding regiment, had been hit in the calf of the leg, after he had led his men into the kraal, and a native boy had been mortally wounded. This poor boy, who was Roach's servant, was hit right through the stomach; in spite of this he went back and brought in Roach's rifle, which he had dropped when hit; he died in great agony the same evening: the other boys buried him, and not only him, but also all Roach's horse brushes, etc., with him. This boy was quite a character, and had caused us much amusement on the march up country. Roach would say, "I say, John, where *is* my horse's nose bag, I must have one"; the next day some one would be short of a nose bag, but Roach's horse *had* one. Again it would be, "John, my rug is gone, *must* have a rug," and sure enough his horse would be comfortably rugged up the next morning, and someone else's would be shivering. When the owners of these articles complained to Roach, as they sometimes did, "John" would be had out by Roach, and threatened with the biggest licking he ever had if it "occurred again": it *did* occur again, but I can't say I ever saw "John" get his licking. He was indeed a good active service servant to

"JOHN."

his master, and Roach was quite down on his luck at his death. We found Tennant thinking of starting to visit some kraals down the Ruya, but I suggested that it would be as well to complete the work at Simbanoota's first. So there we went.

The kraal is situated among a mass of huge

granite boulders and thick bush, on the Ruya River, and has water on three sides of it, while a small stream runs through the middle, dividing it into two parts. The whole kraal is built on solid rock, on which stand large granite boulders that lend themselves admirably to the jack-in-the-box sort of fighting that the Mashona loves. The portion nearest the Ruya was that taken on the 10th.

When we arrived on the river bank opposite to the kraal, there were no signs of the enemy, and a shell or two fired, and the shouting of the Native Contingent, failed to produce a sound from it beyond the barking of a dog. The Salisbury Rifles, now commanded by Captain E. Finucane, and Pilson's section of the Irish company Mounted Infantry, then crossed the river and advanced on the kraal. Major Tennant, Nicholls, Fox, and I, followed them; we had just crossed the river and were beginning to think that the kraal had been deserted, when "boom" went a family gun from the second part of it. "Ah! there they are," said Tennant, and went ahead to join his men. Although we (Nicholls, Fox, and myself) were merely spectators, for I did not in any way interfere with Tennant's command of the patrol; having come so far we were bound to go on, and soon were in the first portion of the kraal. Here things were pretty warm, as bullets and pot legs were singing about in all directions, and I heard one, which had evidently been fired out of a cave straight up into the air, fall "fut," into the ground behind us. Under these circumstances it was difficult to tell where one was safe, so we joined Pilson's men behind a low stone wall. Here we found the body of poor Johnson of the Salisbury Rifles, who had just been shot through the chest and killed. He had been caught by a trap in the shape of a goat tied up in front of a concealed loop hole. Poor chap! his troubles were over, and as one watched the colour dying out of his hands and face, and gave orders for the latter to be covered over, it was impossible not to think "who next?" It is far better to be an actor than a spectator when there are bullets in the guns. A little later on I had a near go of being laid out by the side of poor Johnson. I was looking over the wall, admiring the cool way in which Pilson was handling his men, behind another wall, a little way in front, when "smack!" came something against the stone under my chin, and at the same instant I found there was blood on my cheek. A bullet, fired from a cave behind some bushes about 20 yards off, had apparently hit the stone, and then it, or a piece of it, had grazed my cheek. I was pretty quick in bobbing down behind that wall! and *very* cautious how I looked over it in future. While I abused myself for being such a fool as to play spectator at such an ungentlemanly game.

The worst part was that, having got into the

middle of it, we could not in common decency leave till it was over.

Gradually Tennant worked his men up to the kraal, and presently they rushed the last wall and were on the top of the rock underneath which were the few remaining defenders. Now began a fight very much like that between people on the roof of a house and those inside, the one firing up the chimney, the other down; jumpy work, as neither could tell when the other was going to fire. In this fighting Mr. Colin Harding, who had just come up to Salisbury, and who is now an Inspector in the British South Africa Company's police, particularly distinguished himself, and paid no more attention to the Mashona bullets than if they were snowballs.

I also admired the way in which Captain Finucane took the Salisbury Rifles into the kraal, "Come on, ye lazy beggars: I'll make ye smell powder!"

This would not quite do at Aldershot now-a-days perhaps, but it was effective, and he certainly led them where they had every chance of doing what he promised. With such men to lead the fighting, it was small wonder that the fire of the defenders was soon silenced, and that there was nothing more for us to see, and for me to do, but congratulate Major Tennant on the way he had handled his men; so, leaving a party to demolish the kraal, we returned to his laager, and thence rode back into Salisbury.

L

That night I had the honour of attending the Pioneers' smoking concert (those men who trekked up to, and built Fort Salisbury in 1891 meet each year), and I was pleased to tell them that I had that day seen imperial troops and local troops fighting side by side, under, and excellently handled by, a Salisbury man.

This announcement was received with cheers, and I think it did a good deal to strengthen the good feeling which already existed between the two forces.

It was during the fighting at Simbanoota's that "Tommy Atkins" was first heard to make answer to the expression sounding like "my way!" referred to on page 90, which the Mashonas used when a bullet went near them, when a shell burst, or when they were otherwise surprised. Tommy's retort was, "No! you—— it's *our*——way this time!"

Among the patrols which went out in September, Nos. 14 and 15 are worth notice. The former, under French, made the Mazoë Fort its headquarters, and from there visited and destroyed Amanda's and other kraals, and probably made the natives decide on commencing the "indaba" of which more hereafter. No. 15 patrol, under Pilson, went to Norton's farm, where the murders had been committed on the 17th June, and burnt the kraals near there, killing a few of the enemy, and collecting some two or three waggon loads of grain.

On September 21st Judge Vintcent, Sir Thos. Scanlan, Mr. Marshall Hole, and myself rode out to the Golden Stairs (the entrance to the Mazoë Valley) to "indaba" with Chidamba, and other Mazoë chiefs who had informed Lieut. Fairbairn, commanding the fort, that they wanted peace; whether this was true or not I do not, even now, in the least know, but if not, then they certainly are wonderful actors. They undoubtedly appeared desirous of peace, and gave up on the spot one Mazwe, who was an ex-native policeman, much to his disgust. It was arranged that they were to give in their arms the next day, and the Judge and Hole remained at the fort to be present, while Sir Thomas and I rode back to Salisbury.

Late the next night the Judge came back very much disgusted; not a single arm had come in! The chiefs said their young men would not come in because they thought we had killed Mazwe and they wanted first to see him alive; so the ex-policeman was sent out under escort, with no result, as far as the arms coming in was concerned, but with the very unfortunate one for us, that he escaped during the night! He was under a guard inside the fort, tied to one of them in fact, and yet he got loose without disturbing this man, and, evading all the sentries and the outlying piquets, got clean away. We only had the very poor compensation of trying the non-commissioned officer in command of the guard.

Unless you have brick walls and iron bars it is almost impossible to keep a Mashona prisoner, and this is only one of many cases of prisoners escaping. Their hands are so small that they can slip off any ordinary sized handcuff, while with their teeth and feet they seem able to undo almost any knot.

After this incident it was no good to think of peace for the present, and I sent orders to McMahon to attack Chidamba and the others, sending him a reinforcement at the same time.

McMahon had left Salisbury for Mazoë on the 18th with a patrol (No. 16, Part III., Appendix C), and had assisted Fairbairn in arranging the preliminaries of the above mentioned "indaba." The doings of his patrol and the result of his attack on the Iron Masque Range he tells himself in the next chapter.

When the result of the indaba was known in Salisbury, all of us "Indabarers," particularly he Judge and myself, got unmercifully slated by the *Rhodesia Herald* and the *Financial Times*, the two local papers, who called us all sorts of names, the least abusive of which was "the peace-at-any-price party." The *Nugget* (a cyclostile paper), in particular, was very rabid; said that we ought to be tried by court martial, and brought out a cartoon showing the Judge and myself in petticoats and early Victorian bonnets (the editor was no doubt even then thinking of the Jubilee!) in a supplicating attitude before a most ferocious-looking Mashona. It was undoubtedly a clever picture, as most of the *Nugget's* were, and under the circumstances the hit was a fair one—as paper hits go. The proprietor of the *Nugget* was his own editor, artist, printer, or rather cyclostile writer, and office boy, and the production certainly did him credit, though the same could not always be said of the tone of his articles.

McMahon's Mazoë patrol was the last of the September ones, and, looking back on the month, I cannot say that I was satisfied. We had certainly hunted the Mashonas about a bit, burnt their kraals, taken a few of their cattle, and got them into such a state of respect for our "impi" that they would not show at all in the open. This last was unfortunately the principal reason that we did not seem much nearer the end, for since Makoni's we had never been able to really get at them. So little was I pleased with the results up to date, that in a conversation over the telegraph wire, about this time, with Colonel Baden-Powell (Chief Staff Officer to Sir Frederick Carrington), I told him somewhat as follows: "I should like to say that I am not at all satisfied with the way we are able to carry on operations here. We have plenty of men to go into any two or three districts at the same time, and to destroy the kraals in them and drive the natives out. What in my opinion is then required is to leave from

50 to 100 men in the district, according to its size and the numbers of the natives, with orders to give the natives no rest and to prevent them sowing their crops. We have neither the men, the supplies, nor the transport, to do this and still be in a position to go into other districts."

Colonel Baden-Powell's reply was that they, in Matabeleland, were met at every turn by the same difficulties. In fact, the question throughout Rhodesia, and I think especially in Mashonaland, at that time was not the enemy so much as *supply* and *transport*.

Further, the time available, before the rains set in and made operations difficult, and in some parts of the country impossible, was getting short, and with the rains would come fever for the men, and horse sickness for the horses. Both the Imperial Authorities and the Company, especially the latter, were anxious to get the imperial troops out of the country before the rains, while Sir Frederick Carrington was anxious for me to complete the circle of operations round Salisbury before they came. Thus time also came in very much as a factor to be considered when making plans.

Now these three factors—*supply*, *transport*, and *time*, or rather the shortness of them—were all against us, and in favour of the Mashonas. For generations they had been used to being periodically raided by the Matabele, who made rushes into the country, seized all the women, children, and cattle, and killed all the men they caught in the open, and then went away. During these raids the Mashonas went to their caves and calmly waited till the clouds rolled by, knowing that the Matabele, who rarely made determined attacks on the caves, would not stop long.

Now here were we, through want of *supply*, *transport*, and *time* (I do not say want of men, because they could have been got had we been able to feed them), playing just the same game as the Matabele, inasmuch as in only one district (the Mazoë) had we left men behind us. The worst of it was that we knew that this was a game which did not frighten the Mashona much, when once he had got away from the district we were in at the time, and into a cave in some other one, in which he sat and probably said to himself: "Oh they are just like the Matabele, here a week or two, and then on they go." And yet, from the reasons given above, we were unable at this time to play a better game. There was another thing which also appeared probable, and that was that many of the kraals that we were destroying would shortly after our departure be built up again and re-occupied. Grass huts are easily built and cost nothing, when the material grows on the spot, and the labour is unpaid! The same also applies to stone walls and stockades.

September having been unsatisfactory, it will be

well to turn over a leaf, and begin a fresh chapter with October.

Before doing so it may be interesting, and help to show the state of affairs at the end of the former month, if I give some of the current prices then prevailing in Salisbury. I jotted them down in my diary at the time, and here they are:

Bread (⅔ rice),	2/	per lb.
Flour,	240/	„ bag.
Tea,	7/6	„ lb.
Milk (no fresh),	7/6	„ tin.
Butter (no fresh),	7/6	„ tin.
Whiskey,	30/	„ bottle.
Brandy,	40/	„ bottle.

It might also be added that, by way of helping things along, the telegraph wire to Charter, and thence to Buluwayo, was down for some days on several occasions during this month. That it kept up so well as it did was, considering the state of the poles, a wonder.

On the last day of this month I returned from visiting McMahon's patrol in the Mazoë Valley, feeling very much better for the four days out of the office and on the veldt.

I was pleased to find that the half of the English company Mounted Infantry (sent from Maritzburg, where the English and the Highland companies had been moved) had arrived in Salisbury, Harland and Hare being the officers with them. Besides ours, their horses, who had

had mealies all the way up country, looked quite pictures, but, alas! they also very soon assumed the depressing hat-stand-like look. I was also glad to hear that poor Evans, whom I had specially asked for, as I wanted to have him as second in command, and Surgeon Captain Hilliard, C.M.G. Army Medical Staff (I had asked for an extra medical officer), had arrived at Umtali.

This last day in September we had a warning, in the shape of a very heavy thunder and rain storm, that the time before the wet season came was getting short.

CHAPTER XI

CLEARING THE GRANITE RANGE IN THE MAZOË VALLEY

By Captain Sir Horace W. McMahon, Bart., D.S.O.

ON the 17th September, Colonel Alderson gave me his instructions for a patrol, which was to start the next morning for the Mazoë district, about twenty-eight miles from Salisbury, under my command. His orders were that we were to go to the Mazoë Fort, which is situated a few hundred yards from the Alice Mine, and was at that time garrisoned by about thirty Salisbury Rifles under Lieut. Fairbairn, and, in conjunction with the latter, to try and arrange a meeting for Judge Vintcent with some chiefs who were reported to be willing to surrender. If we were successful, Judge Vintcent and the Colonel would ride out and explain to them, at whatever place had been agreed upon, the terms upon which peace could be made. In the event of our being unable to communicate with the rebels, they were to be attacked and driven from their position without delay. Next day the following troops, which were to form the patrol, started from Salisbury. Two sections of my Irish company Mounted Infantry (Royal Irish— Lieut. French, and Royal Irish Rifles—Lieut. King-Harman); the Artillery Troop of the Rhodesia Horse; one seven-pounder—Lieut. Ashe; the Dismounted Troop Rhodesia Horse—Lieut. Ross, and a detachment of the Native Contingent, consisting of Shangaans: total, about 150 men. We halted for the night at Forbes' farm, which is about half a mile from the Granite Range, the stronghold of Chidamba, who was supposed to be the most influential chief in the district, and to whom it was our intention to try and explain our mission.

On the following morning we passed close under the Granite Range and were inspected by hundreds of the natives from the top of the rocks, both sides displaying the greatest curiosity but without a shot being fired. Fairbairn met us a few miles further on, and whilst the column proceeded to the fort, he, French, and myself, with three of the Native Contingent, one of whom was to act as interpreter and spoke tolerably fair English, returned to the Granite Range to commence negotiations. This proved a most tedious process. Each day that we held communication with the niggers our conversation commenced by shouting in a sort of sing-song voice at a distance of about half a mile, and as soon as the meaning of our message was grasped, it had to be conveyed, even further back, to the chiefs before any answer could be obtained. Gradually more confidence would be established, and two or three would eventually pluck up enough courage to come down and talk with us, but even then they insisted on the negotiations being carried on across a small stream. It was also necessary to leave our horses at a distance, as the natives are very nervous about being pursued, far more so than of being fired at, this fact no doubt accounting for their sense of safety when conversing with us over a stream about 8 feet wide. One day we experienced some of the inborn treachery of the Mashonas, as whilst we were engaged shouting to the top of the hill, one of our black boys detected three of the rebels stalking us through the long grass along the banks of the stream. As soon as they saw that we knew of their whereabouts, they made off, dragging their rifles behind them; but as we were still anxious to get the chiefs down, we did not fire at them. We waited some time longer, but in the end had to give it up, as this event seemed to have upset them for the day.

Next morning we determined to explore a district about twelve miles north of Mazoë, where it was reported that the natives were massing from all sides with a view to attacking the Mazoë Fort, whilst Fairbairn with a small escort was to persevere with Chidamba. We did this more in the hope of procuring some food for our horses than in the belief that we should find any large number of rebels. From this point of view we were successful, as, having taken possession of a kraal rather larger than usual, our starving horses were treated to a grand feed of mealies, and several sackfuls more were taken back in the waggons, one shot only being fired at us from a cave in some of the neighbouring rocks. This cave we were unable to locate, and so were compelled to leave our enemy there undisturbed. We returned to the fort after the usual midday halt, the larger part of which on this occasion had to be spent by the Artillery in repairing the dissel-boom (pole) of their gun limber, which broke on the way down from the kraal. This operation speaks volumes for the handiness of the Rhodesian troopers, as it was performed with the aid only of an axe, a branch of a tree, and a piece of raw hide, and was so thoroughly successful that the gun travelled over the roughest country in the same state for the next fortnight without a hitch of any kind. In our absence Fairbairn had been most fortunate in his negotiations, and had managed to induce Chidamba and about half a dozen less important chiefs to promise to meet him on the following morning at the foot of the Granite Range, and then to proceed to the Golden Stairs, which is a peculiarly rough road, ascending a hill at the entrance to the Mazoë valley, and about eighteen miles from Salisbury. At this spot they were to interview the Great White Chiefs (*i.e.* Vintcent and Alderson), who would there hold a conference with them. As the undertakings of these gentry are not always performed with the punctuality promised, it was thought advisable not to send into Salisbury until Fairbairn had actually got them on their way to the Golden Stairs. In the morning, however, they appeared at the tryst, and a message was at once sent on to Colonel Alderson asking him to come out with the Judge as soon as possible. When I arrived at the top of the Stairs I found Fairbairn sitting alone with Chidamba. On one side, several hundred yards off, was Fairbairn's escort, whilst several other chiefs squatted at about the same distance on the other. On the hills from over half a mile off we could see a number of the natives, evidently watching the scene with interest. From time to time Chidamba would move off and consult with the chiefs, and several times messages were sent by them to their people.

Whilst this was going on a short but sturdy young nigger came up to us with a rifle, and had some conversation with Fairbairn, who then explained that he was one of the Chartered Company's Police who had deserted at the outbreak of the rebellion, and who was suspected of being the murderer of the Native Commissioner of the Mazoë District. This native's name was Mazwe. He approached us with the greatest assurance, which we afterwards attributed to the fact that, owing to his being a good shot, and well acquainted with white men's ways, he had on his return to his kraal been looked on by his people as a great warrior, and had consequently been sent by them as their representative. In fact, he was probably really more influential than any of the chiefs present on this occasion. It was impossible for us to make him a prisoner at the moment, as, even if we could have kept him in the face of the number of rebels looking on, it would at once have ended all chance of our holding any more intercourse with the chiefs, and Judge Vintcent would have come out from Salisbury to no purpose. We therefore told him that if he waited he could be present at the meeting, and could hear all that was said, and this he eventually did. After waiting for about six hours, the party from Salisbury came in sight. It included, besides the Judge and the Colonel with his staff and an escort of twenty men, Mr. Hole, resident magistrate at Salisbury, Sir Thomas Scanlan, and Mr. Campbell, N.C. In order not to frighten the natives, all the escort and horses were left at a distance. The Judge, Colonel Alderson, and Sir T. Scanlan, with Fairbairn and the black interpreter, then sat down on a rock, with the chiefs and Mazwe on the ground in front of them, all others being excluded from the proceedings, as it was thought that the chiefs would talk with greater freedom and confidence if they were allowed to converse through the people who had persuaded them to come, and whom they knew.

This, at the time, gave great offence to several of the Salisburians, who, for various reasons, were anxious to be present, and who afterwards found relief by publishing a few caustic letters in the Salisbury papers on the subject. The terms offered, and to which the chiefs agreed at this conference, were chiefly the following : That all arms were to be surrendered at the Mazoë Fort the next day. That in future the natives were to live in the places selected for them by the Chartered Company. That all murderers, and the deserters from the police, were to be handed over for trial. After these terms had been accepted, Judge Vintcent insisted on Mazwe being then and there handed over as a prisoner for trial, to show that they meant to act up to their word. This was at once done, and Mazwe was forthwith marched off to Salisbury by Colonel Alderson and his party. The Judge, Hole, and Campbell came back with us to the fort to superintend the surrender of arms on the following day.

In the morning, after waiting in vain for several hours for the arrival of the arms, Fairbairn started off to the Granite Range to find out what was delaying matters. There he was told that the natives believed Mazwe had been shot, and that they would not give up their arms until they had seen him alive. On hearing this the

Judge decided to return to Salisbury, leaving word that we should receive orders next day.

Having again run short of food for our horses, which were rapidly diminishing both in size and numbers, we spent the next day in search of grain, but were not so lucky on this occasion, and had to return without any.

As I was not feeling my best when we turned our heads for home, I decided to get into a waggon with Newnham, who was in medical charge of our party, and whose horse was unable to carry him further. All the waggons being empty we trotted most of the way. Newnham, who had been in the country some time, lay like a log and slept through the journey, whilst the only rest that I obtained was on the rather frequent occasions that we fetched up with a bump against a tree, which then had to be cut down before we could proceed, there being little hope of backing a South African waggon with a span of fourteen mules attached to it. It is difficult to describe the comfort of a drive in one of these empty vehicles, but I can safely say I never before nor since have enjoyed so lively an experience. On arrival at our camp I found Roach, Intelligence Officer on Col. Alderson's staff, who had been sent out in charge of Mazwe, with orders for us to show him to his friends, and then to return him with the same escort to Salisbury.

Next morning, after placing Mazwe on one

of the horses, and making arrangements to keep him in his position there, we started off to exhibit him at the Granite Range. Not being accustomed to horse exercise, and his riding costume consisting only of two pieces of ragged fur draped from a string round his waist, the long ride of the previous day had made a great impression on him, and at his urgent and repeated requests he was permitted to descend from his perch and perform the rest of the journey on foot, handcuffed to one of the men's stirrup irons. We spent all the morning conversing with the natives, but none of the chiefs would come down. They tried to induce us to take Mazwe up into the hills with various ingenious excuses, so we told them finally that at the expiration of twenty-four hours they would be attacked, unless before then they had surrendered their arms. Mazwe also before we left was allowed to converse with his wife at a distance of quite a quarter of a mile, in order to convince her that he was still alive, and she in return sent him down his dinner, a horrible looking compound, which he devoured with the greatest zest. At daybreak next morning I was horrified at being awakened by the non-commissioned officer commanding the guard, which had charge of the prisoner, with the news that during the night he had escaped. Search parties were of course at once sent in all directions, but no one could hit off his tracks and we were compelled to give it up and own ourselves beaten. He had been confined in the fort itself, which was an ordinary earth breastwork with a ditch outside about six feet deep, having barb wire entanglements to increase the difficulty of getting over it. The original orders were that the sentry was to stand at the door of the small galvanized-iron shed in which the prisoner and the remainder of the guard were to rest, and that Mazwe was to be handcuffed to one of the men of the guard. This however was found impossible, as a handcuff which will fit a nigger cannot be got on to the wrist of a white man, and so Mazwe had the handcuffs put on both his wrists in the ordinary manner, and was further tied to one of the guard by a stout piece of cord. Evidently he had contrived to untie this cord and slip past the sentry. His foot-prints over the parapet were found, but how a man could be clever enough with both hands handcuffed to get over the loose earth and stones, not to mention the barbed wire, without being heard by the sentry, and pass close to another sentry who was outside the fort, almost defies comprehension. A cat could not have done it better. Naturally the imperial troops who formed the guard came in for a great deal of abuse in connection with this unfortunate event; but as the majority of people imagined, in spite of one of the guard being tried by court martial afterwards, that we had not been able to resist the temptation of taking Mazwe out quietly and shooting him, we got off with less than we should otherwise have done.

As soon as the search for the fugitive had been given up, we moved our camp to Forbes' Farm again, and at twelve noon four parties went out to reconnoitre the enemy's position from different directions. These parties all brought in valuable information regarding the enemy and how they were placed; several outlying posts were driven in; a few small kraals burnt, and, better still, some cattle were captured, giving us fresh meat for a day or two.

When daylight appeared next morning we found ourselves moving to the attack of Gaderra's kraal, which lies on the northern side of the range, and which we had chosen as the best point at which to commence operations. We were all on foot and left only a small party to look after the waggons and horses, as the camp would be well within our view. We had hardly commenced the ascent of the hills before firing commenced. It was with some difficulty that the seven-pounder was dragged up into a position from where the kraal could be shelled, and after a short bombardment, which could not have had much more effect than of frightening our enemy, the Mounted Infantry and the Rhodesia Horse advanced up the hill. The position was a dense mass of rocks and trees, and the ascent was so steep that it was only with the greatest difficulty that bodies of men could be kept together. The firing increased tenfold as soon as the enemy saw our men coming up to them, but it was almost impossible to detect the position of the firers, not only on account of the trees and rocks, but chiefly because the majority of the rifles in the hands of the enemy were of a small-bore pattern and were fired out of caves some distance back from the entrance to them.

Eventually, after several hours' fighting, Ashe, with some of the Rhodesia Horse, effected an entrance into Gaderra's kraal, whilst French and King-Harman with their sections kept up a continuous fusillade, directed on the heights above, to subdue the fire from that quarter, which otherwise would have rendered Ashe's position untenable. The seven-pounder was now powerless to help owing to the close proximity of our men to the enemy. For half an hour after Ashe and his men gained a footing in the kraal, they were evidently having some sharp fighting, judging from the amount of firing going on inside, but gradually this ceased, and he signalled down for mining materials. These were sent up in boxes carried by the Shangaans. These warriors going up, came in for a fresh outburst of firing, and the boxes were constantly placed on the floor whilst the bearer returned to some position more agreeable to himself. The difficulty of persuading them to persevere increased after one of them was wounded, but finally the cases reached their destination in safety. After the customary warning, which was always given before using explosives, that all women and children who came out should be allowed to go free, and that the men might surrender and only those convicted of crime should be punished, the mines were fired and it was decided to return to the camp for the night. No sooner had this course been commenced than the enemy's fire was redoubled, as we suppose they imagined that we had been beaten back. The Mounted Infantry still kept up their fire to cover the party retiring from the kraal, but as soon as they in their turn commenced to retire, each position as they vacated it was reoccupied by the enemy. When, however, they arrived at the position where the gun was, the enemy showed that they had no inclination to tackle us in a more open country and ceased following us.

In this retirement, which was made more difficult by our having to drive some cattle, which we had captured, in front of us, Lieut. French, Royal Irish regiment, serving with the Mounted Infantry; Corporal Tully, Rhodesia Horse, and one of the Native Contingent were wounded. Late in the evening Roach and Harding arrived from Salisbury, saying that more men and rations would arrive next day. Owing to this we decided not to continue the attack on the stronghold until they arrived, and we consequently spent the next day reconnoitring the rear of the enemy's position, with the double object of gaining information concerning their line of retreat, and if possible of preventing their fleeing in a north-east direction, should they be showing any signs of doing so. We saw numbers of natives, but they were all up in the hills, evidently on the look-out, and we could find no tracks other than those of the ladies who had, according to their custom, come down during the night to fetch water for their husbands.

During the afternoon the reinforcements arrived under command of Lieut. Pilson, who had just returned from a successful patrol in the neighbourhood of Norton's Farm. The troops under him consisted of the remainder of my company (*i.e.* 1st section Royal Irish Fusiliers, Lieut. Southey; 1st section Royal Dublin Fusiliers, Lieut. Pilson); the Salisbury Rifles under Lieut. Finucane, and a detachment of the Native Contingent of about fifty Zulus. Also another seven-pounder with a detachment of the Royal Artillery, and Surgeon-Captain Hale, Army Medical Staff, accompanied by a few men of the Medical Staff Corps. In all about 140 men. Captain Moberly of the Rhodesia Horse arrived at the same time to take command of the guns. The wounded were sent into Salisbury during the day.

At sunrise next day I attacked with the whole force from the same direction as on the previous occasion, and at first met with slight opposition. Evidently the sight of our increase of strength had been too much for our opponents, as there were undoubted signs of numbers having moved off northwards during the night. This was most disappointing. On our ascent we were fired at from time to time and from different positions, but we were obviously only fighting with outposts who retired as we advanced. This of course was a very slow proceeding, not only on account of the difficult climbing, but also from the necessity of making sure that we left none of the enemy in our rear. On our way we burnt several kraals and mined some of the more important caves. The Salisbury Rifles and Zulus on the right with Harding and Ashe, both most valuable officers, whose coolness and daring on every occasion it would be hard to beat, came in for most of the fighting, and drove the enemy back from one position to another, until a determined stand was made in Chidamba's kraal. In this kraal was the cave of the famous witch-doctress Nyanda, who was reported to be the cause of most of the discontent prevailing in the district and whose capture we were consequently most anxious to effect. It took some time to find the entrance to the kraal, and after heavy firing on both sides it was rushed by Lieut. Pilson and the Royal Dublin Fusiliers section. The natives pursued their ordinary tactics and retired into their caves, which on this occasion were even more extensive than usual, and from which it was hopeless of thinking of dislodging them with the mining material in our possession. However, we captured many arms and cattle and a quantity of property which had been taken by the natives from their murdered victims, all of which were concealed in Nyanda's cave, but unfortunately the witch was gone. This cave we determined to destroy completely, in order to show the natives that the white man had little respect for Nyanda's power. After a party, which had been sent to warn everybody to come out of the cave, had returned and reported that all was clear, the mines were fired and the place blown to pieces.

We then turned for our camp, as the sun was low, and were moving off when a terrible scene met our view. Behind us a practically nude figure, apparently blind, covered with dirt and blood and crying out for water, came hurrying up to us in a more pitiable condition than I can describe. For some seconds one could not think what it meant, but we soon saw that it must be one of our own people who had in some way or other been injured by the explosion. By some mischance the poor fellow had been concealed behind a rock when the party went in to order all out of the cave, and had met with this terrible accident. He was one of the Salisbury Rifles, named Day, and it turned out afterwards that he had found a £5 bank-note and was diligently hunting for more, quite innocent of his danger. He had been blown out of the cave and fell through a tree, which no doubt saved his life, a distance of at least thirty feet. Curiously enough he had put his £5 note in his trousers' pocket, and these garments were taken completely off him by the explosion. As soon as his loss became generally known, it was curious to find how many of his friends, and their name appeared to be legion, were anxious to go next day to try and recover his rifle for him, this weapon having of course been his companion during his search in the cave and probably therefore in pieces. I am glad to say that after being taken to Salisbury Hospital, and placed under the care of Dr. Fleming, Mother Patrick, and the Jesuit Sisters —to whom numbers in Rhodesia, including myself, owe a lasting debt of gratitude—except for being slightly deaf, he came out little the worse for his terrifying experience.

When we arrived at our camp, which was reached without further fighting, we found that Colonel Alderson, with Nicholls and Wilson-Fox of his staff, had come out to see how things were going. As rations were short with us, and all available food at Salisbury was required for the laager expedition to the Hartley Hills, it was decided not to follow up the Mazoë rebels at present, and so after another day at Forbes' Farm, which was utilized by the Colonel in going to inspect Mazoë Fort and the Granite

Range, and by the troops in two parties under Pilson and Moberly in further patrolling the scene of the late operations, to make certain that the enemy had finally vacated the position, we commenced our return march to Salisbury to prepare for our trip to Hartley.

CHAPTER XII

THE HARTLEY HILLS

THE early days of October were spent in endeavouring to obtain some reliable information about the Hartley district, and the roads to it. There were no dependable maps, and none of the many men, miners, prospectors, and traders that I interviewed, really knew the country well. Most of these *said* they did, but when it came to taking the map and asking them: "Now what's the country like between here and there?" the answer was nearly always, "Oh, I don't know that bit."

However, by putting the pieces known together, by taking the mean of the various accounts, and with the help of a skeleton map from the Survey department, we managed to compile what we thought was a fairly accurate map, but which we afterwards found did not bear much comparison with the ground it was supposed to represent. However, it was sufficiently good to talk over plans with, or, to use correct language, for "strategical purposes."

Jenner had taken a copy of the early edition of this map with him to Charter, so that he and I, and any one at Charter with local knowledge, could talk over (on the wire) the combined movement on the Hartley Hills. We had this talk on October 3rd, and some of it may be interesting, especially perhaps to non-military readers, as showing how things had to be worked out. The Mr. Keith, with whom I talked with after my conversation with Jenner, was a local man supposed to know the country well, and the conversation seems to prove that this supposition was right. It will be noticed that I, to a certain extent, cross-examined him in order to prove this.

Conversation over the telegraph wire between Colonel Alderson, at Salisbury, and Major Jenner, at Charter.

Col. Alderson—I presume you are ready to start at short notice? we are waiting arrival of convoy.

Major Jenner—At present there are only thirty bags mealies in store; we expect waggons back from collecting to-morrow, otherwise I am ready, except seven-pounder ammunition, which you know about.

Col. Alderson—I hope to start Monday, in that case you would have to start Tuesday. I must think over the question of the roads and wire you definitely; I am inclined to think the middle road is the best to prevent escape to Lomagundi's, and every one here tells me it is the best road. I have some socket signals to send up at night, when I think you should be in a position to see them; they throw red and white stars. Please instruct your sentries to look out when near Mashangombi's. Have you anything to answer with?

Major Jenner—Sorry to say I have not.

Col. Alderson—You could fire a blank charge from the seven-pounder, or perhaps Charter has a few rockets, or you might improvise some.

Major Jenner—I will see what I can do and let you know.

Col. Alderson—Don't forget that on the map the road from Mashangombi's to Beatrice Mine is on the wrong side of river.

Major Jenner—Yes. Keith is here now and can speak if you wish it.

Conversation over the telegraph wire between Colonel Alderson and Mr. Keith.

Col. Alderson—I should like to speak to you. Does not the south road run through a deal of swamp?

Mr. Keith—Yes; not at this time of year.

Col. Alderson—Is it not at this time of year very much cut up and are there not a great many ruts?

Mr. Keith—When I went along last it was all right.

Col. Alderson—When was that?

Mr. Keith—Last year, September, October.

Col. Alderson—Is there much bush?

Mr. Keith—Yes; there is a good bit.

Col. Alderson—And are there not long distances between water?

Mr. Keith—No, not very long, the longest is thirteen miles? no others longer than nine miles.

Col. Alderson—Is there plenty of water?

Mr. Keith—Yes, lots.

Col. Alderson—Will it be possible to leave the road immediately north of Mashangombi's and strike the road on the west of it?

Mr. Keith—You would leave the road by the old Matabele raiding track.

Col. Alderson—Have you been along that path?

Mr. Keith—Yes; on foot.

Col. Alderson—Will it take waggons?

Mr. Keith—My boys have taken my waggons, but I never have myself, so can give no particulars.

Col. Alderson—Do you know anything of the country the other side of river, immediately south of Mashangombi's?

Mr. Keith—I know the country both sides of the river immediately south of Mashangombi's.

Col. Alderson—Could Major Jenner leave the Charter Road south of Mashangombi's and go straight to the kraal?

Mr. Keith—Major Jenner leaves south-east of

Mashangombi's kraal and crosses the Umfuli River on the dotted red line.

Col. Alderson—Do you notice anything wrong with the map between Mashangombi's and Beatrice Mine?

Mr. Keith—The Beatrice Mine is marked correctly, but there should be a road running parallel to the river on the south from the Beatrice Mine to the red dotted line.

Col. Alderson—Does it cross the river at the red dotted line?

Mr. Keith—Yes.

Col. Alderson—And that is where you propose Major Jenner should cross?

Mr. Keith—Yes.

Col. Alderson—In your opinion, you think the south road would be best for the Salisbury column?

Mr. Keith—Yes.

On October 4th, the news of Captain Pease's operations at Chipara's and Manyerbeera's, near Marandellas (Patrol No. 17, Part III., Appendix C), arrived. At the taking of the former kraal another piece of heroism on the part of a local force officer occurred.

Lieut. Leigh Lye, Umtali Rifles, was severely wounded close to the entrance of a cave unseen before the shot was fired. Lieut. Morris, of the same corps, who was near by, at once went to his assistance, picked him up, and was carrying him out of the line of fire from the cave, when he himself was dangerously wounded by a shot fired from a rifle which was poked out of a crack in the rock, and of which the muzzle almost touched him. Both officers were got out of their dangerous position and taken to the hospital at Marandellas, where Lieut. Morris died the same evening from incontrollable hemorrhage. Another gallant life lost, in a gallant action, in this miserable cave fighting!

While making final preparations for the move on Hartley, we were given another blow by the everlasting supply question, Fox informing me that, owing to the non-arrival of an expected food convoy, he could only give us fourteen days' rations of "bully beef," and we wanted a month's! This would of course entail the sending back for more, and must, more or less, act as a tether to our movements; but there was no help for it, and on the 5th, taking what we could get, we actually made a start on this much put off "patrol."

The force (see Patrol No. 18, Part III., Appendix C), being a much mixed one, I merely ordered for the first day's move a rendezvous by four P.M. at a stream four miles from Salisbury, having learnt from experience that, under similar circumstances, an early simultaneous start meant long waiting for the punctual ones, and bad packing of waggons, and vexation for all.

On riding out in the evening to join the

column, we (*i.e.* myself, with Godley and Roach as Staff Officers, and Nicholls, Fox junior, Harding, and Robin Grey, as gallopers) found them well settled in a diamond-shaped laager, which we had decided to adopt, instead of the square one we had used hitherto. Godley had carefully worked out the details of this laager, and had published, with the orders for the patrol, an excellent plan, showing the position of each unit and each waggon belonging to it. The result of this was that, even on this, the first evening, the laager had been formed quickly and without any bother. Though it is somewhat technical, the reproduction of this picture may be interesting (see opposite page).

It will be seen that the men slept outside this laager; this was due to the fact that the horses completely filled the inside.

Sleeping on the outside and running *back* to man the waggons, in case of alarm, is a very different thing to sleeping inside and jumping *up* to man them, and having in view this, and also the crowd of horses inside, I decided that in this instance the men should, in case of an attack, fight where they slept. If not quite so well placed to stop a sudden rush, as they would be on the waggons, they would be far safer from chance shots fired at night, and in any case were only doing what had been done in the Soudan, without any waggons at all, against far more formidable enemies.

THE LAAGER

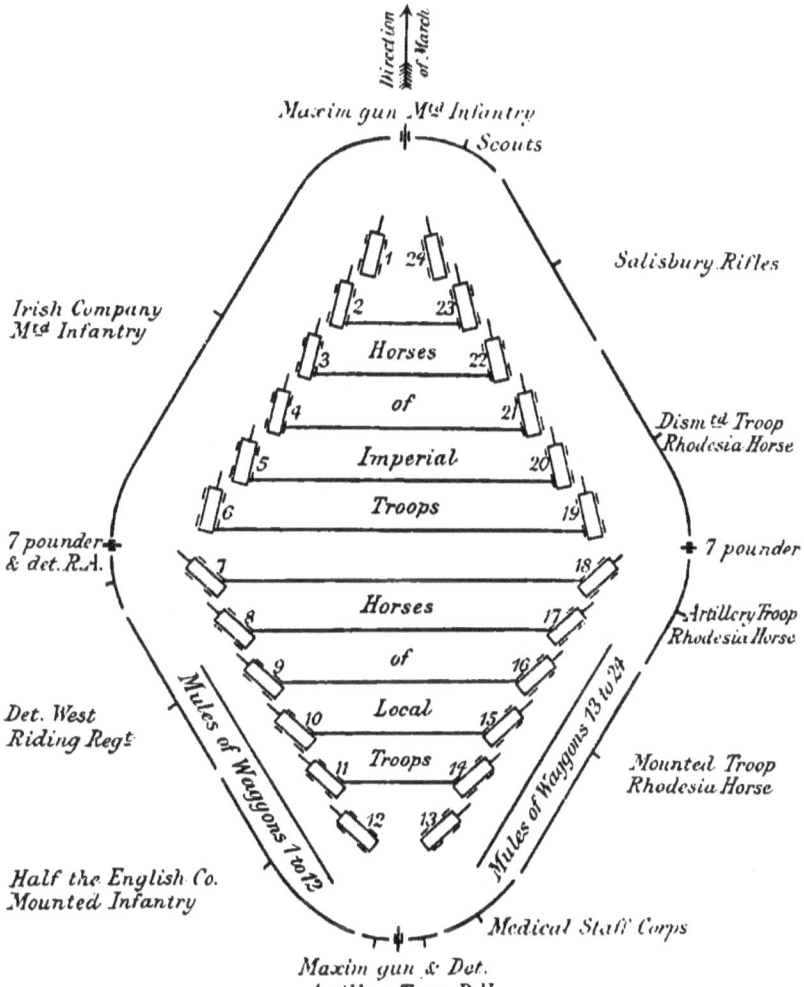

The shape of this laager lent itself much more readily to quick formation on a badly shaped or cramped piece of ground than the square one, as, no matter how distorted or elongated it had to be, each waggon could still go into its accustomed place. This was still the case even if the waggons were only drawn up on each side of a road, as might possibly be necessary in thick bush, or among trees.

CROSSING THE HUNYANI.

On the 6th we were off soon after daybreak, and reached the Hunyani River a little before sunset. While the waggons were crossing the steep and sandy drift, having to double span in many cases, a shot was fired at McMahon, who was making good the ground on the far side of the river with the advanced guard.

THE WITCH-DOCTOR PUZZLED

On cantering on to see what was up, I found that a few natives had been chased into or through (for they had miraculously disappeared) a small kraal upon a kopje in the bush. This kraal was destroyed and some ten head of cattle captured. Two or three of these were said to have belonged to Norton, whose farm was close by. It was on this day that Jenner marched from Charter, in order to meet us at Mashangombi's.

On the 7th we were at the Sirua River, and on the 8th at the Zimbo. On the 9th we left the road in the morning and struck almost due south across the veldt. Later in the day we cut into the Hartley Hill—Beatrice Mine road (see Map), and turned east along it, outspanning for the night about three miles *west* of Mashangombi's main kraal. After dark we sent up socket signals (a sort of rocket throwing coloured stars), and these were answered by star shells from Jenner's column, which was then where we wished, and expected it, about four miles *east* of Mashangombi's.

No doubt the latter gentleman saw, and was somewhat perturbed at, these signs of our presence, which his witch-doctor must have been hard put to to explain.

Leaving a sufficient laager guard, we moved off early the next morning for Mashangombi's. After going about two miles natives were heard shouting to each other in some kopjes just ahead, and we detached two sections of the Irish company Mounted Infantry, the Salisbury Rifles, and the Native Contingent, to clear them. This they very soon did, and, following up the enemy quickly, they got into and captured the main kraal without further assistance.

The natives were either taken by surprise, or (knowing they had stronger places) did not intend to hold this kraal, and, though they appeared to enter them, they did not remain in its caves, and all of these which could be located were blown up.

About 11 A.M. we effected a junction with Jenner, who was "marching to the sound of the cannon" from the east. Later in the day many other kraals were taken and burnt without opposition. These included Tora's, Quata's, Morumba's, and Inyoka's, the latter being the celebrated native general. From the shields, head-dresses, and assegais found, it was evident that many Matabele had been in the kraals.

The following casualties occurred during the day: Severely wounded—Lieut. R. F. Ashe, Artillery Troop, Rhodesia Horse; No. 5357, Private F. Colin, 1st Battalion Royal Dublin Fusiliers, serving with the Mounted Infantry. Slightly wounded—Sergeant A. Feltham, Artillery Troop, Rhodesia Horse.

Lieut. Ashe had his left arm nearly blown off by a shot fired through a crack in the rock up which he was climbing.

A very brave and kindly deed was done this day by Mr. Colin Harding, who was with us as a volunteer and was attached to my staff. He, with several others, was outside the entrance to a cave from which several "family guns" had been fired. Some of the Mounted Infantry were ordered to fire volleys into this cave. Just before the order was carried out a child's voice was heard crying inside. Mr. Harding then asked leave to go in, and bring it out before the volleys were fired. Should the Mashonas be still in the cave this might mean certain death to him, but in he went, and came out with a little, perfectly blind, Mashona child in his arms. This is how the "brutal soldier and volunteer treats the unfortunate native!" (Exeter Hall please note). I had subsequently much pleasure in bringing this act to the notice of the Royal Humane Society, but unfortunately their rules do not provide for a case of this sort.

That night Jenner's column laagered close to Mashangombi's kraal, and mine returned to where we had left the waggons. The next day (October 11th) we worked the two columns in such a manner as to thoroughly scour the whole district. Threw them into the immense covert of bushes and boulders, like a pack of hounds in fact, with a view to find the kraals and locate the bulk of the natives. Equally like a pack of hounds, when once in the covert, they scattered and were out of hand, and I could only ride about like a huntsman and endeavour to make my way at times to where the greatest volume of the "cry" (represented by rifle shots) seemed to come from.

It was not till the afternoon that we heard in the distance, apparently down by the river, the repeated "crack, crack" of Lee-Metford rifle volleys in the same place, which seemed to indicate that something had been run to ground. Turning in the direction of the sound we made our way there as quickly as possible, and this was not very fast, for care had to be exercised in passing under, or between, the many ugly looking kopjes and boulders, and through the dense bush. As we went we gathered up any of the scattered pack that we came across.

After about half an hour's riding we struck the Umfuli River, and there we found McMahon, with three sections of his company, baying in front of the kraal shown on the opposite page and also on page 203. He had, with his usual go-a-headness, gone for it directly he came across it, and had got half way across the river, but then found the fire too hot, and wisely decided to wait for reinforcements.

In getting back to the north bank of the river McMahon was hit in the foot, but, in spite of this, he remained with his company until I sent word that he must go to the ambulance.

The kraal was known as Chena's, and, as will be seen by Hare's excellent sketch, it appeared an ugly place to tackle. By the time

THE WESTERN PORTION OF CHEVA'S KRAAL AS SEEN FROM THE NORTH SIDE OF THE UMFULI RIVER

we had collected and concentrated a sufficient force to attack it with, the sun was beginning to set, and, seeing the size of the place and the thickness of the bush and of the boulders round it, we decided that it would be better to wait until the next day. I should have liked to have placed piquets round it; but its size, the distance we were from the laagers, the work done by the men during the day, and also the fact that the natives would think we were afraid of it, and therefore be sure to stay there, made me consider that that game was not worth the candle. So, having fired some shells into it, with the result of setting a portion on fire, we began our march back to the laager just as the sun disappeared behind the western line of bush.

Much to my regret I found that we had again had several casualties. These were: Killed—Trooper J. S. Coryndon, Salisbury Rifles. Severely wounded—No. 4213, Private B. Byrne, 1st Royal Dublin Fusiliers; and No. 4014, Private J. M'Kay, 1st Royal Irish regiment, both serving with the Mounted Infantry; Captain Sir H. McMahon, Bart., Royal Welsh Fusiliers, commanding the Irish company Mounted Infantry. Slightly wounded—One man, Native Contingent. One horse killed.

Many kraals had been taken and burnt, and some 100 head of cattle captured; but I doubt if the enemy had lost many men, they took such precious good care to keep under cover!

Poor young Coryndon (a brother of the well-known, in Rhodesia, "Bob" Coryndon, a great hunter and a friend of Mr. Rhodes) had, like Johnson at Simbanoota's, been caught by one of the many traps set; in his case it was a rug, placed in front of a crack in the rock, and had been shot through the head. A fine, cheery, dare-devil boy he was.

The following day, October 12th, we rendezvoused early outside Jenner's laager, and moved off at once to Chena's. There were several among those I talked to on the subject who were against going to this kraal again, arguing that as we had set it on fire (I am told that the burning of a kraal is an accepted sign of defeat among the natives), there was little more that we could do. Personally, though very anxious to keep down the number of casualties, I did not see it in this light, and considered that you cannot claim to have taken a kraal unless you actually go into it.

Directly we debouched from the mass of kopjes, opposite to the kraal on the north side of the river, we found that our surmise—that the natives would stay there—was correct, as their bullets began to sing over our heads. As Hare's sketch only shows the part of the kraal which he could see from the spot on which he drew it, perhaps the very rough one which I drew at the time will help to make our movements clear.

In the first instance, we concentrated the force

behind the big kopje, the position of which is shown in the sketch, but which is not drawn in, because it obstructs the general *coup d'œil*. I then rode about looking at the place from various points, and finally crossed the river to the west, and rode through the bush close up to the south side of the kraal. I found that this, though by

CHENA'S KRAAL, TAKEN OCT. 12TH.
(The kopje on which the kraal is built is about a thousand yards long, it was fortified more or less, and was all held.)

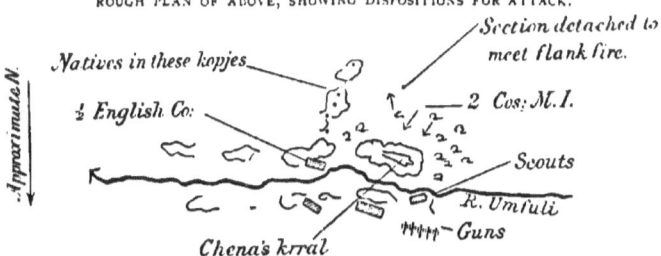

ROUGH PLAN OF ABOVE, SHOWING DISPOSITIONS FOR ATTACK.

no means nice, could be more easily assaulted than the north side. I then directed Jenner to move the Rifle and the Irish companies Mounted Infantry round to the south, by the drift on the east, while the Natal Troop, and the Mounted Troop Rhodesia Horse, crossed to the west. The Mounted Infantry were to assault, with the Natal Troop in reserve, and the Rhodesia Horse to guard the horses. While these movements were going on, the remainder of the force got into the positions in which they are shown on the small plan below the sketch. When all were in position, I sent the order for the guns to open, and this was the signal for all the troops, on the north side, to begin a heavy and continuous fire, in order to attract the enemy's attention to that side.

This fire was kept up for some ten minutes, and when it ceased, by prearranged signal, the Mounted Infantry, who had been lying down at the edge of the bush on the south side, at once commenced their advance. Directly they appeared in the narrow strip of open, between the edge of the bush and the foot of the hill on which the kraal was built, they were fired at from the kopjes· (shown on both sketch and plan), running at right angles to the one they were attacking. To meet this flank fire a section was detached, as quietly as if on a field day, and the rest of the two companies continued their advance, scaled the kopje and took the kraal, with the loss of one of Honey's men killed, and two Mounted Infantry men wounded.

Directly the first men of the Mounted Infantry appeared on the top of the kopje, where shown

THE NORFOLK AND THE HAMPSHIRE SECTIONS OF THE ENGLISH COMPANY
MOUNTED INFANTRY GETTING INTO THE EAST END OF CHENA'S KRAAL
"WHEN WILL A 'FAMILY GUN' GO OFF?"

on the sketch, many natives showed themselves among the bush and boulders on the lower north side, and the troops on the far side of the river at once opened on them, causing them to scatter and disappear. Very soon Jenner's men were running about in all directions, setting fire to the huts and stockades, and the whole of the kraal on the west end of the kopje was shortly in a blaze.

While this had been going on, the half English company had worked, from the position it is shown in on the plan, into the portion of the kraal on the east end of the kopje. In doing this they had some very awkward work, as will be seen by the sketch on the next page, and great credit is due to Lieutenants Harland and Hare, and the men under them, for the way in which they did it. How "jumpy" the work was, one instance will show. Private C. Grapes, of the Norfolk section, English company, Mounted Infantry, having climbed into the kraal, was walking across it, when "bang" went a rifle, fired up through one of the cracks in the rock underneath his feet. The bullet entered the upper part of the underneath side of his thigh, and, going upwards, inflicted a most horrible wound, from which he died some eight days afterwards. Poor lad! a nice, fresh, typical eastern counties' boy he was. That this sort of way of being wounded did not make them show signs of "jumpiness," says a great deal for the nerve of the young soldier. But, in this kind of work, and in all kinds of chancey and go-a-head work, the young soldier seems better than the old; in the same way as the young and impetuous hunter is better than the old and perhaps stale one, when hounds really run, and the ground is hard and the fences are blind, for he does not refuse from "knowing too much," or because he is afraid of hurting himself when he lands, but throws his heart over and jumps all he knows after it.

It is when sitting still under fire, and seeing men hit around him, or when retreating, and things look black, that the experience of the old soldier comes in; because he is able to say to himself, "I was in just as bad a place at so and so, and came out all right." In the same way as the old hunter, on the top of a trappy bank, thinks, "If I change my feet quickly here I shan't go down like I did as a four-year-old at so-and-so."

But I am off the track, and bringing the play of hunting into the work of fighting.

When the fire started by the half English company, flared up and joined those lighted by the Irish and the Rifle companies, the whole of the kraal, or rather kraals, for there were several detached clusters of huts, were in a blaze, and we could say that Chena's was taken. I then sent the Native Contingent in to complete the incendiary work, which was a congenial operation to them, as it meant loot as well. In this case, however, they did not find the job as pleasant as usual, for they were several times fired at by lurking Mashonas, who had remained hidden in the innumerable caves and crannies while the Mounted Infantry were in the kraal.

The advance of the Native Contingent on the kraal was, as usual, very funny. Once told to attack a place, or that the enemy is anywhere near, loose off their rifles they *must*, up in the air, into the ground, at every rock or boulder, and over each other's, or any one else's, heads. It does not matter so long as a *noise* is made. This is supposed to put fear into the heart of the enemy, and no doubt it did make many a Mashona think twice before he put his head out of his hole to fire. And goodness knows, that with the Native Contingent, or "Black Watch," as we called them, attacking, no one *anywhere* within range was safe.

At this time the "Black Watch" was commanded by Captain Brabant, and a more wonderful man with natives I never saw. When in charge of the Charter district he had been known by the natives all over Mashonaland as "Makabere," *i.e.* "the man who knows everything." Certainly with the "Black Watch" he could *do anything* and make them *go anywhere*. Did a man hang back when attacking a kraal, or get out of line when skirmishing in the bush, Captain Brabant had only to turn his horse towards him to make him run in the required direction, as if ten thousand devils were after him! Before this officer took command, the "Black Watch" were like a herd of sheep, and always in the way; now they were handy, mobile, and very useful.

While the "Black Watch" were having their run through the kraal, a few caves, including that from which poor young Grapes had been shot, were mined and destroyed. But they were much too numerous to be all treated in the same way, and, as I have before said, it was doubtful if in such a honeycombed place the mining of one cave did not make another equally good one.

What had been the result of the day's work? The kraal had been taken and burnt, a few caves destroyed, and a considerable number of natives killed. (Seven dead were counted in one small outer kraal, and many seen in the main kraal, while many were no doubt pulled into the caves.) Was this decisive? It undoubtedly would have been had we been able, there and then, to build a fort on the kopje opposite to the kraal on the north side of the river, and leave in it a garrison of about 100 white men and 50 Native Contingent, with orders to fire at any natives seen in or near the kraal, and to so patrol the mealie gardens in the district that they should be unable to sow. This must have obliged them to leave the district, or to surrender.

Establish this fort at that time we could not. We might, at a pinch, have spared the men (though we had Lomagundi's, Mapondera's, and other districts to visit before the rains), and other difficulties in the way, such as terms of service (for the garrison must come from the local forces), medical arrangements, clothing, etc., etc., might have been overcome. The real stopper was the old question—supply. We ourselves could not provision the fort, and we knew that Salisbury, even if we sent back there, was equally powerless in this respect. Once the rains set in, communication between Salisbury and Hartley was uncertain, owing to the rivers, and the softness of the soil over which the track passed. We were told that waggons had been known to be three weeks waiting to cross the Hunyani in the rainy season. To leave a garrison at Hartley to which we could not even give a fortnight's rations was therefore not to be thought of.

Our casualties during the day had been: Killed—Trooper P. J. Botha, Honey's Scouts. Dangerously wounded—No. 3925, Private C. Grapes, 2nd Norfolk regiment, serving with the Mounted Infantry. Severely wounded—No. 8224, Private T. Boardman, 4th K.R.R. Corps, serving with the Mounted Infantry; two men, Native Contingent. Slightly wounded—No. 7745, Private A. Harding, 4th K.R.R. Corps, serving with the Mounted Infantry; No. 3931, Private H.

Everett, 2nd West Riding regiment. Two horses killed and one wounded.

Fifteen casualties in the three days. Quite enough, considering the size of the force, to give me plenty to think about as we rode back to the laagers that evening. It was during this ride that I realized how much *less pleasant* it is to direct operations, and to say to one officer, "Take your men there," to another, "Attack that kopje," etc., than it is to receive such orders and then to say to your own little lot of men, "Come on." The latter is exhilarating, like a good run with hounds in a stiff country; the former is like seeing a dear friend ride a steeplechase over a severe course on a bad horse.

One thing in the three days' fighting I am sure of, and that is, that the wounded could not under the circumstances have been picked up quicker, or made more comfortable than they were under the arrangements made by Surgeon-Captain Hale.

That night I had a talk with Mr. Arthur Eyre, Captain Brabant, and others with knowledge of the natives and their ways, and their universal opinion was that, as we could not establish a fort, we should do no good by remaining longer in the district, from which they considered that the bulk of the natives had fled. The latter idea was certainly borne out by the reports of the mounted patrols, which we had daily sent out, all of which stated that there were numerous tracks of natives going towards Thaba Insimbi Hill, and the Iron Mine Hill, south-west of Charter. The patrols had followed up some of these tracks, but the natives had too much start, and they only succeeded in overtaking and capturing a few stray women and cattle.

All the above, coupled with the facts that time was getting short, that we had no mealies for the animals, and that the grass and the water where we were were bad, made me decide to make a move the following morning.

CHAPTER XIII

THE UMVUKWE MOUNTAINS AND EYRE'S FARM

ON the 13th October we moved to the Zimbo River, where the grass and water were good. During the following day we remained halted in order that the men might rest and wash and the animals graze, and all these were badly needed.

A convoy was organized, and the wounded, under charge of Surgeon-Captain Saw, Army Medical Staff, left for Salisbury with the Natal Troop, and the detachment West Riding regiment as escort. Several small patrols were sent out during the day, and burnt some three or four kraals of 150 to 200 huts in all, but saw no natives.

On the 15th we moved along what is locally known as the north Hartley-Salisbury road to Matibo's kraal. This was deserted, and had apparently been left in a hurry, for the grain had not, as usual, been hidden, and we got about a waggon-load.

During the 16th and 17th we continued our

march to the Hunyani River through a most fertile-looking and well-watered country, full of game of all sorts, sable and roan antelope, hartbeest, hares, pheasants, partridges, and water fowl of various sorts, while a few ostriches were seen by the scouts and flanking parties.

Midday on the 17th saw us at the Hunyani, which we struck about three miles west of its junction with the Gwebi (see map), and which we reached by leaving the road and striking across the veldt for some ten miles. That afternoon was spent in constructing a "drift" over the river, in bathing, and in dynamiting fish.

"Most unsportsman like," did you say? Well, perhaps so, but there was no one to catch them in the orthodox way, and we were only too glad to give the men a change from "bully beef," no matter how. The operation was most successful, and every one had fresh fried fish for tea, rather muddy-tasting and bony, perhaps, but nevertheless quite a treat. They were of various sorts, some rather like bream, others more like trout in shape, with beautiful red and yellow stripes, locally known as "tiger fish."

The next day, the 18th, I decided to again detach Jenner's column, and send it to destroy some kraals about fifteen miles down stream, while mine crossed the river and moved in a N.N.E. direction along the east side of the Umvukwe Mountains, making its own road as it went. We thought we had made the "drift" rather well, but it took us an hour to cross even with the aid of much shouting and little pulling on the part of the "Black Watch."

During this day's march the flanking parties burnt two kraals, captured two native women and a few cattle and goats, but saw no men. That night the horses ate the last of the mealies found at Matibo's, and so were again reduced to indifferent grass. Not only was it a case of no food, but it was also a case of no road, and consequently, for the mules, of dragging the heavy waggons through scrub and grass over the, at times, soft veldt. Small wonder that when we arrived near Eyre's Farm, on the evening of the 20th, both mules and horses were much done up.

During the march on the 20th, Eyre took me over the Umvukwe Mountains and showed me in the distance the kraals whose inhabitants had murdered his brother. Most treacherously too. A body of them went to the farm in the early days of the rising (June 21st was the actual date), and told poor Herbert Eyre that they wanted work. While talking about this, one of them went behind him, stunned him with a battle-axe or a knob kerrie, and the rest at once set on him. This is the story told to his brother, Arthur Eyre, by a native servant who was present, and who managed to escape. We had much satisfaction in routing out these

Mashonas and destroying their kraals two days later!

Since leaving the Zimbo on the 15th we had moved with parties some five to ten miles wide on each flank, so that a strip of country fifteen to twenty miles wide was thoroughly swept. In this way, though few natives were seen, many kraals were found and burnt.

On the 21st we remained halted, and Jenner's column, which had been following in our tracts, rejoined. During the morning I went up to his house with Arthur Eyre. A comfortable, roomy building it is, in a charming site. Half way up and with its back to the mountain, it has grand views to the west, north, and east, so that from it Eyre can see the greater part of his farm. It would be well to explain that the word "farm" does not, in Rhodesia, necessarily mean cultivated or arable land; it is used in talking of any piece of ground that a man possesses. In Eyre's case there was only an acre or so of cultivated ground, a lot of grand grazing, and a good deal of wood and mountain.

Poor Herbert Eyre had been sitting on the steps of the house when so treacherously attacked, and on them we saw the marks of his blood. Inside, the Mashonas had slashed and hacked things about in the same way as they had done at the Headlands' store. The Salisbury-Sinoia and Ayrshire Mine road runs just below the house, and across this the Mashonas had taken trouble to build a fairly solid stone wall, three feet six inches to four feet high. Up on the hill sides above this were stone schances commanding the road each way. While looking about outside the house I picked up Herbert Eyre's diary, the last entry being on the 19th June, two days before he was murdered.

On the 22nd, Jenner's column rested, and I marched with the combatants of mine at three A.M. for the kraals which Arthur Eyre had shown me in the distance on the 20th. He acted as our guide, with no small satisfaction I should imagine, though he said very little. We had a long day's work in a difficult and thickly-bushed country, and, for most of us, it was not very exciting; for, though we found and burnt seven large kraals and many small detached ones, we did not see a single native.

A detached party, however, under Captain Daly, Rhodesia Horse (and late 15th Hussars), did find a considerable number in Zimba's kraal, which they took, burnt, and destroyed. In attacking this kraal, Captain Edward Finucane, commanding the Salisbury Rifles, was hit in the leg by a big bullet (Eyre thought very probably fired from one of his large bore rifles, which the Mashonas had looted), and, though at once attended to, the shock, the loss of blood, and the nine or ten miles back to the laager on a stretcher, were too much for him, and he died the same evening. This officer was one of the best in the local forces, and a pluckier, more cheery, or a better rough-and-tumble soldier, it would be impossible to find.

The following day we remained halted, and the whole force attended poor Finucane's funeral. We buried him below Eyre's, and the Salisbury Rifles put up a cross and built a stone wall round his grave. That afternoon we had a heavy thunder and rain storm, the feature of which was a very big "devil," which drove right through the laager, and took rugs, helmets, loose coats, and everything at all portable, some hundred feet up into the air, and dropped them again all over the veldt. A South African "devil" is a little whirlwind which may start on the spot, or may be seen coming across the veldt a long way off. It is a most objectionable thing to come into a laager, particularly a dusty one, or if you have got all your papers out.

In the evening, four waggons, escorted by the Natal Troop, arrived at Salisbury, bringing "bully beef," biscuits, etc., and also some very acceptable letters.

On the 24th I again divided the force, sending one portion under Jenner to strike across country for Mapondera's, and thence to the Mazoë district. The other, under Godley, to Sinoia's and the Ayrshire Mine. The latter tells his own story in the next chapter, and of the former more hereafter.

When the order for these movements was issued a new difficulty cropped up. I was told that it was impossible for many of the men to go because their boots were totally worn out. We then had a general turn-out and inspection of *all the boots and shoes*[1] *everybody had*, and by

TOMMY ATKINS' FIGHTING KIT ABOUT THE END OF OCTOBER. RATHER "PART WORN."

dint of taking from those, all over the force, who had more than one wearable pair, and much

[1] We had luckily drawn a pair of these for each man before leaving Cape Town. They were carried one on the outside of each wallet, and were by this time the only footgear that many of the men had, shortness of transport having prohibited the carrying of a second pair of boots. For the same reason the men had, throughout the operations, very little but what they stood up in, and their kits were by this time considerably "part worn" (*vide* sketch).

chopping and changing, we managed to rig every one out somehow. Anyhow, the columns marched.

At the same time I started for Salisbury with the Natal Troop and the empty food waggons, Nicholls, Roach, Grey, and Arthur Eyre accompanying me. The horses of the three former had knocked up, and they were reduced to walking, not a dignified mode of progression for staff officers!

On the 25th I left the waggons and my walking staff, rode through to Salisbury with Eyre, and took over the command there from Watts, who returned to the line of communications.

CHAPTER XIV

THE SINOIA AND THE AYRSHIRE MINE PATROL

BY BREVET-MAJOR A. J. GODLEY

ON October 24th, having seen Colonel Alderson off to Salisbury, and Jenner to Mazoë, I started in the afternoon with a column for the Lomagundi and Sinoia district. The force was composed as follows :

	All Ranks.
Staff,	8
Scouts,	12
Irish company Mounted Infantry with Maxim,	109
Medical Staff Corps,	6
Mounted Troop Rhodesia Horse,	30
Artillery Troop Rhodesia Horse,	30
(One seven pounder and two Maxims).	
Salisbury Rifles,	35
Native Contingent,	76
Total,	306

with 21 mule waggons.

Colonel Alderson had kindly lent me Wilson, Fox, and Harding from his staff, to act as gallopers; Lieutenant (now Brevet-Major) Pilson, of my regiment, was in command of the Mounted Infantry company, and acted as staff officer; Captains Daly (late 15th Hussars), and Moberly (late R.A.), were in command of the cavalry and artillery of the Rhodesia Horse, and with Captain Brabant to lead the Native Contingent, and Surgeon-Captain Hale, D.S.O., to look after the medical arrangements, I considered myself very lucky in my command. The only difficulties were mealies and boots. We had a long way to go in a certain time, with no mealies for the mules and uncommonly little for the horses, and, in the event of much rain, with consequent heavy roads and swollen rivers, it would be touch-and-go whether the animals would last long enough to enable us to visit as much country as the Colonel wished. The question of boots was a serious one too. Many of the Salisbury Rifles, and the dismounted party of the Mounted Infantry, whose horses had died, were already almost barefooted, and one could hardly have wondered if they had grumbled at being now ordered to turn their heads away from Salisbury, and start on a practically fresh expedition. However, so far from grumbling, every one had made shift to get himself some sort of foot-covering. The Colonel, and one or two other officers who had them, had supplied lawn-tennis shoes, the sick going back to Salisbury had contributed anything they had, and the

Natal Troop, who were to escort the Colonel, had taken their boots off, and exchanged them for the "remnants" of their foot-slogging friends. Those who had not been able to cover their feet in any other way had sewn strips of horse or ox-hide across the holes, and so we set off. We had hardly started when down (without any warning, as is the way of them in South Africa) came a terrific rain and hail storm, and, as I watched the mules straining up the hill by Eyre's Farm, and the foot-sloggers toiling and slipping in the mud, I must confess to having felt rather down-hearted at the prospect of a rainy trip. However, the men didn't seem to mind, and we contented ourselves with a short trek for the first day.

We had to do a long march next day, so—after a very windy and uncomfortable night, fortunately the rain had stopped—we inspanned at three A.M., and by nightfall had reached and laagered up at a valley near the Bluecoat Mine. We had travelled all day through thick bush without seeing a sign of a kraal or a nigger. Our marching troubles had begun though: the road was very rough and sandy, we had just enough more rain to make it heavy, the crossing of the Maninie River (where we outspanned in the middle of the day) proved fatal to the dissel-boom of one of the waggons, and there were four mules less at evening roll-call than had started in the morning. Still, we had done fourteen miles, and the weather was looking brighter.

On the 26th we came upon the first traces of the murders in the Lomagundi district. Our midday outspan was near the Sange River, and there we found two skulls, some bones, and some partly burnt letters from Jameson, the Mining Commissioner of the district, who was supposed to have been murdered. Hale pronounced one of the skulls to be that of a white man, so we took it with us and buried it next day at the store.

In the afternoon Pilson, with some Mounted Infantry and Scouts, went on to Deary's store at the Doondu River to take over and make an inventory of the contents, while Harding and Southey with another party went to the Mining Commissioner's camp and collected all his papers and effects. I followed later with the column, and on arrival collected all papers of importance from the parties which had gone on in advance, and "commandeered" and divided equally among the troops what stores had been found. The rebels had left practically nothing though but a few bottles of pickles, sauce, etc. Both camp and stores were completely wrecked and looted, and there were abundant traces that they had been living in the huts. In one of them they had killed a buck, apparently only the day before we arrived, and there was fresh spoor all round the place leading into the bush. Two diaries were found in the Mining Commissioner's office, one written up to June 21st and the other up to June 22nd. We either burnt or brought away papers or letters, according as they appeared important or not. We had now done only twenty-six miles, the Rhodesia Horse had finished their mealies, and I wondered how many horses would get back to Salisbury. There were signal fires at night on the Sinoia Hills, and they, coupled with the desertion of this place, made us afraid that the niggers intended "clearing" before us, and that we should not have a fight.

However, the caves of Sinoia had to be visited, as it had been reported that the rebels were living in them, so I decided to leave all the weakest horses and mules with most of the waggons here, and make a flying visit to the caves. Our road to the Ayrshire Mine, which was another object of the patrol, branched off from here, so it seemed only an unnecessary waste of energy to drag all the waggons, etc., to Sinoia and back. We started with a few waggons, the best of the mules, and four days' rations, leaving the Salisbury Rifles, some casuals of the various detachments, and the Mounted Infantry Maxim to guard the laager and look after the weak horses. Lieut. Elphinstone-Dalrymple of the Salisbury Rifles remained in charge.

On arrival at the Hunyani River we outspanned and decided not to go on to the caves at once, but to rest for the remainder of the day so as to have the horses fresh for the job, and a whole day available if necessary. One of the first sights that greeted our eyes on arrival at the river was a huge crocodile, which effectually did us out of the bathe to which we had been looking forward. The Scouts had reported seeing plenty of spoor of niggers on the Sinoia road, so we hoped that they might be waiting for us.

On the 28th we started early with the Scouts, as many of the Mounted Infantry as we could find horses for, the seven-pounder, and one of the Maxims of the Artillery Troop Rhodesia Horse, the Mounted Troop of the Rhodesia Horse, and the Native Contingent, leaving twenty-five dismounted Mounted Infantry men and one of the Artillery Troop Maxims with a gun detachment for it, under command of Lieut. Stockley, M.M.P., to guard the laager. The drift across the Hunyani was a bad one, and we were delayed by the darkness and by some of the horses being swept off their legs, but fortunately we had no waggons to get over, and, long before daybreak, were well on our way. The distance was much further than I had been led to expect though, and when at last the guide reported that we were within sight of the caves it had long been daylight. However, it did not matter, as, on two sections of Mounted Infantry and the Native Contingent going to explore and occupy the caves, they found them full, not of niggers, but of baboons.

From the spoor seen and intelligence received before starting, I knew there must be rebels in the neighbourhood, so I had the guns outspanned, off-saddled what horses were not required, and started off the Mounted Infantry and the Mounted Troop Rhodesia Horse in four different directions to scour the surrounding country. They burnt a lot of kraals which showed traces of recent occupation, and in one of them found an old woman, whom they brought back. She said that all Sinoia's people and all the natives of the district had "cleared" into the fly-belt towards the Zambesi on hearing of our approach, and that she had been left because she was too old to move quickly. She knew all about our fight at Mashangombi's, and confirmed the report that his brother had been killed in the action there, and that Mashangombi himself with most of his people and cattle had escaped to Thaba Insimbi and Iron Mine Hill. She also told us that it was people from Zimba's and Sinoia's kraals who had murdered the whites at Deary's store and the Ayrshire Mine.

On the return of the parties they off-saddled their horses for a bit, ate the half-day's rations which they had carried on their saddles, and we all took the opportunity of exploring the far-famed caves of Sinoia. People who have seen them both say that they are far prettier than the blue grotto at Capri, and certainly the main cave was quite beautiful; the hole goes down perpendicularly from a flat level surface, and is a tunnel, narrow at the opening and widening out as you get into the cave. At the end of the tunnel is a pool of clear blue water, with a tree growing in front of it, and as you go down you see its reflection in the water, which is very deep, and most vivid blue. The effect is beautiful. On arrival at the pool you see that the hole of the cave is circular, about 100 feet in diameter and about 150 feet high, with the same diameter right up to the sunlight. The clear blue sky appears through the green branches of the tree spreading overhead. The whole cave is composed of marble, and the effect of the blue sky seen through the green branches above, the clear blue water below, and the surrounding walls of marble, is more lovely than I can attempt to describe.

On the far side of the pool are black and gloomy caverns, which appear to lead into the bowels of the earth.

We returned in two parties, the guns with a section of Mounted Infantry as escort going by the road, and the rest of us taking a short cut through the bush. The former party saw a few armed natives running away into the bush about five hundred yards from them, but the horses of the escort were so done up that they could not catch them. We had to leave a good many horses on the road before we got back to laager, but they were recovered in the cool of the evening. All the horses which had been out round Sinoia's were very much done up, chiefly, I think, from want of water and the great heat. We had not been able to find any water for them between the Hunyani and Sinoia's, and at the latter place they could not get at it.

Next day we trekked back to the Doondu, leaving behind the bones of three of our best mules, one of which had strayed and been taken by a lion the previous night. On arrival at the store the laager there was broken up, and the force, again re-united, trekked a short way along the road to the Ayrshire Mine. Two horses and two mules died, however, and at the rate they were going it seemed as if we should not have many to show on our return to Salisbury.

All this time we had excellent shooting, and the Scouts and flank guards had pretty well kept the column supplied with fresh meat. One of the Scouts had shot a beautiful water-buck, and Southey and King-Harman, two of the Mounted Infantry subalterns, had been very successful among the smaller buck and guinea-fowl and partridges. I forget whether it was on this patrol, or before we left the Colonel, that our bill-of-fare for dinner at the headquarter mess one night was: Venison soup, barbel (a very good fish that we used to blow out of the rivers with dynamite, no time for catching them by more legitimate methods), roast eland (the best eating buck in South Africa), roast guinea-fowl, omelette of ostrich egg (some one had picked one up), and tinned peaches. Could any gourmand want more, especially when washed down with a little of our precious stock of "dop" (Cape brandy)? I am bound to say, though, that "bully beef" and biscuit was our more common fare.

October 30th found us at the Ayrshire Mine after a hard march. We had a rainy, windy night, and, starting at three A.M. in rain and cloud, had made little progress at first. This was chiefly owing to the very thick bush, the difficulties of keeping to the so-called track, and the necessity for incessant halts to clear the bush and cut down trees which obstructed the waggons. We had no moon now either, but the transport riders and conductors were unanimous in their opinion that, if we were to do the job with no food for the animals, we must do all the marching possible in the cool of the evening or early morning, and give them the whole day to graze. The day at Sinoia's when we had been out for so long in the heat of the sun had knocked the horses up more than all the rest of the marching we had done put together. Two more of them and a mule had succumbed to this march, but when we outspanned we had the satisfaction of finding that we had done twelve miles, and had unexpectedly arrived at the Native Commissioner's camp.

In the afternoon I went with a small escort to the Ayrshire Mine, while Hale and Fox explored the Native Commissioner's camp. We found the store and all the huts at the Ayrshire looted, and nothing of any value left. The mining camp is quite a large colony of well-built huts, and must have been most comfortable; it was very sad to see everything so completely and wantonly wrecked, the machinery being apparently the only thing which the niggers had left untouched. One of the Scouts, who had heard stories of untold gold and treasure having been thrown down the main shaft by the fugitives after the outbreak, lowered himself down with a rope, but found there was too much water to allow of investigations, and our only spoil eventually consisted of some specimens of quartz, and some tobacco, cigarettes, and cocoa, which my escort divided among themselves; the tobacco was a godsend, as most of the column had been reduced to smoking tea or not smoking at all.

On our return, we found that the party to the Native Commissioner's camp had found and buried the skulls and bones of two Europeans, which were supposed to be those of Maynhardt, the Native Commissioner, and Carr or Suter. They had also found and brought away a quantity of papers. The Native Contingent had, in the meantime, been spending the day in scouring the surrounding country, and had burnt four deserted kraals. They had not met any rebels, but had come across a lot of lately-planted mealies and a great deal of fresh spoor, and, in following this up, had seen a party of natives on the top of a high kopje about 800 yards from camp. These were seen again from the laager just before sunset, so Moberly fired a few rounds of common shell at the place, which apparently had the effect of dispersing them.

Owing to some of the men and horses having had such a long day, and to the indications of rebels about, we did not start till daybreak the following morning. Our way now lay towards Salisbury again, and along the main road from the mine. The road was very sandy and heavy, and the bush very thick, and we could find no water till we struck the Maninie River again, having had to leave five horses, twenty-four mules, and one waggon, on the road. Most of the mules were recovered in the evening. The only way by which we could hope to get any horses back to Salisbury now was to take the men off their backs; so I had nearly everybody dismounted, most of the saddles put on the waggons, and the horses driven like a flock of sheep. It was a most melancholy sight to see the poor brutes tripping over every little stump or rise in the ground, then falling and simply unable to get up from starvation and exhaustion. Among them

TOWARDS THE END OF THE PATROL. THE RESULT OF NO MEALIES!

had to go one of mine which I had hitherto ridden more than the others. The flanking parties, on coming in to the outspan, reported having burnt some deserted kraals, and found a complete skeleton of a murdered Zambesi boy. They had seen a good deal of spoor but no natives.

On Sunday, November 1st, the Scouts found some very good grazing a short way off the track, so we had a day's rest, and sent all the horses and mules there, and were all glad of plenty of time for a good wash and what change of clothes we could muster. A great part of the day was spent in trying to get the horses and mules, which had fallen down, on to their legs again; but, notwithstanding our exertions, when we moved the laager across the drifts in the evening, we had to leave three horses and four mules behind. The Native Contingent had gone out to try and find the bodies of some white men who were supposed to have been murdered near here on their way to Salisbury, and found two, which, as far as we could make out from the papers on them, were those of Drysdale and Briggs. They were buried where we found them.

Next day found us back at the same place where we had outspanned on the first night after leaving Eyre's Farm, but minus five more horses and three mules, and on the 3rd we crossed the Umvukwe Mountains, and met a convoy from Salisbury with rations and mails for us. They were Natal Troop and West Riding men, and from them we heard the sad news that poor Evans had been killed in an attack on Gatzi's kraal near Marandellas, the same place where Barnes, A.S.C., had been killed before we got to Salisbury. We were very glad of the rations and boots which they brought, as may be imagined.

Our journey back, as far as Mount Hampden, was uneventful. Some more deserted kraals were burnt, a good many more horses and mules succumbed, some men who went back to one of the outspans found some niggers there, and exchanged shots with them, without any harm to either side, and the Native Contingent found one day the skeleton of a murdered Shangaan.

On arrival at Mount Hampden, we were met by a most welcome waggon-load of mealies and some "dop," which the Colonel had thoughtfully sent out. Just as we were laagering up, a muledriver, who had gone about a mile off the road to look for a stray mule, which had been left by the escort which took Colonel Alderson into Salisbury, staggered in all covered with blood. It appears that he had been attacked by some Mashonas, who jumped up out of the long grass and assegaied him in the thigh, inflicting a nasty wound. They then ran away in the direction of Mashangombi's. The Native Contingent went after them, and found their spoor and some blankets, mealies, etc., which they had evidently dropped; but after following up the spoor for some way, they saw that it would be hopeless to come up with them, and had to give up the chase.

The Scouts also came upon some fresh spoor, and followed it up till they came to a brand new kraal in the Mazoë direction, which showed traces of having been recently occupied. This they burnt, and came back without having seen a nigger.

On the morning of November 8th we met the Colonel, who had ridden out from Salisbury to see us, and by ten A.M. the column had dispersed to their different camps and laagers about the town, and I had to return, reluctantly, to my office stool. We had been on our own resources for sixteen days, and during that time had covered 140 miles, gone considerably farther north than anybody else in the course of the campaign, and thoroughly explored the Lomagundi district. We were of course very much disgusted at not having had a fight, but from all one saw and heard, there was no doubt that most of the rebels in that country had cleared before us into the "fly." There were evidently armed parties of them hiding in the bush, but one's chance of coming across them was practically *nil*.

It had been a most interesting trip otherwise, the country being so different to most of the rest of Mashonaland. Instead of kopjes and comparatively open country, we had been travelling, except at the Ayrshire where there were kopjes, through flat country with dense bush, and the scenery at the Hunyani and Maninie Rivers, and the caves of Sinoia, was worth a trip from Europe to see alone. The only unpleasant feature had been watching the horses and mules dying daily. We had lost twenty-seven horses and twenty mules altogether. The men had a lot of very hard marching, but, notwithstanding their bootless condition, had tramped most cheerfully, and nobody could have had a nicer command, or have given it up with more regret than I did.

CHAPTER XV

FIGHTING ON THE LINE OF COMMUNICATIONS
MR. RHODES TAKES OUT A PATROL

WHILE we had been away on the Hartley Patrol, a good deal had been going on in the line of communications. About October 15th Major Evans, who had moved up from Umtali, had proceeded with a detachment of the line of communication troops, from Marandellas to a spot in the bush about ten miles off the road to the south, where some 1000 natives were supposed to be massed. When he arrived there the birds had flown, and apparently scattered. He then went on to Cheri's kraal, which was deserted as he approached, and after burning it and some others, he returned to Marandellas.

On the 19th he moved to Gatzi's, which we had burnt on the 10th August, and where the natives were reported to be collecting. Reaching there at daybreak, Evans at once rushed the kraal, the natives as usual retiring to the caves. It was whilst reconnoitring these, that poor Evans was shot through the heart and died instantly. In the rush on the kraal Trooper H. P. Earnshaw, Umtali Rifles, accidentally shot himself dead, and Trooper C. Seigert, Matabeleland Relief Force, was seriously wounded. After Evans' death Captain Pease, King's Own Light Infantry, who was attached to the detachment of the West Riding regiment, assumed the command, and after blockading the caves for five days, either took, destroyed, or drove the natives out of them all. In these operations Pease was ably assisted by Captain Ludlow, Army Service Corps (who, by the way, had really no business to be there at all!). The caves were found to be very extensive, and had water running right through them. The kraal had not been rebuilt since we burnt it, but all the grass and poles for this purpose were found stacked ready inside it. On the conclusion of the operations, the units composing the force returned to their several stations on the line of communications, a portion of them burning Soswie's kraal on the way.

Poor Evans' death was a great blow to me. He was one of my best friends in the service, and we had done a good deal of soldiering and hunting together. Apart from my local rank, he was senior to me in the army; he had, however, especially asked to be allowed to come out with his Mounted Infantry company, and I could not have had a more sincerely loyal second in command, both in the Mounted Infantry and in the Mashonaland Field Force. His body was taken to Marandellas and buried in the little cemetery there, beside poor Barnes, Morris, and others, and we, of the Mounted Infantry, subsequently sent a stone to be erected to his memory.

We found the food question at Salisbury somewhat improved; some of the extra mules and waggons which the company had purchased in Natal and elsewhere were already at work on the Umtali-Salisbury road, and convoys were arriving fairly regularly. But still it was not yet certain whether enough food could be put into the country before the rainy season began, though Fox was very sanguine (results later on proved that he was right).

As it appeared probable at this time that the imperial troops would remain in the country during the rains, it was necessary to make arrangements for their being properly housed, and this was one of the reasons why I had returned to Salisbury from Eyre's. The first idea was to have a camp of mud and straw huts in the open outside Salisbury, but it appeared doubtful whether the native labour necessary for the construction could be obtained. It then occurred to me that the "Cecil Hotel," a large incomplete building in Salisbury, might be utilized. It was then without a roof and would probably suffer much damage from the rains. Owing to the rinderpest and the rising, the company who were building the hotel were unable to get the iron for its roof up country. On sounding the representative of this company, I found that he would be only too glad to let the troops use the building, if that would cause it to be roofed before the rains. Eventually the British South Africa Company and the Hotel Company came to an arrangement in the matter, in which the former were to assist with material, etc., for the roof, and the latter were to so far complete the inside of the building that it would be habitable for the troops.

All the local troops likely to be in Salisbury would fit into the (so-called) Rhodesia Horse Barracks, or improvised additions to them, where it appeared that there would also be sufficient stabling for all the horses likely to be left alive by the time the rains might be expected to begin.

The above arrangements disposed of a serious question, for, during the rains, men under waggons or canvas would surely get fever, and horses in the open would equally surely die of that curse of a great part of South Africa, horse sickness. Another question which had to be gone into, and telegraphed about, was that of clothes, boots, etc., for the imperial troops. As has already been said, shortness of transport prevented them bringing up much kit, and what they did bring was now entirely worn out.

There was no time to be lost if fresh supplies were to reach Salisbury before the rains.

On the 31st of October, Jenner's column arrived near the Mazoë Fort, having visited Mapondera's and other districts north of Mazoë. All of these were deserted, the tracks pointing, as in the case of Godley's patrol, to the natives having gone to the "fly" country. I sent Jenner orders to remain at Mazoë for a few days, in order to assist in moving the fort to a new site, which I rode out to select, nearer to the Granite Range and to the large mealie gardens in the valley.

When the orders were issued for the moving of this fort an incident, which could only happen with irregulars, occurred. The garrison of the old fort sent in a round robin to their commander, Lieut. Fairbairn, stating that they were not going to work at building a new fort, as they did not consider that this was a part of the "soldiering" for which they had "signed on." Fairbairn brought this precious document to me, and I told him to take it back, parade them all, and tell them from me, that they had "signed on," and were paid 10/- a day to do as they were told, and that they might think themselves very lucky to get the round robin back instead of finding it used as evidence against them on a court of officers (this is the name given to what applies to a court martial, in the British South Africa Company's Volunteer Act of 1895, under which the men were). Apparently the men thought better of it; any way, no more was heard of the matter, and they *did* build the new fort.

On the 31st we received the news that Mr. Rhodes, then on his way to Salisbury from Buluwayo, when passing Enkeldorn, had taken out some thirty of the Dutchmen composing the garrison, and visited, taken, and burnt Singala's kraal. One man, named Swart, was wounded and some thirty rebels killed.

It was characteristic of the man (Rhodes) to go and risk his own life at the head of thirty Dutchmen, in taking a cluster of straw huts! And one could not help thinking—"What difference would it have made to South Africa in general and to Rhodesia in particular if he had been killed?"

There was one amusing result of this impromptu "patrol," rumour in Salisbury having it that I had threatened to or had put Mr. Rhodes under arrest for having taken out men who were under my command without referring to me!

On November 4th Mr. Rhodes arrived in Salisbury, and a few days later he met the principal business men and property owners. A certain section among these had been for some time threatening him with all sorts of penalties, and other unpleasant things, if he did not do just what they wished regarding the railway and other matters when he arrived in Salisbury. It was amusing to read in the local papers the accounts of the interview. According to these accounts, all these lions of the past became veritable lambs when in the presence of the man they had metaphorically threatened to tear in pieces. The only man who, judging by the accounts, seemed to stick to his guns, was Mr. W. E. Fairbridge, editor of the *Rhodesia Herald*.

It was about this time that Captain Hon. F. W. Eveleigh de Moleyns, 4th Hussars, who was to be the Lieutenant-Colonel Commandant of the new Mashonaland Police, arrived in Salisbury; at present he had no men, though 200 were on their way from Cape Town. He had been serving on Sir Frederick Carrington's staff in Matabeleland. The last time we had met was when I spent a very pleasant six weeks attached to the 4th Hussars at Aldershot. On November 8th, Godley's column arrived in Salisbury from Sinoia's and the Ayrshire Mine. His horses and mules were looking better than I expected, considering they had had nothing but grass for the last three weeks or more. He had had no fighting, and, like Jenner, reported that the natives had gone to the "fly" country.

On the 12th a large convoy left Salisbury for Umtali, and among those who went down were, much to my regret, Judge and Mrs. Vintcent. He had indeed earned a rest. Ever since the rising commenced the whole responsibility of the administration in Mashonaland had been on his shoulders, and, prior to my arrival in Salisbury, he had had the direction of military matters also. To be suddenly pitchforked from the position of senior judge into a double-barrelled one of Administrator and Commander-in-Chief would be trying to a Napoleon.

It must have been specially so in a community like that at Salisbury, which was so small that every man almost could make his voice heard, and where it appeared that all were determined to do so. The worst part being that all had different ideas, and each one grumbled if his own plan was not adopted!

Through the troublesome early days of the rising, when questions of whether this or that patrol could be sent out—questions of life and death for some, in fact—had to be decided; through the times when food was short, and people said the Government (*i.e.* the Company) ought to feed them; settling this big, or that little, question in a kindly, gentlemanly manner— while he saw every one, no matter who, and listened to their story; authorizing this or that expenditure,—through all this the Judge steered the ship. Personally, I naturally saw a great deal of him, and I know I can safely say that the British South Africa Company may think themselves lucky if all their servants are half as keen about their interests, as conscientious, and as hard working, as Mr. Justice Vintcent.

Mr. Milton, who had come up specially from

Cape Town to re-organize the Company's civil service, took over the administration from the Judge.

On the 13th we had a very heavy wind, rain, hail, and thunder storm, much glass was broken, and several roofs taken off. Among the latter were the roofs of two stables opposite to the house we were then in. I happened to be looking out and saw them lifted up and taken bodily off, one after the other. This storm necessitated the putting off, for a couple of days, of the patrol under Jenner, which was going to Chiquaqua's and Kunzi's. It also caused the principal medical officer to write an official letter, pointing out the inadvisability of sending men out on what might be a fourteen days' patrol, when more such storms were probable. This could not, however, be allowed to make any difference; the work had to be done whatever the weather, and on the 15th this patrol (No. 26, Part III., Appendix C) started.

On the 18th Jenner sent in a report that he had had a satisfactory "indaba" with Chiquaqua, who said he wanted peace. This was followed on the 22nd by a similar report regarding Kunzi.

On the 19th Sir Frederick Carrington, whom I rode out to meet, arrived in Salisbury, and he and his staff went into the quarters we had had arranged for them in the Commercial Hotel, the landlord of which, Mr. Rosenthal—like so many other men in South Africa—had served under the General in one of the many irregular corps he had commanded.

This did not, however, prevent mine host from running them up a tremendous bill, I think it was over £250—this for five of them for eleven days! But then it must be remembered that they always had eggs for breakfast, and occasionally had chickens, and eggs and chickens were at that time luxuries only dreamt of by us.

With the General were Colonel R. S. Baden-Powell, chief staff officer; Major Vyvyan, brigade major; Captain Ferguson, A.D.C.; and Surgeon-Colonel Gormley, principal medical officer. Lord and Lady Grey, Lady Victoria Grey, the Hon. Hubert Howard, and Mr. H. C. Lister, who had all been travelling with the General, also arrived at the same time—Lord Grey, of course, taking over the administration from Mr. Milton.

This brings us almost to the last scene, and it would perhaps be well to begin a new chapter.

CHAPTER XVI

THE "IMAGE OF WAR," AND THE BEGINNING OF THE END

ON November the 23rd we had, much to our delight, a look at what Mr. Jorrocks calls the "h'image of war," the hounds meeting at the Judge's house (now occupied by Mr. Rhodes) at six A.M.

These hounds, now only some five and a half couple, had been originally given to Salisbury by Lord Grey. During the hard times of the laager, and of the following two months, they had been devotedly looked after by Mr. Graham (Salisbury's post-master), who was master, and they now came out for the first time that season, looking well, though decidedly on the fat side. A field of about thirty were, as "Trivy" would say, "at the fixture," including Lord Grey, Lady Victoria Grey, the General, Mr. Rhodes, Colonel Baden-Powell, Mr. Wilson Fox, and a smattering of soldiers, both imperial and local. We went to draw for a jackal but found a diuker (a small buck), and he very quickly ran the over-fat hounds out of scent. When I left, having to get to the office, they were still drawing for the second time.

The next day the wire to Buluwayo, and thence to Cape Town, went down, much to the General's annoyance, as he wanted to get the question of whether the imperial troops were to stay in the country through the rains or not settled as soon as possible. We at once sent off a party to find the break, but it was not until the 26th that communication was restored. That day the hounds met at Lord Grey's (Mr. Pauling's) house, and we had a fast thirty-five minutes after a jackal, but lost him. Riding home, Mr. Graham asked me if I would hunt them in future. Wouldn't I just! Nothing I like better than having *anything* to do with hounds of *any sort*. As a boy I had been whip to a pack of beagles, and during my soldiering had been lucky enough to hunt three packs of hounds—the Shorncliffe, and the Staff College Drag Hounds, and the Cape Jackal Hounds. Now here was another pack! I had thus hunted hounds in June, fought till the end of November, and then taken hounds again. What more could a soldier possibly want? For the bringing in of this bit of personal history, enthusiasm for the chase must be my excuse, which I hope the reader will accept?

On the 28th the General issued orders for 150 of the Mounted Infantry, and the detach-

THE SITUATION IN MASHONALAND

ment Royal Artillery, to move down to Umtali, so as to be in readiness to move on to rail head (now Bendulas), and thence to Beira, for re-embarkation.

As this was the beginning of the end, as far as the imperial troops were concerned, it would be well to briefly survey the situation at this date, and, in doing this, it will be best to look at the map. If we start with Simbanoota's, and other kraals near the Salisbury-Umtali road, on the south-east of Salisbury, and go on with the sun to those on the Ruya and Hunyani Rivers to the south, then to Umtegeza's, to Mashangombi's, and many other kraals in the Hartley Hills, thence to the Umvukwe Hills, to Eyre's, Sinoia's, the Ayrshire Mine, Mapondera's, Mazoë, and finish up with Kunzi's, Chiquaqua's, and Chishawasha, it will be seen that a complete circle had been made round Salisbury by "patrols." All of these (except in the case of Kunzi and Chiquaqua, with whom apparently satisfactory "indabas" had been held), had inflicted defeats, more or less severe, on the Mashonas, had taken and destroyed their kraals, and brought away all the cattle and grain which could be found.

On the line of communications, *i.e.* on Mashonaland's one line of supply, Makoni was dead, and, though his son was alive and hostile, his people were scattered; Umtassa, once doubtful, was supplying carriers; Marandellas', Mangwendi's, Gatzi's, and numerous other kraals, had been taken or burnt. The only chief likely to give trouble remaining being Tandi (subsequently visited by, and surrendered to, a patrol under Captain Pease).

To pass to the question of men. The General had asked me to estimate the number of police that the Company ought to have if the imperial troops left the country. This I put down at 600 whites, with 200 to 300 Native Contingent. The Company thought this an excessive number, and it was eventually cut down to 580 whites and no natives.

These I proposed to station as follows:

Umtali,	30
Devil's Pass,	15
Fort Haynes,	30
Headlands,	25
Marandellas,	40
Salisbury,	150
Charter,	30
Victoria,	50
Enkeldorn,	30
Hartley,	75
Mazoë,	40
Chiquaqua's,	20
Chishawasha,	5
Law's,	20
Hunyani,	10
Norton's,	10
	580

Taken generally, this distribution was approved of, though the Company still thought it excessive, especially in the case of the 150 men at Salisbury.

THE QUESTION OF POLICE

In making my estimate I had given the numbers with which I would have taken over the country myself. With less than the 580 this was cut down to I certainly would not have taken the responsibility, and I considered that it was most important to have at least 100 men in Salisbury, exclusive of the garrison, who could be moved anywhere at short notice. Had this number been in Salisbury in June '96, instead of the five (!) police then there, it is scarcely likely that the rising would have become general. Some of those who desired to cut down the numbers of the police at this time must have forgotten that no peace had been made with the Mashonas like it had with the Matabele. They appear to have forgotten also that though Salisbury and the other large stations were in no danger of being attacked, and though the country was comparatively safe for even small parties of five to ten men to move about in the open, there must still be desultory fighting, and that convoys, traders, farmers, and others could not move about without escorts.

The Company could easily make up more than the 580 armed whites from its own resources. Nearly all the men of the local forces were willing to re-engage to the 31st March, 1897, while 200 of the new police were already at Beira.

Our old bug-bear—supply—was, thanks to Mr. Fox and Lieut.-Col. Beal, now dead; sufficient food stuffs were in the country to feed the population until the next dry season, and there was enough transport to distribute them.

Under these circumstances it did not seem necessary to keep the imperial troops in the country. The imperial authorities wished to get them out, and the Company were naturally anxious to do so, so that they might be able to say that Rhodesia was quite able to take care of herself. Certainly none of us had any wish to sit in Salisbury during the rains, and see the men get fever and the horses die. So the General's order of the 28th November suited all parties. I have referred above to no peace having been made with the Mashonas, and would now say that to make a general peace with them will probably be found difficult. Unlike the Matabele, the Mashonas have no great national chiefs whom they obey, but each petty chief goes his own way. The result of one of these making peace *and handing in his arms* would probably be that his next-door neighbour would attack him and "eat him up."

On the 29th the General inspected the imperial troops in the afternoon, and directly afterwards the Rifle Company and the half English company Mounted Infantry, with the detachment Royal Artillery, and a convoy of sick, marched for Umtali in a tremendous thunder and rain storm. The latter, which wetted one through in about two minutes, kept on during the greater part of the night, and the marching troops must have had a very uncomfortable time.

On the 30th the hounds met at Lord Grey's house at 5.30 A.M., but with a catchy scent we did not do much. At eleven A.M. the General inspected the local forces in the Rhodesia Horse Barracks. The rest of the day was spent in making arrangements for the garrison which the General wished sent out to Hartley. On Dec. 2nd the General and his staff left for Umtali, *en route* for Beira and Cape Town, and thence home. Before they went, Colonel Baden-Powell handed me what must be a quite unique specimen of the *multum in parvo* sort of instructions. They were exactly seven short lines in length, but contained all one wanted to know, and in other things left me a free hand. Only those who have experienced it can tell what a blessing it is not to have instructions, *trop détaillées et très précises*, when the man who issues them will soon be hundreds of miles away. This last order was characteristic of the way I had been treated throughout the operations, and I shall always be grateful for the amount of "rein" given me.

Lord and Lady Grey and Lady Victoria Grey also left on the 29th—the former to visit Umtali, the two latter *en route* for England. Each down-going convoy was now taking passengers, and Salisbury was getting empty indeed. Nicholls, who had been in the country some five or six years, and was quite played out, went down with one of these convoys. I was very sorry indeed to lose him; we had got to know each other well, and the way in which he looked after me and anticipated my wants was wonderful.

On the third we had another hunt, and had a fast forty minutes with one buck, then unfortunately changed on to another, which ran us out of scent in an hour. This afternoon we had some excitement in the shape of a report from the driver of the Charter post-cart, that his oxen had been stolen by Mashonas while outspanned near the Hunyani. King-Harman was sent out with his section to investigate. He took the driver with him, and soon discovered that there were no Mashonas in the case at all. The two drivers had gone to sleep and the oxen had strayed; then, being frightened, they made up the story to cover themselves. Truly, this was a real case for the sjambok!

On the 17th we had a real good hunt. Meeting at five A.M., we found a diuker at once, and ran him hard and straight for fifty minutes; then, just as he was beat, we changed. Rough on the hounds this, and rough on me too, as I had made all sorts of vows to Diana if we killed him—among them being one to have his head mounted with silver!

On the 8th the Irish company Mounted Infantry and the remaining details of the imperial troops marched for Umtali, in order to catch the "Pembroke Castle," which was expected at Beira about the 27th. I remained to settle up, hand over to de Moleyns, etc., etc. During these last few days, my diary shows that we did much dining-out, and also did a little entertaining at what we were pleased to call the headquarter mess, which we had now established in Pauling's House. Among other entries are—" Dined with Fox, A1 dinner and wine," and "Dined with Harding at the Commercial Hotel, mine host Rosenthal excels himself"; also "Bowen, Fleming, Harding, Godley, junior, and Roach dine with us."

On the 10th we had our last hunt, and did find a jackal, but it was a very bad scenting day, and we did nothing.

The next day there was packing, and that evening the last orders of the Mashonaland Field Force appeared. No. 1 ran as follows: "On the departure of Lieut.-Colonel Alderson from Salisbury to-morrow, the Mashonaland Field Force will be broken up.

"Lieut.-Colonel Hon. F. R. W. Eveleigh de Moleyns, commanding the Rhodesia Mounted Police, will assume command of the British South Africa Company's forces in Mashonaland. His office will be the same as the present office of the Mashonaland Field Force."

On the 12th December, Godley, Turner, Ludlow, Harbord, and I (we persuaded Harbord, who was over-working himself in the company's pay-office, to come down with us) left Salisbury at seven A.M. with our horses and servants, two waggons, and a cape-cart. The two Foxes, Godley, junior, and several others rode as far as Beesas' kraal with us.

Of Salisbury itself as a place, now that the rains were coming on, we were not sorry to see the last; but there were many among its inhabitants whom we were really sorry to say "Farewell" to. While from the whole of them we had received nothing but kindness, hospitality, and consideration; and if everlasting "bully beef" and biscuit had made the place somewhat pall on us, those who lived in it had done their very best to make us take away pleasant memories of them, and they certainly succeeded.

There were also many officers of the local forces, all of whom had served me so well, that I was very sorry to say "Good-bye" to.

One institution in Salisbury I had much pleasure in writing officially to the Administrator about, and that was the hospital. A list of the casualties which occurred during the operations is given in Appendix B.

Nearly all those shown as wounded in this list, as well as the sick, were treated in the Salisbury Hospital, and I attribute the rapid, and in some cases wonderful, recoveries that almost all of them made in no small degree to the skilful treatment they received from Dr. Fleming, and to the good and attentive nursing of Mother Patrick and those under her.

CHAPTER XVII

WHOO! WHOOP!

WE had a very peaceful and uneventful journey down country; Godley, Turner, Ludlow, and Harbord shot, especially Ludlow, who was very keen, and always found us fresh meat of some sort. I sketched the road (I luckily had brought a cavalry sketching case up with me) right down to Bendulas, which was then rail-head, at an inch to the mile; this worked out over 200 inches in length. We reached Umtali on the 20th December. On the 21st I see the entry in my diary is—"Umtali, very hot, flies bad"; and on the 22nd—"Umtali, and wish we were out of it! Very hot, flies *awful!*"

On the 23rd we were on the move again, and outspanned for the night on the site of new Umtali. The company are going to move the township on account of the difficulty of getting the railway to the old town. As this entails compensating all the owners of buildings in the latter, it must mean a good round sum.

The new site is much more in the open and much prettier than the old one. Lord Grey and Howard dined with us that evening, and took us all over the site of the new township, showing us where the hospital and other public buildings were to be.

That night I heard, much to my grief, that the rinderpest regulations would not allow me to land my horses in Natal, where we were going. Poor "Grimstone" and poor "Makoni," you had indeed done me well, never been sick or sorry, and never given me a fall, though I had galloped you both over all sorts of ground; now you must remain behind, perhaps to die of horse sickness (which both did within two months!).

Lord Grey kindly approved of the company buying both at the valuation put on them by a board of officers, and he took "Grimstone" for his own riding.

There is no doubt that in the matter of buying our private horses, of allowing us extra pay, and in various other ways, the British South Africa Company treated us with great liberality, and this prevented our being out of pocket with the famine prices at which we had for some time been living.

Christmas Eve saw us at Massikessi, where I called on the Portuguese Commandante, who kindly regaled me with champagne, which, as I had just finished sketching some twenty miles of road in a very hot sun, was most acceptable.

Christmas Day '96 *was wet*, so wet that my sketching paper went to pulp, and I had to give it up and be content with merely taking notes of the road. During the afternoon we passed the Rifle company, plodding along in the mud, drenched to the skin, but all as merry as crickets. That night saw us outspanned at Bendulas, in a very feverish-looking spot, with rank and dank vegetation all round.

At four P.M. on Boxing Day we were in the train; the line was covered with young locusts, and this meant the men getting out and pushing the train up all the hills.

"Christmassing" demoralized the railway employees, and it was the evening of the 28th before we reached Beira. Since we left there in July the pier had been finished, and our train was run right on to the head of it, from which, to the "Pembroke Castle," was a short trip in lighters.

For once I was glad to be on board a ship!— to get decent food, and be able to sit still, was indeed delightful.

Next day I went ashore to call on Colonel Machado and Mr. Carnegie Ross, Her Majesty's Consul; and the Irish company arrived in the middle of the night. On the evening of the 30th the detachment West Riding regiment arrived, and about 12.30 P.M. the next day we sailed—an appropriate ending to a year which had been, for many of us, eventful.

We had a very smooth and comfortable voyage to Durban, where we arrived on the 2nd January, 1897, and at once went up to Pietermaritzburg by train. Here we were most hospitably received, both by the 9th Lancers and the 2nd Battalion West Riding regiment. All the barracks being full, we had to go under canvas; this at a time of year when one day there was heavy rain and the next a hot sun! This, no doubt, brought out the fever which had been contracted while marching down to Beira in the rains, and, in ten days' time, we had nearly fifty per cent. of both officers and men in hospital. However, very few of the cases were severe ones, and a few weeks or so more saw the percentage of sick being steadily reduced.

Poor Swanson of the West Riding, however, died; while I was unfortunate enough to be among the few severe cases, and, after coming off the sick list, had a relapse, which necessitated my being invalided home in February.

No soldier likes being invalided, but this hit me particularly hard, for it meant leaving the corps I was so proud to command behind me. (By the *corps* I now mean the Mounted Infantry.) Not one iota of trouble had they given me in any way *whatever*, and scarcely a man of them had come before me as prisoner. Always willing, cheerful, giving their full attention, both at drill and in the field, and ever ready to catch the least hint of what was wanted of them—they were indeed a charming command.

It is not the fashion in the army to bestow much praise, and though I often think that it would be better if this powerful lever were more used, I will not say any more myself; but I should not be doing the officers and men justice if I did not quote a few of the things that other people said of them. In his book, *The Campaign in Matabeleland*, 1896, Colonel Baden-Powell says: "The Mounted Infantry corps from Aldershot was probably the finest of its kind that had ever taken the field. It was employed entirely in Mashonaland, where its doings in the field drew unqualified praise from Colonials and Dutch alike."

Several men in the local forces in Mashonaland said to me: "We thought we could shoot, but we ain't a patch on your men."

In writing of them to me, Lord Grey said: "I hear nothing but good of them."

The Times correspondent, in an article which appeared on the 24th March, 1897, after having remarked that the work done by the Mounted Infantry would tend to restore the prestige of the British soldier in South Africa, went on to say: "Even Dutchmen acknowledged that these Mounted Infantry could shoot, and were astonished at the precision of the volleys which they poured in on the enemy's positions."

While before they left Pietermaritzburg, the General Officer commanding the troops there wrote as follows: "The Major-General commanding Natal and Zululand requests that you will convey to the officers commanding the several battalions represented in the Mounted Infantry battalion his high appreciation of the excellent conduct and soldierly qualities displayed by all ranks, both while serving under his command, and also when on active service in Rhodesia.

"The good behaviour on all occasions of the companies in Mashonaland has been testified to by Earl Grey, Administrator of Rhodesia, who also recently telegraphed in warm terms regarding the fifty N.C.O.'s and men transferred to the British South Africa Company's Police in April last."

Small wonder that I, who knew so well that all the above, and a good deal more besides, was perfectly true, should be down on my luck at leaving such a command behind me.

There is little more to be said. The corps, under Captain G. R. Tod, Seaforth Highlanders, remained in Maritzburg till the end of May, when it sailed for England in the S.S. "Dunera." The evening of Jubilee day, 1897, saw them in the Solent, and me waiting for them in Southampton Docks. The following day I saw, with the most sincere regret, the officers and men who had, one and all, served me as well as any man ever was, or ever will be, served, leave Southampton to rejoin their respective regiments, and the Mounted Infantry battalion of 1896 was, in its turn—like the Mashonaland Field Force—no more.

APPENDIX A

MOUNTED INFANTRY FOR SOUTH AFRICA.[1]

STAFF.

1 Commanding Officer, Capt. (temporary Lieut.-Colonel) E. A. H. Alderson, 2nd R. West Kent regiment, and soldier servant.
1 Adjutant—Capt. A. J. Godley, 1st R. Dublin Fusiliers.
1 N.C.O. as Q. M. Sergeant and O. R. Sergeant (from M. I. Aldershot).
1 Saddler Sergeant (from M. I. Aldershot).
1 Sergeant Cook—Lance-Sergeant Willis, 7th Hussars.
1 Veterinary Officer—Veterinary-Major G. D. Whitefield, A.V.D.
1 Farrier Sergeant as his Assistant.
1 Medical Officer—Surgeon-Captain Saw, A.M.S.
1 Sergeant (or N.C.O.) Medical Staff Corps, as his Assistant.
1 Field Forge.

No. 6 COMPANY (ENGLISH). COMMANDED BY MAJOR F. S. EVANS, 1ST BATTALION DERBYSHIRE REGIMENT. *To embark on 2nd May.*

Detachments.	Officer's Names.	Co.-Sergt. Major.	Sergeants.	Corporals.	Shoeing Smiths.	Buglers.	Privates.	Saddler.	Sergt. Farrier.
2nd Norfolk regiment,	Lieut. R. W. Hare,	—	2a	1	1	—	27	—	⎫
2nd Hampshire regt.,	Lieut. B. Harland,	—	1	2	1	1	19	—	⎬ 1
1st S. Lancashire regt.,	2nd Lieut. A. H. Bailey,	—	1	2	1	—	27	—	⎭
1st Derbyshire regiment,	2nd Lieut. P. M. Dove,	1	1b	1b	—	—	23	1	1
		1	5	6	3	1	96	1	1

[1] This detail is a copy of that given to me at the War Office.   *a* Includes Co.Q.M.S.   *b* Paid Lance-Sergts.

266 APPENDIX A

No. 7 COMPANY (RIFLE). COMMANDED BY CAPTAIN A. V. JENNER, D.S.O., 4TH BATTALION RIFLE BRIGADE. To embark on 2nd May.

Detachments.	Officers' Names.	Co.-Sergt. Major.	Sergeants.	Corporals.	Shoeing Smiths.	Buglers.	Privates.	Saddler.	Sergt. Farrier.
3rd K.R. Rifle Corps,	Lieut. G. S. St. Aulyn (4th Battalion),	—	1	2	1	—	25	—	} 1
4th K.R. Rifle Corps,	Lieut. C. L. E. Eustace,	—	2a	1	1	1	25	1	
2nd Rifle Brigade,	Lieut. R. B. Stephens,	—	1	2	1	1	25	—	
4th Rifle Brigade,	Lieut. H. E. Vernon,	1	1	1	1	—	25	—	
		1	5	6	4	2	100	1	1

No. 9 COMPANY (HIGHLAND). COMMANDED BY CAPTAIN G. R. TOD, 1ST BATTALION SEAFORTH HIGHLANDERS. Embarked 25th April.

Detachments.	Officers' Names.	Co.-Sergt. Major.	Sergeants.	Corporals.	Shoeing Smiths.	Buglers.	Privates.	Saddler.	Sergt. Farrier.
2nd Royal Highlanders,	Lieut. C. E. Stewart,	—	1	2	1	—	25	—	} 1
1st Seaforth Highlanders,	Lieut. E. Cox,	1	1	1	1	—	25	—	
2nd Gordon Highlanders,	Lieut. Hon. R. F. Carnegie,	—	1	2	1	1	25	1	
1st A. and S. Highlanders,	Lieut. A. J. Campbell,	—	2b	1	1	—	25	—	
		1	5	6	4	1	100	1	1

No. 11 COMPANY (IRISH). COMMANDED BY CAPTAIN SIR H. W. McMAHON, BART., 2ND ROYAL WELSH FUSILIERS. To embark on 2nd May.

Detachments.	Officers' Names.	Co.-Sergt. Major.	Sergeants.	Corporals.	Shoeing Smiths.	Buglers.	Privates.	Saddler.	Sergt. Farrier.
1st R. Irish regiment,	Lieut. G. S. French,	—	1	1	1	1	26	—	} 1
1st R. Dublin Fusiliers,	Lieut. A. F. Pilson,	—	2b	1	1	—	26	1	
2nd R. Irish Fusiliers,	Lieut. C. E. Southey,	—	1	2	1	—	23	—	
1st R. Irish Rifles,	Lieut. W. A. King-Harman,	1	1	1	1	—	24	—	
		1	5	5	4	1	99	1	1

a Includes Co.Q.M.S.   b Includes Q.M.S.

LIST OF CASUALTIES

APPENDIX B

LIST OF CASUALTIES
(WHITE MEN)
DURING THE MASHONALAND RISING, 1896.

NOTE.—*This List only refers to Mashonaland, and does not include Matabeleland.*

SUMMARY OF CASUALTIES UP TO 6TH DECEMBER, 1896.

	Deaths.	Wounds.
Killed in action,	14	—
Died of wounds received in action,	5	—
Wounded in action,	—	59
Reported murdered or missing,	118	—
Accidentally killed,	4	—
Accidentally wounded,	—	2
Wounded at the commencement of rising,	—	9
Died from other causes,	9	—
TOTALS,	150	70

Total Number of Deaths and Wounds, ... 220

NOTE.—*The above Summary refers only to casualties the immediate result of the Mashonaland Rising.*

SECTIONAL SUMMARY.

	Civilians.		Local Forces.		Imperial Troops.		TOTAL.
	Deaths.	Wounds.	Deaths.	Wounds.	Deaths.	Wounds.	
Killed in action,	—	—	9	—	5	—	14
Died of wounds received in action,	—	—	3	—	2	—	5
Wounded in action,	—	—	—	41	—	18	59
Reported murdered or missing,	114	—	3	—	1	—	118
Accidentally killed,	1	—	3	—	—	—	4
Accidentally wounded,	—	—	—	2	—	—	2
Wounded at commencement of rising,	—	8	—	1	—	—	9
Died from other causes,	2	—	6	—	1	—	9
	117	8	24	44	9	18	220

In the following Lists (M.I.) denotes Mounted Infantry.
„ „ (S.R.) „ Salisbury Rifles.
„ „ (R.H.) „ Rhodesia Horse.
„ „ (S.F.F.) „ Salisbury Field Force.
„ „ (M.R.F.) „ Matabeleland Relief Force.

KILLED IN ACTION.

List of Officers, Non-Commissioned Officers, and Men killed in Action in the Mashonaland Rising of 1896.

No.	Name.	Rank, Corps, when and where Killed.
1.	Barnes, William E.,	Lieutenant, Army Service Corps, August 13, Gadzi's kraal.
2.	Botha, Philip J.,	Trooper, Honey's Scouts, October 12, Chena's kraal,
3.	Coryndon, John S.,	Trooper, Salisbury Rifles, October 11, Chena's kraal.
4.	Evans, Francis S.,	Major, Derbyshire regiment (M.I.), October 19, Gadzi's kraal.
5.	Gwillim, William H.,	Trooper, S.F.F., July 20, 2nd Hartley Patrol.
6.	Haynes, Aubrey E.,	Captain, R.E., August 3, Makoni's kraal.
7.	Jacobs, Gileam,	Trooper, S.F.F., June 20, Mazoë Patrol.
8.	Johnson, Edward,	Trooper, S.R., Sept. 12, Simbanoota's kraal.
9.	Joliffe, Michael,	Conductor, Transport, August 17, Marandellas' kraal.
10.	M'Geer, Christian,	Lieut., S.F.F., June 20, 1st Mazoë Patrol.
11.	Stevens, Charles T.,	Guide, S.F.F., June 25, Chishawasha.
12.	Van Staaden, H. J.,	Trooper, S.F.F., June 20, Mazoë Patrol.
13.	Vicars, Smith,	Private, King's Royal Rifles (M.I.), Aug. 3, Makoni's kraal.
14.	Wickham, William,	Private, Royal Irish regiment (M.I.), August 3, Makoni's kraal.

DIED OF WOUNDS RECEIVED IN ACTION.

No.	Name.	Rank, Corps, when and where Wounded, and Date of Death.
1.	Finucane, Edward E.,	Captain, Salisbury Rifles, October 22, Eyre's Farm, died October 22.
2.	Frost, William,	Private, King's Royal Rifles (M.I.), Sept. 3, near Graham and White's, died Sept. 14.
3.	Grapes, Charles,	Private, Norfolk regiment (M.I.), Oct. 12, Chena's kraal, died October 20.
4.	Michell, John B.,	Trooper, Umtali Contingent, June 19, 1st Hartley Patrol, died June 27.
5.	Morris, Herbert J.,	Lieutenant, Umtali Rifles, October 2, Manyabera's kraal, died October 3.

WOUNDED IN ACTION.

No.	Name.	Rank, Corps, Date, when and where Wounded, etc.
1.	Arnott, Sydney N.,	Sergeant, S.F.F., July 27, 2nd Hartley Patrol.
2.	Ashe, Robert F.,	Lieutenant, Artillery Troop, R.H., October 10, Mashingombi's kraal; arm amputated.
3.	Berry, H. J.,	Trooper, S.F.F., June 20, 1st Mazoë Patrol.
4.	Boardman, Thomas,	Private, King's Royal Rifles (M.I.), October 12, Chena's kraal.
5.	Bottomley, Wm. G.,	Trooper, Natal Troop, June 20, 1st Hartley Patrol.
6.	Broad, Richard,	Private, Rifle Brigade (M.I.), August 3, Makoni's kraal; leg amputated.
7.	Brown, William H.,	Trooper, S.F.F., July 23, Makombi's kraal.
8.	Burton, Archer,	Trooper, S.F.F., June 20, 1st Mazoë Patrol; permanently injured.
9.	Byrne, Peter,	Private, Royal Dublin Fusiliers (M.I.), October 11, Mashingombi's kraal; very severe.
10.	Colin, Frederick,	Private, Royal Dublin Fusiliers (M.I.), October 10, Mashingombi's kraal; very severe.
11.	Colling, William B.,	Sergeant, S.F.F., September 2, 3rd Chishawasha Patrol; hand amputated and permanent injury to other arm.
12.	Coode, Percival,	Lieutenant, West Riding regiment, September 12, Simbanoota's kraal.
13.	Creswick, James E.,	Corporal, Dismounted Troop, R.H., September 9, Simbanoota's kraal; very severe.
14.	Eastwood, Ernest,	Trooper, Mashonaland Column of M.R.F., July 29, near Marandellas; severe.
15.	Eustace, Chas. L. E.,	Lieutenant, King's Royal Rifles (M.I.), Oct. 9, Mashingombi's kraal; very severe.
16.	Everett, Henry,	Private, West Riding regiment, October 12, Chena's kraal.
17.	Feltham, John P.,	Sergeant, Artillery Troop, R.H., October 10, Mashingombi's kraal.
18.	Ferreira, Thomas I.,	Commandant, Enkeldoorn Garrison, June 23, Sigara's kraal.
19.	Finucane, Edward E.,	Sergeant, Umtali Contingent, June 19, 1st Hartley Patrol.
20.	Fitzpatrick, H. A.,	Trooper, S.F.F. (Beal's Column), July 12, Hunyani River.
21.	Franklin, Edward,	Lance-Corporal, West Riding regiment, Sept. 12, Simbanoota's kraal.
22.	Fraser, Jock,	Sergeant, S.F.F., July 23, 2nd Chishawasha Patrol.
23.	French, Sampson G.,	Lieutenant, Royal Irish regiment (M.I.), September 26, 3rd Mazoë Patrol.
24.	Grey, Henry H.,	Surgeon, Natal Troop, June 20, 1st Hartley Patrol; very severe.
25.	Hamilton, John,	Corporal, Mashonaland Column of M.R.F., July 29, near Marandellas.
26.	Harding, Alfred,	Private, King's Royal Rifles (M.I.), October 12, Chena's kraal.
27.	Hendrikz, Charles,	Trooper, S.F.F., June 20, 1st Mazoë Patrol; severe.
28.	Hobson, Frederick P.,	Corporal, Natal Troop, Sept. 20, Gona Hills.
29.	Holman, George,	Trooper, S.F.F., June 17, Abercorn Laager.

APPENDIX B

No.	Name.	Rank, Corps, Date, when and where Wounded, etc.
30.	Janki, John C., .	Trooper, White's Scouts, August 24, Hunyani River.
31.	Judson, Dan, .	Lieutenant, S.F.F., June 20, 1st Mazoë Patrol.
32.	Kerr, Robert A.,	Trooper, S.F.F., July 20, 2nd Hartley Patrol ; very severe.
33.	Lea, St. John W.,	Trooper, White's Scouts, July 20, 2nd Hartley Patrol ; severe.
34.	Leigh-Lye, Frederick,	Lieutenant, Umtali Rifles, October 2, Manyabera's kraal ; very severe.
35.	Lock, Henry, .	Private, King's Royal Rifles (M.I.), Aug. 3, Makoni's kraal.
36.	Mackey, William,	Private, Royal Irish regiment (M.I.), Aug. 3, Makoni's kraal ; severe.
37.	Mahoney, Thomas, .	Private, Royal Irish regiment (M.I.), Sept. 2, 3rd Chishawasha Patrol ; arm amputated.
38.	McKay, James, .	Private, Royal Irish regiment (M.I.), October 11, Chena's kraal.
39.	McMahon, Sir Horace W., Bart.,	Captain, Royal Welsh Fusiliers (M.I.), October 11, Chena's kraal ; severe.
40.	Miller, James, .	Trooper, S.F.F. (Beal's Column), July 23, 2nd Chishawasha Patrol.
41.	Montgomery, Foster K. W. L.,	Captain, S.F.F. (Beal's Column), August 14, 2nd Mazoë Patrol ; very severe wound in head.
42.	Niebuhr, Richard, .	Trooper, S.F.F., June 20, 1st Mazoë Patrol.
43.	Ogilvie, Ogilvie II., .	Lieutenant, S.F.F., June 20, 1st Mazoë Patrol.
44.	Rainey, Richard,	Private, Royal Irish regiment (M.I.), August 19, Gwandula's kraal ; leg amputated.
45.	Seigert, Charlie,	Trooper, Mashonaland Column, M.R.F., Oct. 19, Gatsi's kraal.
46.	Shannon, John, .	Trooper, Natal Troop (formerly West Riding regiment), August 23, Hunyani River.
47.	Smith, James, .	Private, Royal Dublin Fusiliers (M.I.), September 19, Villam's kraal.
48.	Swartz, Gideon J.,	Trooper, Enkeldoorn Garrison, October 31, Sango's kraal.
49.	Taylor, John F.,	Captain, Natal Troop, Aug. 23, Hunyani River.
50.	Taylor, John F.,	Captain, Natal Troop, Sept. 20, Gona Hills.
51.	Trevor, Roger, .	Corporal, White's Scouts, August 24, Hunyani River.
52.	Tully, George, .	Corporal, Dismounted Troop, R.H., September 26, 3rd Mazoë Patrol.
53.	Van Niekerk, John, .	Trooper, Charter Garrison, July 20, Umtigesa's kraal.
54.	Van Reit, William, .	Trooper, S.F.F. (Beal's Column), July 24, 2nd Chisawasha Patrol.
55.	Watson, James, .	Trooper, S.F.F., August 13, 2nd Mazoë Patrol.
56.	White, George, .	Lance-Corporal, 7th Hussars, serving with M.R.F., July 29, near Marandellas.
57.	Wood, Alfred H.,	Sergeant-Major, Umtali Rifles, September 3, Makoni's kraal.
58.	Wray, William, .	Trooper, Mashonaland Column, M.R.F. (formerly West Riding regiment), July 20, near Marandellas.
59.	Young, David D.,	Trooper, Umtali Rifles, Aug. 3, Makoni's kraal.

PERSONS MURDERED OR MISSING 271

LIST OF PERSONS REPORTED MURDERED OR MISSING.

NOTE.—*In the following List of Murdered and Missing no hope is entertained for any of those returned as "missing." All bodies that have been found have been buried.*

No.	Name.	When and where Murdered, etc.
1.	Alexander, James M.,	June 17, Porta farm (Norton's), Hunyani River; farm assistant. Body found.
2.	Annesty, Charles,	about June 19, Mazoë District; prospector, last seen at Chipadza's, June 13, going to Mazoë.
3.	Angelbrecht, Michael,	about June 20, near Enkeldoorn; farmer, believed to have been murdered at Marooma's kraal.
4.	Austin, Frank,	about June 21, Makombi's, Abercorn; prospector; believed to have been murdered at Makombi's kraal.
5.	Basson, Nicholas,	about June 18, Headlands District; last heard of trading at Chiduka's kraal.
6.	Behr, Johannes P.,	about June 20, Charter District; farmer, believed to have been murdered five miles from Enkeldoorn Laager.
7.	Behr, Michael,	
8.	Bent, Francis L.,	about June 20, Mazoë District; engineer, Great B. Syndicate, known to have been with Henckens, prospecting near Mazoë River.
9.	Beyer, David J.,	June 19, Salisbury District; murdered at Native Commissioner Campbell's camp.
10.	Birkett, William,	about June 18, Salisbury District; murdered near Salisbury Reef. Body found Aug. 5.
11.	Botha, Christian,	about June 20, Charter District; murdered ten miles north of Enkeldoorn. Body found June 22.
12.	Blakiston, John L.,	June 18, Mazoë District; telegraphist, murdered whilst returning from duty at Telegraph Office. Body found.
13.	Box, Duncan,	about June 20, Lomagundi District; believed to have been murdered at the Eureka mine.
14.	Box, James,	about June 20, Lomagundi District; believed to have been murdered at the Eureka mine.
15.	Bredenbach, Jacob,	about June 20, Charter District; farmer, believed to have been murdered seven miles south of Enkeldoorn.
16.	Bredenbach, Harry,	about June 20, Charter District; farmer, believed to have been murdered seven miles south of Enkeldoorn.
17.	Bremner, Harry,	about June 20, Marandellas; Lieutenant and Adjutant, 20th Hussars, murdered at White's farm, twelve miles from Marandellas. Body found August 5.

APPENDIX B

No.	Name.	When and where Murdered, etc.
18.	Briggs, John W.,	June 22, Lomagundi District; engine-driver employed at Ayrshire mine, murdered while on his way into Salisbury at the Menene River. Body found October 27.
19.	Briscoe, John D.,	about June 18, Salisbury District; farmer, believed to have been murdered on or near his farm about eight miles from Salisbury.
20.	Burton, George W.,	about June 18, Mazoë District; prospector, known to have been with Mr. Tom Salthouse, who left Chipadza's, June 17.
21.	Calcott, Henry R.,	about June 18, Salisbury District.
22.	Campbell, George D.,	June 19, Salisbury District; farmer, murdered at Native Commissioner Campbell's camp.
23.	Care, William,	June 21, Lomagundi District; miner at Woodbyrne mine, Ayrshire, murdered at camp of Native Commissioner for Lomagundi.
24.	Cass, Edward T.,	June 18, Mazoë District; farmer, murdered at the Salvation Army camp, Mazoë Valley. Body found.
25.	Carrick, Edward T.,	June 19, Hartley District; Mining Commissioner, murdered on his way in to Salisbury from Hartley Hills. Body found July 21.
26.	"Charlie,"	June 25, Matatima camp; German by birth, murdered with Capt. M'Cullum at the telegraph construction camp.
27.	Crouchley, Thos. W.,	about June 20, Abercorn District; prospector, last seen at Abercorn store, June 19.
28.	Curtis, Thomas H.,	about June 17, Mazoë District; surveyor, believed to have been murdered at Gutama's kraal. Reported by Mrs. Cass, who saw him on June 14.
29.	Dickenson, James,	June 18, Mazoë District; Mining Commissioner, murdered near the Salvation Army camp, Mazoë Valley. Body found.
30.	Dickinson, Adam J.,	June 19, Salisbury District; tailor, murdered near Law's store, on Umtali Road.
31.	Dovenbrock, R.,	About June 20, Salisbury District; missing from Cattlethorpe, near Enterprise mine.
32.	Dougherty, John,	May 31, Lomagundi District; miner, murdered by his natives at Alaska mine.
33.	Dryden, John,	about June 20, Abercorn District; last seen at Fletcher's camp, near Chipadza's kraal, on June 18.
34.	Drysdale, John H.,	June 22, Lomagundi District; blacksmith, murdered on Menene River, on his way in to Salisbury. Body found Oct. 27.
35.	Eaton, George St. J.,	about June 19, Abercorn District; prospector, believed to have been murdered at Chipadza's kraal.
36.	Eyre, Herbert H.,	about June 21, Lomagundi District; farmer, murdered on his farm, Umvokwe Mountains. Body found Oct. 22.

PERSONS MURDERED OR MISSING

No.	Name.	When and where Murdered, etc.
37.	Fairweather, L. M.,	June 17, Salisbury District; nurse to Mrs. Norton, murdered at Porta farm, Hunyani River. Body found June 18.
38.	Faull, William,	June 18, Mazoe District; bricklayer, murdered near Salvation Army camp whilst attempting to escape in to Salisbury. Body found.
39.	Fletcher, John,	June 21, Abercorn District; murdered at Abercorn store. Body found same day.
40.	Fourie, Benjamin J.,	about June 16, Salisbury District; trader, murdered at Villam's kraal on Hartley Road.
41.	Fraser,	Abercorn District.
42.	Fuller, George L.,	about June 20, Charter District, murdered at Jinganga's kraal.
43.	Gambier, J. Cecil,	June 22, Lomagundi District; assayer and surveyor at Ayrshire mine, murdered on Menene River, on his way into Salisbury.
44.	Gibson, Thomas J.,	about June 20, Abercorn District; carpenter and prospector.
45.	Graham, Harry,	about June 19, Salisbury District; storekeeper, Graham & White. Body found August 3.
46.	Grant, Henry J.,	about June 18, Charter District; farmer, murdered at Altona farm.
47.	Gravenor, Harry,	June 17, Salisbury District; farm assistant, murdered at Porta farm, Hunyani River.
48.	Gray, Harry,	about June 19, Salisbury District; miner, murdered at Gloucester Reef and body thrown down shaft.
49.	Greyling, Amelius,	about June 20, Charter District; farmer.
50.	Harry, Ernest W.,	about June 21, Abercorn District, reported by Zambesi boy to have been murdered at Quadzuda's kraal.
51.	Harvey, John L.,	June, Salisbury District.
52.	Heine, Corlina M.,	
53.	Heine, Frederick,	about June 20, Charter District; murdered twenty miles from Charter.
54.	Heine, Mary,	
55.	Heine, Thomas,	
56.	Henckens, Anton H.,	about June 20, Mazoë District; prospector, known to have been with Bent prospecting near Mazoë River, last seen at Mazoë store about June 12.
57.	Hepworth, John C.,	June 17, Hartley District; mine manager, Renny Tayleur Concession, believed to have been killed at Wallace's farm, Hartley District.
58.	Hermann, Louis,	June 21, Abercorn District; prospector, murdered at Makombi's kraal.
59.	Hermiston,	July 24, Charter District; trooper, Mashonaland Column, M.R.F., lost on March between Charter and Marandellas.
60.	Hitchman, Henry A.,	about June 20, trader. Body found at Nedizwi's kraal, five miles from Headlands, Aug. 20.
61.	Hodgson, Alfred,	about June 21, Lomagundi District; manager, Deary's store; murdered near store.

S

APPENDIX B

No.	Name.	When and where Murdered, etc.
62.	Ireland, George,	about June 21, Lomagundi District; prospector, believed to have been murdered at the Eureka mine.
63.	Jameson, Arthur J.,	about June 21, Lomagundi District; Mining Commissioner, believed to have been murdered at M.C.'s camp, Lomagundi.
64.	Joubert, J.,	about June, Salisbury District.
65.	Keatinge, Frank,	June 18, Lomagundi District; corporal, M.M.P., murdered at the Gwebe River, real name was Frank Gilbert Keating Jackson.
66.	Kerr,	June 20, Lomagundi District; prospector.
67.	Koefoed, S.,	June 16, Salisbury District; prospector, murdered at the Beatrice mine by M'slopa's people. Body thrown down well.
68.	Law, Horace,	about June 20, Salisbury District; storekeeper, murdered near Native Commissioner Campbell's farm. Body supposed to be his found July 25.
69.	M'Cullum, Capt. W.,	June 25, Lomagundi District; telegraph constructor, murdered at his camp, Matatima.
70.	M'Gowan, James,	June 21, Lomagundi District; prospector, murdered at or near Deary's store.
71.	Metcalf, Samuel,	about June 20, Headlands; trader. Body found August 20 at Nedziwi's kraal.
72.	Milton, William,	about June 20, Salisbury District; transport rider. Body found on Umtali Road, August 3.
73.	Moore, John,	about June 20, Salisbury District; storekeeper. Body found near Umtali telegraph line on August 3.
74.	Mynhardt, A. G. F.,	June 21, Lomagundi District; Native Commissioner, murdered at his camp. Body supposed to be his found October 30.
75.	Moony, David E.,	June 15, Hartley District; Native Commissioner, murdered at Mashingombi's kraal.
76.	Nelson, Thomas,	about June 20, Hartley District; prospector, believed to have been murdered near Umswezwe's kraal.
77.	Noble, Andrew,	about June 20, Abercorn District; last heard of May 22.
78.	Norton, Joseph N.,	about June 17, Salisbury District; farmer, murdered at or near his farm Porta.
79.	Norton, Caroline,	about June 17, Salisbury District; wife of above, murdered at or near his farm Porta.
80.	Norton, Dorothy,	about June 17, Salisbury District; daughter of above.
81.	Phillips, Henry O.,	about June 20, Salisbury District; last heard of at Graham and White's stores.
82.	Pollard, Henry H.,	about June 18, Mazoë District; Native Commissioner, last heard of June 14, at Tamaringa's kraal.
83.	Richards, G.,	about June 20, Headlands District; trader, murdered at Nedziwi's kraal. Body found August 20.

PERSONS MURDERED OR MISSING 275

No.	Name.	When and where Murdered, etc.
84.	Routledge, T. G.,	about June 18, Mazoë District; telegraphist, murdered whilst returning from duty at the Telegraph Office. Body found.
85.	Ruping, Henry H.,	about June 24, Abercorn District; Acting Native Commissioner, M'topo's, murdered by his police at M'lewa's kraal.
86.	Saddler, Henry,	about June 20, Salisbury District; trader, left Salisbury for Hunyani River on June 13.
87.	Sagar, Robert,	about June 20, Abercorn District; fitter, known to have been with Crouchley.
88.	Salthouse, Elijah T.,	about June 18, Mazoë District; prospector, known to have been with Burton—they left Chipadza's kraal June 17.
89.	Saunders, William,	about June 20, Salisbury District; transport rider.
90.	Schooter, Frederick,	June 21, Lomagundi District; Homan's storekeeper, murdered at Native Commissioner's camp, Lomagundi. Body supposed to be his found October 30.
91.	Shapiro, Reuben,	about June 20, Abercorn District; jeweller, believed to have been murdered at Umlewy's kraal.
92.	Shell, A.,	June 15, Hartley District; murdered at Mashingombi's kraal.
93.	Short, Henry,	June 23, Charter District; trader, believed to have been murdered on Charter Road.
94.	Smit, Cornelius,	June 20, Charter District; farmer, murdered at Van der Merwe's farm.
95.	Smith, Arthur,	about June 18, Salisbury District; believed to have been murdered near Ballyhooley.
96.	State *alias* Steyte,	June, Lomagundi District.
97.	Steele, James,	June 21, Abercorn District; known to have been with Austin. (See No. 4.)
98.	Steele, William,	June, Abercorn District; carpenter, last heard of May 22.
99.	Stopforth, Jan M.,	June 20, Charter District; murdered at his farm ten miles from Enkeldoorn. Body found.
100.	Stunt, John,	June 15, Hartley District; prospector, murdered at Mashingombi's kraal.
101.	Tapsell, Walter,	June 21, Abercorn District; farmer, believed to have been murdered at Makombi's kraal.
102.	Tate, William J.,	June 16, Salisbury District; mining engineer, murdered at the Beatrice Mine by M'slopa's people.
103.	Thurgood, Harry,	about June 15, Hartley District; formerly Native Commissioner, Hartley, murdered at George's kraal.
104.	Tucker, Augustus T.,	June 20, Salisbury District; barman at Ballyhooley, murdered near Law's store. Body found August 3.
105.	Turner, A. L.,	June 19, Hartley District; assistant storekeeper, Hartley Hill, murdered with Carrick on way into Salisbury.

No.	Name.	When and where Murdered, etc.
106.	Van der Merwe, C.,	June 20, Charter District; farmer, murdered at his farm.
107.	Van Rooyen, Robert W. A.,	June 16, Salisbury District; transport rider, murdered near Hunyani River on Hartley Road.
108.	Wallace, James,	June 17, Hartley District; prospector, murdered at his farm.
109.	Watkins, Charles H.,	June 21, Lomagundi District; medical officer, murdered near Deary's store.
110.	Weyers, Jan,	⎫ about June 18, Salisbury District; murdered at Umtali Road. Bodies found June 19.
111.	Weyers (Mrs.), S. S.,	
112.	Child of above,	
113.	Child of above,	⎭
114.	White, James,	July 7, Marandellas District; farm manager, murdered at Wesleyan Mission Station, near Marandellas.
115.	White, Wm. de Coy,	about June 19; Salisbury District; storekeeper.
116.	Wickström, N. A.,	about June 17, Hartley District; prospector, believed to have been murdered near Umsezwe's kraal.
117.	Wills, Franklin,	June 18, Salisbury District; trooper M.M.P., murdered on Gwebi River.
118.	Young, Arthur L.,	about June 21, Lomagundi District; trooper M.M.P., murdered near Eyre's Farm, Umvokwe Mountains.

ACCIDENTALLY KILLED.

No.	Name.	When and where Wounded, etc.
1.	Bester, Susarah,	June 20, Van der Merwe's farm, near Enkeldoorn; wife of Mr. Bester, accidentally shot when natives attacked the farm.
2.	Earnshaw, Harry P.,	Trooper, Umtali Rifles, October 19, Gatsi's kraal; shot himself in action.
3.	Gordon, George,	Lieutenant and Adjutant, Umtali Rifles, Sept. 29, near Headlands; revolver accident.
4.	Jenkins, Henry,	Trooper, Umtali Rifles, August 4, Umtali; revolver accident.

ACCIDENTALLY WOUNDED.

No.	Name.	Rank, Corps, when and where Wounded, etc.
1.	Day, Frederick W.,	Trooper, Dismounted Troop, R.H., Sept. 28, 3rd Mazoë Patrol; dynamite.
2.	Gibbs, Joseph,	Trooper, Mounted Troop, R.H., Salisbury, September; rifle bursting.

WOUNDED AT COMMENCEMENT OF RISING.

No.	Name.	When and where Wounded, etc.
1.	Bester, Barnadus,	June 20, Charter District; farmer, wounded at Van der Merwe's farm.
2.	Broadbent, Edward C.,	June 20, Abercorn District; prospector, on his way to Abercorn store.

WOUNDED AT COMMENCEMENT

No.	Name.	When and where Wounded, etc.
3.	Cape, F. W.,	June, Lomagundi District; prospector, on his way to Salisbury.
4.	Cartwright, Charles,	Trooper, M.M.P., June 15, Lomagundi District; wounded at Drake's farm.
5.	Krook, Otto,	June, Lomagundi District; prospector, on his way to Salisbury.
6.	Deane, Joseph F.,	June 19, Abercorn District; prospector, on his way to Abercorn store.
7.	Stockfelt,	June, Lomagundi District; on his way to Salisbury.
8.	Stroyan, James,	June 19, Abercorn District; prospector, on his way to Abercorn store.
9.	Van der Merwe, H.,	June 20, Charter District; farmer, wounded at Van der Merwe's farm.

DIED FROM OTHER CAUSES.

No.	Name.	Rank, Corps, from what Cause, etc.
1.	Beaty, John,	Private, Medical Staff Corps, October 29, Marandellas Hospital; rheumatic fever and heart disease.
2.	Caplen, Henry S.,	Sergeant-Major, Umtali Garrison, July 18, Umtali Hospital; fever.
3.	Hodgson, Robert,	Trooper, Natal Troop, July 14, Salisbury Hospital; fever.
4.	Hunt, C.,	Trooper, Artillery Troop, R.H., November 28, Salisbury Hospital; fever.
5.	McGowan, James,	Trooper, Artillery Troop, R.H., November 18, Salisbury Hospital; fever and jaundice.
6.	Noy, Richard,	about June 18, Salisbury District; miner, on his way to Salisbury; fever.
7.	Rowland, John R.,	July 14, Abercorn District; exhaustion, on his way into Salisbury after being rescued.
8.	Slade, William G.,	Bugler, White's Scouts, about July 2, Enkeldoorn, Laager; dysentery.
9.	Zboril, Adolph,	Volunteer, serving with Natal Troop, June 27, Salisbury Hospital; effects of the sun.

APPENDIX C

PART I.—PATROLS SENT OUT FROM SALISBURY BEFORE THE ARRIVAL OF THE IMPERIAL TROOPS.

Where Sent.	Strength and Composition.	Commander.	Duration.	Actions.	Result, Loot, Etc.	Casualties.	Remarks.
1. Umfuli	6 Volunteers	Lieut. Christison, Rhodesia Horse	June 16th to June 18th	Nil	Met Capt. Turner's column from Natal at Umfuli	Nil	Went on with Capt. Turner's patrol towards Hartley
2. Norton's Farm	7 M.M.P.	Capt. Nesbitt, M.M.P.	June 17th	Nil	Found and buried bodies of Norton's household	Nil	Nil
3. Mazoë	9 Volunteers	Mr. Judson, Inspector of Telegraphs	June 18th	Fought from Cass' Farm to Alice Mine, Mazoë	Went into laager at Mazoë	1 white man wounded; 1 horse killed	Some rebels killed
4. Beatrice Mine	36 Natal Troop; 8 Umtali Contingent; 6 Lieut. Christison's Patrol; 1 Maxim	Capt. Turner, West Riding Regiment	June 18th to June 25th	Fought from 9 a.m., 20th, to 1 p.m., 21st	Burnt M'Slopa's kraal, where murderers of people at Beatrice Mine were	1 white man died of wounds; 3 white men wounded; 2 Native Contingent killed; 7 horses killed; 5 horses wounded; 1 mule killed	This patrol went eight miles beyond M'Slopa's, but was forced to retire, owing to being attacked and surrounded by very large bodies of rebels. Number of enemy killed impossible to estimate, but a good many dead bodies seen

PATROLS SENT OUT

5. Mazoë	13 Volunteers	Capt. Nesbitt, M.M.P.	June 19th to June 20th	Fought their way to Mazoë and back	Relieved Judson's patrol and Mazoë laager, and brought them into Salisbury	3 white men killed 5 white men wounded 8 horses killed 7 horses wounded	Brought three women back in armour-plated waggon, and killed a good many rebels
6. Chishawasha	40 mounted men, S.F.F.	Capt. St. Hill, Salisbury Field Force	June 23rd to June 24th	Collin's Farm and near Chishawasha	Two waggon loads of mealies	Nil	Returned to Salisbury without having succeeded in reaching Chishawasha, owing to rebels being in too great strength to get through them
7. Haupt's Farm	34 dismounted men 15 mounted men, S.F.F.	Capt. Stamford Brown, S.F.F.	June 24th	Nil	Collected 3,500 bundles of forage	Nil	Nil
8. Chishawasha	21 Natal Troop 14 S.F.F. 8 Umtali gun detachment with 1 Maxim	Capt. Taylor, Natal Troop	June 25th	Fought their way back from Chishawasha	Relieved laager of Jesuit Fathers, and brought in 18 whites and 20 friendly natives	1 white man killed 1 horse killed	Nil

APPENDIX C

Where Sent.	Strength and Composition.	Commander.	Duration.	Actions.	Result, Loot, Etc.	Casualties.	Remarks.
9. Edmond's Farm	70 dismounted men 30 mounted men, 1 Maxim gun and detachment S.F.F.	Capt. Nesbitt, M.M.P.	June 26th	Nil	Collected one waggon load of forage, 2½ waggon loads of mealies, and one waggon load of provisions	Nil	Nil
10. Umvukwe Mountains	2 white guides 40 Native Contingent (Zulus)	Mr. Duncan (Australian prospector)	June 27th to July 2nd	Drake's Farm	Brought in wounded white man from Lomagundi district	Nil	Native Contingent promised reward of £5 a piece
11. Drake's Farm	40 Natal Troop 1 Maxim gun and detachment S.F.F.	Capt. Taylor, Natal Troop	June 27th	Nil	Relieved 5 whites	Nil	Nil
12. Charra's kraal	17 mtd. men 27 dismounted men S.F.F. 100 Native Contingent 1 Maxim and detachment S.F.F.	Capt. Nesbitt, M.M.P.	June 29th	Charra's kraal	Kraal and a lot of grain burnt. Collected 40 bags grain, 2 cows, and 30 sheep and goats	Nil	Four rebels seen dead, and many others believed killed

PATROLS SENT OUT

13. Chirimba's, Beesa's, etc.	30 Natal Troop 40 dismounted men S.F.F., 1 Maxim and detachment S.F.F. 163 Native Contingent	Capt. Taylor, Natal Troop	July 1st	Chirimba's	Burnt several kraals, killed 6 natives, and brought in 4 waggon loads of grain	Nil	Nil
14. Briscoe's Farm	20 Natal Troop 20 dismounted men and 1 Maxim, and detachment S.F.F. 100 Native Contingent	Capt. St. Hill, S.F.F.	July 3rd	Briscoe's Farm	Brought in 3,000 bundles of forage and one waggon load of mealies	Nil	30 or 40 rebels killed
15. Brown's Farm	30 mounted men S.F.F.	Capt. Moberly (late R.H.), S.F.F.	July 7th	Nil	Collected three waggon loads of mealies	Nil	Nil
16. Webb's Farm	25 mounted men S.F.F.	Capt. Harrison, S.F.F.	July 10th	Nil	Collected one waggon load of mealies	Nil	Nil
17. Abercorn	40 Natal Troop 25 mounted men S.F.F. 1 Maxim gun and detachment S.F.F.	Mr. A. H. F. Duncan	July 11th to July 17th	Two skirmishes on way out, Tsapu's kraal, Mazoe Valley, and Mount Hampden on way back	6 white men rescued, 1 white man buried, 61 head of cattle captured	Nil	A good many natives killed

APPENDIX C

Where Sent.	Strength and Composition.	Commander.	Duration.	Actions.	Result, Loot, Etc.	Casualties.	Remarks.
18. Brown's Farm	5 mounted men 20 dismounted men S.F.F. 50 Native Con.	Capt. Moberly, S.F.F.	July 15th	Nil	Collected two waggon loads of mealies	Nil	Nil
19. Hartley Hills	65 White's Scouts, with 1 Maxim 42 Natal Troop 60 dismounted men S.F.F., 19 Artillery S.F.F., with 1 Maxim, 1 7-pounder with gun detachment from Beal's column 40 Native Contingent	Capt. Hon. C. White	July 19th to July 28th	Three miles Salisbury side of Hunyani river, Hunyani river, George's kraal, Umputnela's kraal	Relieved 10 white men of Hartley Garrison. Captured between 400 and 500 head of cattle, 100 sheep and goats, 1 horse, 9 4 mules, 9 donkeys, 13 revolvers, 20 rifles, and a large quantity of ammunition	1 white man killed 3 white men wounded 3 Native Contingent wounded 1 Native Contingent killed 1 horse killed 2 horses wounded 1 mule killed 1 mule wounded	Enemy's loss computed at 137. Twice encountered in the open
20. Chishawasha	133 Beal's Matabeleland Column	Lieut.-Col. Beal, Rhodesia Horse	July 22nd to July 28th	Rupara Valley, Ruoko's kraal, and numerous skirmishes	12 kraals burnt. Collected 200 bags of mealies, captured 50 cattle and 500 sheep and goats	3 white men wounded	10 to 15 natives killed, among them the Chief Chirumbe

PATROLS SENT OUT

21. Law's	68 S.F.F. 4 Scouts 150 Native Contingent	Commandant Smith, S.F.F.	July 22nd to July 26th	Ballyhooley, and near Law's	Collected four waggon loads of grain	1 man Native Contingent killed	21 natives estimated as killed
22. Chishawasha	24 S.F.F.	Capt. Snodgrass, S.F.F.	July 25th to July 26th	Nil	Collected five waggon loads of grain	Nil	Nil
23. Charter	40 S.F.F. 82 Native Contingent	Capt. Judson, S.F.F.	July 27th to Aug. 28th	Shawe's Farm	Captured 12 head of cattle and 50 bags of grain	Nil	Remained for some time at Charter
24. Marandellas	60 men S.F.F. 1 Maxim and gun detachment mounted 50 Native Contingent	Capt. Nesbitt, M.M.P.	Aug. 2nd to Aug. 13th	Nil	Mended telegraph line, and burnt several kraals	Nil	Met Col. Alderson's column
25. Chishawasha	24 dismounted men S.F.F. 30 Native Con.	Lieut. Neale, S.F.F.	Aug. 4th to Aug. 8th	Nil	Collected six waggon loads of grain	Nil	Nil
26. Mazoë	66 White's Scouts and 1 Maxim 44 Natal Troop 131 Beal's Column, with 1 Maxim and 1 7-pounder	Major Hoste, Rhodesia Horse.	Aug. 9th to Aug. 19th	Four days' fighting Chiwe's kraal, Amanda's kraal, and Chidamba's kraal	Burnt about 20 kraals	2 white men wounded 1 mule wounded	Built fort at Mazoë

APPENDIX C

Where Sent.	Strength and Composition.	Commander.	Duration.	Actions.	Result, Loot, Etc.	Casualties.	Remarks.
27. Mazoe	30 S.F.F. 25 Native Contingent	Lieut. Fairburn, S.F.F.	Started Aug. 15th	Nil	Garrisoned Mazoë Fort	Nil	Nil.
28. Charter	40 men S.F.F. 1 Maxim	Capt. Moberly, S.F.F.	Aug. 15th to Aug. 24th	Nil	Nil	Nil	Taking food to Charter

PART II.—COLUMNS AND PATROLS SENT INTO MASHONALAND.

WHERE SENT.	STRENGTH AND COMPOSITION.	COMMANDER.	DURATION.	ACTIONS.	RESULT, LOOT, ETC.	CASUALTIES.	REMARKS.
1. Salisbury (from Buluwayo)	75 mounted men 90 dismounted men R.H. 150 Native Contingent	Lieut.-Col. Beal, R.H.	July 1st to July 17th	Marooma's kraal, Lucas Post Stations, Hunyani River	Burnt about 20 kraals, and captured certain amount of grain	1 white man wounded 2 Native Contingent wounded 3 horses killed 1 horse wounded	Unable to compute number of natives killed, but it was considerable
2. Salisbury (from Buluwayo)	66 mounted men White's Scouts	Capt. Hon. C. White	July 1st to July 10th	Marooma's kraal, Charter District	Burnt a number of kraals about Charter	Nil	
3. Salisbury (from Capetown) via Beira and Umtali	213 I.M.I with 2 Maxims 39 R.E., 14 R.A. with 2 7-pounders 48 West Riding Regiment 17 Medical S. Corps 92 Umtali Vol. 15 Honey's Scouts 15 Deary's Vol.	Lieut.-Col. Alderson, Commanding Mashonaland Field Force	July 31st to Aug. 3rd	Skirmish on Devil's Pass range	Burnt several kraals		Not many natives killed

Where Sent.	Strength and Composition.	Commander.	Duration.	Actions.	Result, Loot, Etc.	Casualties.	Remarks.
4. Makoni's	2 Coys. M.I. with Maxim 22 R.E., R.A. with 2 7-pounders Honey's Scouts 40 Umtali Volunteers	Lieut.-Col. Alderson	Aug. 3rd	Makoni's kraal	Captured 353 head of cattle and 210 sheep and goats Established Fort Haynes	3 white men killed and 4 wounded 1 Cape boy wounded	Enemy's loss estimated at 200, including his witch doctor and 10 of his chief councillors
5. Nidziwe's kraal	2 Sections M.I.	Capt. Sir H. McMahon, Bart.	Aug. 7th	Nil	Collected two waggon loads of oat hay	Nil	Nil
6. Chitsa's kraal	2 Sections M.I. 1 7-pounder and detachment R.A. Deary's Volunteers	Lieut.-Col. Alderson	Aug. 8th	Chitsa's kraal	Captured and burnt kraal	Nil	Nil
7. Gatsi's and Magwendi's	2 Coys. M.I., 20 R.E., detachment R.A. with 2 7-pounders 30 Native Contingent	Lieut.-Col. Alderson	Aug. 10th to Aug. 16th	Gatsi's	Captured and burnt Gatsi's and Magwendi's and numerous other kraals, and got a lot of sheep and goats	1 white man killed	A few rebels killed

PATROLS SENT OUT

8. Salisbury	1 Section M.I.	Lieut.-Col. Alderson	Aug. 15th	Two kraals near Law's	Burnt these kraals and some others	Nil	A lot of wearing apparel, etc., found
9. Marandellas to Salisbury	1½ Coys. M.I. and 1 Maxim Honey's Scouts All R.E. All R.A. and 2 7-pounders 15 Umtali Volunteers and some M.S.C.	Major Jenner, D.S.O., M.I.	Aug. 13th to Aug. 25th	Marandellas' and other kraals	Took and burnt several kraals, and collected a large quantity of oat hay	1 white man killed	Some natives killed

PART III.—PATROLS SENT OUT AFTER THE ARRIVAL OF THE IMPERIAL TROOPS.

Where Sent.	Strength and Composition.	Commander.	Duration.	Actions.	Result, Loot, Etc.	Casualties.	Remarks.
1. Gloucester Reef	Rhodesia Horse Volunteers, Maxim gun detachment, S.F.F., and 16 Native Contingent	Capt. Newman, R.H.	Aug. 19th to Aug. 21st	Nil	Collected two waggon loads of grain	Nil	Nil
2. Garandoola's Kraal	2 Sections M.I. 1 Maxim 7 men S.F.F. 4 Native guides	Lieut. St. Aubyn, M.I.	Aug. 23rd	Garandoola's kraal	Collected six waggon loads of grain	1 white man wounded 3 horses wounded	3 natives known to be killed, probably more
3. Hunyani River, via Umtali Telegraph line	1 Section M.I. 45 Natal Troop 1 Maxim	Capt. Nesbitt. M.M.P.	Aug. 23rd to Aug. 27th	Hunyani River (two actions)	Burnt numerous kraals, captured 8 donkeys, 9 head cattle, 38 sheep	2 white men wounded	About 10 natives known to have been shot
4. Hunyani River, via Six mile Spruit	1 Section M.I. 60 White's Scouts 1 Maxim, 1 7-pounder detachment, Col. Beal's column	Lieut. St. Aubyn, M.I.	Aug. 23rd to Aug. 27th	Sigoko's kraal and others burnt	Three waggon loads mealies and 40 goats captured	2 white men wounded	3 natives shot for certain

PATROLS SENT OUT

5. Chishawasha	2 Sections M.I. 50 Mtd. Trp. R.H. 25 Salisbury Rifles 1 7-pounder Det. R.A. 50 Native Con.	Capt. Sir H. McMahon, Bart.	Aug. 29th to Sept. 8th	Kaheia's kraal Inyagow River Domba Imbutsi	4 cattle, 30 goats, 10 waggon loads grain. Burnt numerous kraals	2 white men wounded	15 natives killed for certain, probably good many more
6. Charter	50 Natal Troop 58 Native Contingent	Capt. Taylor, Natal Troop	Aug. 31st (joined Maj. Jenner)				
7. Charter District	Rifle Companies M.I., and 1 Maxim 8 R.A. and 1 7-pounder 15 Honey's Scouts Capt. Taylor's patrol joined at Charter	Major Jenner	Sept. 1st to Oct. 10th (when patrol joined Col. Alderson's Column at Mashomgombi's)				
8. Sonyobera's kraal	13 men dismounted troop R. Horse	Lieut. Ross, R. Horse	Sept. 3rd	Nil	Collected three waggon loads of grain	Nil	Nil
9. Marooma's kraal	30 Enkeldoorn Garrison	Commandant Ferreira, Enkeldoorn Garrison	Sept. 3rd	Marooma's kraal	Burnt Marooma's, and captured two waggon loads of grain	Nil	20 known to have been killed

APPENDIX C

Where Sent.	Strength and Composition.	Commander.	Duration.	Actions.	Result, Loot, Etc.	Casualties.	Remarks.
10. Makoni's kraal	Umtali Volunteers West Riding	Major Watts, D.A.A.G., Natal	Sept. 4th	Makoni's kraal	Capture of Makoni, kraal and caves	1 white man wounded 1 Cape boy wounded	Nil
11. Chishawasha District	13 dismounted troop Rhodesia Horse	Lieut. Ellett, Dis. Troop R.H.	Sept. 7th	Nil	Two waggon loads grain	Nil	Nil
12. Donga's kraal	20 dismounted troop R.H.	Lieut. Ross	Sept. 8th	Nil	Two loads grain	Nil	Nil
13. Simlanoota's District	1 Section M.I. Detachment West Riding Regiment 30 Art. Troop R.H. 1 7-pounder and 1 Maxim 30 dismounted troop R.H. 25 Salisbury Rifles and 50 Native Con.	Major Tennant, Art. Troop R.H.	Sept. 8th to Sept. 14th	Simlanoota's kraal and others (four days' fighting)	Few head of cattle, two loads grain. Burnt Simlanoota's and other kraals	1 white man killed 3 white men wounded 1 Native Contingent killed	
14. Mazoë	2 Sections M.I.	Lieut. French, M.I.	Sept. 9th to Sept. 14th	Amanda's kraal	10 goats and 12 sheep	Nil	Few natives killed

PATROLS SENT OUT

#	Place	Force	Commander	Dates	Objective	Result	Casualties	Native casualties
15.	Norton's Farm	2 Sections M.I. 1 machine gun Detachment R.A. 1 7-pounder 25 mounted troop R.H. 30 Salisbury Rifles 50 Native Contingent	Lieut. Pilson, M.I.	Sept. 17th to Sept. 24th	(1) Willen's kraal (2) Two miles south of Hunyani River	Burnt several kraals. 3 head cattle, 26 sheep and goats, 17 pigs, 10 waggon loads grain	1 white man wounded 1 Native Contingent killed	Nil
16.	Mazœ	Irish Coy. M.I. Det. R.A., 1 7-pounder, 1 machine gun 30 men dismounted troop R.H. 30 Ar. Troop R.H., 1 7-pounder, 1 Maxim 30 Salisbury Rifles 100 Native Contingent	Capt. Sir H. McMahon, Bart.	Sept. 18th to Sept. 30th	Iron Masque Range (two days' fighting)	Burnt four kraals. Captured large amount of various loot. Few cattle captured	2 white men wounded 1 ditto (accidentally) 1 Native Contingent wounded	A number of natives known to have been killed
17.	Manyerbeera's Kraal	40 men Umtali Volunteers 30 men M.R.F. 10 Umtali Arty. 1 7-pounder	Capt. Pease	Oct. 2nd to Oct. 9th	Manyerbeera's kraal	Burnt several kraals. Captured 50 goats	1 white man died from wounds 1 white man wounded	Killed 15 natives. Many more believed to be killed

Where Sent.	Strength and Composition.	Commander.	Duration.	Actions.	Result, Loot, Etc.	Casualties.	Remarks.
18. Mashangombi's and Lo Magundi Patrol	6 Staff 166 M.I. and 1 Maxim 7 R.A. and 1 7-pounder 20 W.R. Regt. 10 M.S.C. 30 Art. Troop R.H. 1 7-pounder and 2 Maxims 36 mounted troop R.H. 29 dismounted troop R.H. 39 Salisbury Rif. 12 Scouts 100 Native Con. Major Jenner's Column joined 10th Oct. 109 M.I. and 1 Maxim 8 R.A. and 1 7-pounder 5 M.S.C. 33 Natal Troop 12 Honey's Scts.	Lieut.-Col. Alderson	Oct. 5th to Oct. 24th	Mashomgombi's kraal Chena's kraal Zimba's kraal	Burnt a very large number of kraals. Captured a fair amount of grain and some cattle	2 white men killed 1 white man died of wounds 10 white men wounded 1 Native Contingent killed 3 ditto wounded 2 horses killed 1 horse wounded	Enemy's loss difficult to estimate owing to thick bush and numerous caves, but must have been considerable

19. Mapondera's and Mazoë	110 Rifle Coy. M.I. and 1 Maxim 62 English Coy. M.I. 15 R.A. and 2 7-pounders 8 M.S.C. 27 dismounted troop R.H. 10 Scouts 30 Native Con.	Major Jenner	Oct. 25th to Nov. 10th	Nil	Burnt Mapondera's and other kraals	Nil	Built new fort at Mazoë
20. Sinoia's and the Ayrshire Mine	106 Irish Coy. M.I. and 1 Maxim 30 Art. Troop R.H., with 1 7-pounder and 2 Maxims 8 M.S.C. 34 mounted troop R.H. 35 Salisbury Rif. 10 Scouts 75 Native Con.	Capt. Godley	Oct. 25th to Nov. 8th	Nil	Buried remains of several murdered men. Burnt several kraals	Nil	Nil
21. Gatzi's	25 M.R.F. 52 Umtali Vols. 11 Umtali Art.	Major Evans (killed in action). Capt. Pease took over command	Oct. 19th to Oct. 26th	Gatzi's kraal (six days' fighting)	Burnt Gatzi's kraal	1 white man killed 1 ditto (accidentally) 1 white man wounded	16 known to have been killed, and it is believed that many more were killed

APPENDIX C

Where Sent.	Strength and Composition.	Commander.	Duration.	Actions.	Result, Loot, Etc.	Casualties.	Remarks.
22. Sunday Pass	14 Victoria Garrison 20 Native Con.	Capt. Reed, Victoria Garrison	Oct. 27th to Nov. 5th	Gabana's kraal	Burnt numerous kraals	Nil	Killed about 12 rebels
23. From Marandellas down line of communication	20 M.R.F. 52 Umtali Vols. 11 Umtali Art.	Capt. Pease	Oct. 28th to Nov. 2nd	Soswe's kraal	Burnt Soswe's kraal and cleared road	Nil	Nil
24. Sangala's kraal	35 men of Enkeldoorn Garrison	Capt. Ferreira	Oct. 31st	Sangala's kraal	Burnt Sangala's kraal	1 white man wounded	31 rebels reported killed
25. Chiquaqua's and Kunzi's kraals	248 M.I. 13 R.A. 30 Art. Troop R.H. 24 dismounted troop R.H. 41 Natal Troop 23 Salisbury Rifles 91 Native Contingent	Major Jenner	Nov. 15th to	Nil	Successful Indaba with Chiquaqua and Kunzi	Nil	Nil

PATROLS SENT OUT

26. Norton's Farm	25 mounted troop R.H.	Lieut. Aitken, R.H.	Nov. 18th to Nov. 22nd	Nil	Collected iron and wood from Norton's Farm	Nil	Nil
27. Hartley Hills	11 Art. Troop R.H. and 2 Maxims Mounted troop R.H. Dismounted troop R.H. 40 Natal Troop Native Contingent	Capt. Taylor, Natal Troop	Started Dec. 1st				Object: To establish a post at Hartley Hills
28. Tandi's	100 men from L. of C. troops	Capt. Pease, K.O.L.I.		Nil	Burnt Tandi's kraal	Nil	Tandi subsequently surrendered

ATRE
896.

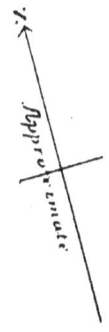

PORTUGUESE

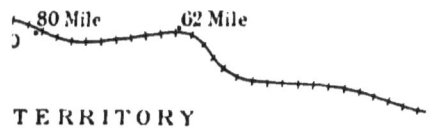

TERRITORY

ximate Scale —
20   30   40   50 Miles

— Main waggon tracks
=== Bye, or indifferently marked waggon tracks
— Rivers
— Railway

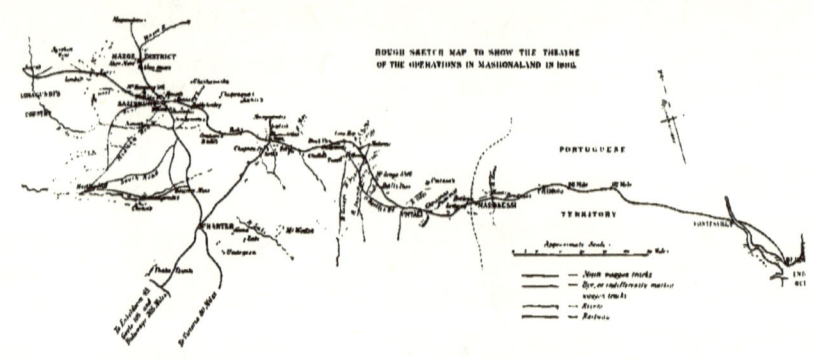

INDEX

A

Abercorn Mine, Mr. Duncan's patrol to, 125, 126, 269, 271-277, 281.

Aldershot, 1, 2, 3, 6, 7, 15, 119, 150, 161, 243, 261, 265.

Alice Mine in Mazoë Valley, relieved by Captain Nesbitt, 122, 123, 126, 170, 278, 279.

Amanda's Kraal destroyed, 130, 162, 283, 290.

"Arab," Mounted Infantry leaving Cape Town on, 16-19, 27, 28, 30, 35, 38, 39, 42, 46, 47, 57, 60.

Army Medical Staff, Medical Staff Corps (see that title).

Army Service Corps forming part of Mashonaland Field Force, 7, 21, 44, 59, 67, 128, 238, 268.

Artillery Troop, Rhodesia Horse, commanded by Major Tennent, 142, 156, 171, 173, 198, 220, 221, 225, 269, 277, 290-295.

Ashe, Lieut., Rhodesia Horse, 171, 181, 184, 198, 269.

Ayrshire Mine, Murders at—Capt. Godley's patrol to, 129, 215, 217, 224, 226, 228-230, 236, 243, 249, 272, 273, 293.

B

Baden-Powell, Col. R. S., Chief Staff Officer to Sir Frederick Carrington, 7, 165, 166, 246, 247, 253, 261.

Balleyhooley, 118, 275, 283.

Barnes, Lieut. W. E., joining Mounted Infantry as supply and transport officer and killed at Gatzi's Kraal, 21, 62, 67, 72, 109, 112-114, 234, 239, 268.

Beal, Lieut.-Col., 12, 116, 117, 120, 121, 126, 128, 141, 251, 269, 270, 282, 283, 285, 288.

Beatrice Mine, Murders by M'Slopa's followers at—Capt. Turner's revenge for, 11, 124, 153, 190, 192, 197, 274, 275, 278.

Beesa's Kraal, 119, 256, 281.

Beira, 11, 19, 21-45, 52, 56-58, 61, 66, 67, 124, 249, 251, 253, 254, 259, 260, 285.

Beira Railway Company, Beira —Fontesvilla Section of, 25, 26, 29, 35, 40-43, 50-59, 61.

Bendulas, 62, 249, 257, 259.
Black Vley, 105.
"Black Watch" or Native Contingent (see that title).
Blue Coat Mine, 222.
Boardman, Private Thos., of King's Royal Rifles, wounded, 209, 269.
Boating Company at Beira, 25, 27, 46, 47.
Botha :—Christian, murdered— Farm of, 107, 271. Trooper P. J., of Honey's Scouts, killed, 209, 268.
Botley's Store, 63.
Bowen, Mr. G., Chief Mining Commissioner in Mashonaland, 21, 47, 255.
Brabant, Capt., commanding Native Contingent, 207, 208, 210, 221.
Bremner, Lieut., of 20th Hussars, murdered, 140, 271.
Bridge, Lieut.-Col. C. H., of Army Service Corps re-organizing Buluwayo Supplies and Transports, 7.
Briggs, Mr., Discovery of body of, 233.
British South Africa or Charter Company, 11, 13, 16-18, 25, 27, 36-38, 40, 45, 53, 59, 65, 67, 69, 99, 102, 117, 125, 138, 140, 142, 161, 166, 174, 176, 239-241, 244, 245, 250-252, 255, 257, 258, 262.
Broad, Private R., of Rifle Brigade, wounded, 95.
Browne, Major Hamilton, Commander of "Umtali Rifles," 65-67, 78, 80, 102, 104.

Buluwayo, 7, 13, 19, 33, 97, 100, 104, 124, 125-127, 131, 136, 141, 168, 242, 248, 285.
Buluwayo Field Force, commanded by Capt. Hon. C. White, 120, 128, 135.
Byrne, Private B., of Royal Dublin Fusiliers, wounded, 201, 269.

C

Campbell, N.C., Mr., 175, 176.
Cape Town, 2, 8-11, 14-17, 26, 59, 61, 66, 218, 243, 245, 248, 253, 285.
Carrington, Sir Fredk., commanding Troops in Rhodesia and Bechuanaland, 7, 13, 40, 45, 121, 131, 143, 144, 165, 166, 243, 245-248, 250, 252, 253.
Charlton, Mr., Railway Manager at Beira, 41.
Charter, 100, 101, 104, 124-129, 132, 140, 141, 143, 144, 146-148, 152, 153, 168, 189-191, 197, 207, 211, 250, 254, 270, 271, 273, 275-277, 283-285, 289.
Chena's Kraal taken, 200-208, 268-270, 292.
Chidamba, Rebel Chief in Mazoë Valley, 130, 163, 164, 171-174, 184, 283.
Chimbi River, 99, 100, 107.
Chimoio, 28, 35, 36, 40-43, 50, 52, 53, 59-63, 128.
Chipara's Kraal, 192.
Chipunza, Chief, 99.
Chiquaqua, Rebel Chief, 130, 141, 245, 249, 250, 294.

INDEX

Chishawasha, 128, 130, 249, 250, 268-270, 279, 282, 283, 289, 290.

Chitza's Kraal burnt, 105, 106, 286.

Chope, Capt., commanding "Arab," 16, 58.

Clayton, Mr., 80.

Colin, Private F., of Royal Dublin Fusiliers, wounded, 198.

Colling, Sergeant W. B., wounded, 136, 137, 269.

Coode, Lieut. P., of West Riding Regt., joining Mashonaland Field Force at Fontesvilla, 59, 99, 157, 269.

Coryndon, Trooper J. S., of Salisbury Rifles, killed, 201, 202, 268.

Creswick, Corporal J., of Rhodesia Horse, wounded, 157, 269.

Christmas Pass, 64.

D

Dafunia, Chief, 98.

Daly, Capt., commanding Mounted Troop of Rhodesia Horse, 142, 216, 221.

Day, Trooper F. W., of Salisbury Rifles, wounded by explosion, 185, 186, 276.

Deary, Mr. H. C., joining Mashonaland Field Force, 71, 72, 285, 286.

Deary's Store, Murders at, 223, 226, 273, 274, 276.

Derbyshire Regt., 1st, 6, 265, 268.

Devil's Pass, 30, 36, 78-80, 96-98, 132, 139, 250, 285.

Dickie, Capt., of steam-tug "Kimberley," 46, 47, 49, 50, 58.

Dismounted Troop, Rhodesia Horse, commanded by Capt. Newman, 142, 171, 269, 270, 276, 289, 290-295.

Doondu River, 223, 228.

Drysdale, Mr., Discovery of body of, 233, 272.

Duncan's, Mr. A. F. H., Surveyor-General to Chartered Company, patrol to Abercorn Mine of, 124, 125, 126, 131, 281.

Durban, 18-21, 27, 38, 40, 47, 61, 260.

E

Earnshaw, Trooper H. P., of "Umtali Rifles," accidentally shot, 238, 276.

Eighty Mile Station on Beira—Fontesvilla Railway, 52, 54.

Elphinstone-Dalrymple, Lieut., of Salisbury Rifles, 224.

Englebach, Dr., in charge of Hospital at Umtali, 68, 69.

English Company of Mounted Infantry, commanded by Major Evans, 2, 6, 7, 168, 204-207, 209, 238, 239, 252, 260-263, 265, 268, 293.

Enkeldorn, 127, 128, 242, 250, 269-271, 275-277, 289, 294.

Eustace, Lieut. C. L. E., of Rifle Company, wounded, 155, 266, 269.

Evans, Major F. S., commanding English Company of Mounted Infantry, killed at Gatzi's Kraal, 6, 169, 234, 237-239, 265, 268, 293.
Everett, Private H., of West Riding Regt., wounded, 209, 210, 269.
Eyre :—Arthur, Farm of, 129, 210, 214-217, 219, 222, 233, 239, 249, 268, 276. Herbert, Murder of, 214-216, 272.

F

Fairbairn, Lieut., commanding Mazoë Fort, 163, 164, 170-176, 241, 284.
Fairbridge, Mr. W. E., 243.
Feltham, Sergeant A., of Artillery Troop, Rhodesia Horse, wounded, 198, 269.
Ferguson, A.D.C., Capt., 246.
Fermaner, Mr. G., Resident Magistrate at Umtali, 36-38, 65, 69.
Fichardt, Lieut., commanding Umtali Artillery, 69.
Finucane, Capt. E., commanding Salisbury Rifles, 159, 161, 183, 216, 217, 268, 269.
Fleming, Dr., of Hospital at Salisbury, 186, 255, 256.
Fontesvilla, 26, 27, 29, 35, 40-42, 49-52, 56-61.
Forbes' Farm, 171, 180, 186.
Fort Haynes, 96, 98, 128, 131-134, 250, 286.
Forty Mile Station on Beira—Fontesvilla Railway, 52.
Fotheringham, Mr., commander at Chimoio, 36, 53.
Fox :—F. Wilson, Mr., 156, 159, 186, 194, 220, 230, 256. H. Wilson, Mr., Attorney-General for Rhodesia, 137-140. 144, 157, 193, 239, 247, 251, 255, 256.
French, Lieut. G. S., of Irish Company, 60, 63, 91, 115-118, 120, 140, 162, 171, 181, 182, 266, 269, 290.
Frost, Private Wm., of King's Royal Rifles, mortally wounded, 147, 268.

G

Gaderra's Kraal taken, 180-182.
"Garth Castle," Mounted Infantry reinforced by men from, 27, 28, 30-35, 39, 59, 60.
Gatzi's Kraal, 108-112, 234, 237, 238, 249, 268, 270, 286, 293.
Godley, Captain A. J., Adjutant to Mounted Infantry, and Staff Officer to Mashonaland Field Force, Patrol to Sinoia and Aryshire Mine of, 6, 18, 45, 55, 62, 87, 92, 98, 102, 106, 116, 120, 121, 157, 194, 217, 220-236, 241, 243, 255, 257, 265, 293. Richard, Quartermaster of B.S.A. Company's Mashonaland Police, 102, 255, 256.
Golden Stairs, Entrance to Mazoë Valley so-called, 163, 173, 174.
Gona Hills, 152, 269, 270.
Goodenough, Major-General Sir W. H., K.C.B., Commander of Troops in S. Africa, 8-10.
Gormley, Surg.-Col., 246.
Graham, 116, 268, 274.

INDEX

Graham, Mr., Postmaster at Salisbury, 247, 248.
Granite Range in Mazoë Valley, 164, 170-187, 241, 291.
Grapes, Private C., of English Company Mounted Infantry, mortally wounded, 205, 208, 209, 268.
Grey:—Lord, 121, 131, 246-248, 253, 258, 261, 262. Robin, 194, 219.
Gwebi River, 213, 276.

H

Hale, Surgeon-Captain C. H., of Army Medical Staff, joining Mashonaland Field Force at Fontesvilla, 59, 183, 210, 221, 223, 230.
Hamilton, Mr., Acting Medical Officer to Mashonaland Field Force, 69.
Hampden, Mount, 119, 234, 281.
Harbord, Mr., fighting in Mazoë Valley, 123, 124, 255, 257.
Harding:—Colin, Mr., Inspector in British South Africa Company's Police, 161, 182, 184, 194, 199, 220, 223, 255. Private A., wounded, 209.
Hare, Lieut., of English Company Mounted Infantry, 168, 200, 202, 205, 265.
Harland, Lieut. C., of English Company Mounted Infantry, 168, 204, 205, 265.
Harrison, Mr., British South Africa Company's Agent at Beira, 25, 39.

Hartley, 11, 124, 126, 129, 130, 138, 139, 144, 153, 186-212, 237, 249, 250, 253, 268-270, 272-276, 278, 282, 295.
Hawes' Store near Revue River, 63.
Haynes, Capt. A. E., of Royal Engineers, joining Mashonaland Field Force at Beira, and killed at Makoni's Kraal, 27, 28, 31, 58, 60, 62, 73, 93, 95, 96, 98, 268.
Headlands' Store, 30, 101-104, 128, 132, 215, 250, 271, 273, 274, 276.
Highland Company of Mounted Infantry, commanded by Capt. Tod, 2, 6, 9, 15, 168, 262, 266.
Hilliard, Surg.-Capt. C. M. G., of Army Medical Staff, 169.
Hole, Mr. Marshall, 163, 175, 176.
Honey's, Mr. Wilfred, scouts joining Mashonaland Field Force, 19, 38, 39, 44, 57, 72, 73, 79, 81, 82, 84, 85, 95, 96, 104, 123, 124, 128, 144, 147, 154, 204, 209, 220, 223, 225, 228, 230, 233, 235, 268, 285-287, 289, 292.
Hoste, Major, establishing Fort in Mazoë Valley, 126, 137, 141, 283.
Howard, Hon. Hubert, 246, 258.
Human, Mr., Chief Waggon-Conductor of Mashonaland Field Force, 76.
Hunt, Capt., commanding H.M.S. "Widgeon," 22, 25-27, 32-34, 43, 49, 50, 54, 58.

Hunyani River, 11, 130, 135, 196, 209, 213, 224, 225, 228, 236, 249, 250, 254, 269, 270, 271, 273, 275, 276, 282, 285, 288, 291.

Hussars, 4th, 7th, 13th, 15th, and 20th, 7, 140, 143, 216, 221, 243, 265, 270.

Hutton, Col. E. T. H., C.B., A.D.C., 1.

Hylands, Mr., Chief Engineer of Beira-Fontesvilla Railway, 53.

I

Inyampombere River, 80.
Inyoka's Kraal taken, 198.
Irish Company of Mounted Infantry, commanded by Capt. Sir H. McMahon, 2, 6, 7, 15, 17, 44, 60, 62, 73, 81, 82, 84, 85, 88, 91, 95, 98, 104, 108-110, 113, 128, 159, 171, 180, 182, 183, 198-201, 203, 204, 206, 207, 220, 221, 223, 225-227, 254, 259-263, 266, 268-270, 286, 291, 293.

Iron Mine Hill, 211, 226.

J

Jameson :—Dr., 12, 120, 121. Mr., Charter Company's Agent at Durban, 18, 19, 38. Mining Commissioner, 223, 224, 274.

Jenner, Captain, commanding Rifle Company Mounted Infantry—Patrol to Umtegeza's and Gona Hills of, 6, 15, 45, 57-59, 64, 72, 73, 87, 88, 92, 109, 116, 130, 137, 140, 141, 144-151, 155, 189-192, 197-199, 202, 203, 205, 213, 215-217, 220, 241, 243, 245, 266, 287, 289, 292-294.

Johnson, Trooper Edward, of Salisbury Rifles, killed, 160, 202, 268.

Jolliffe, Mr. J. B. S., killed, 141.

Judson's, Mr., patrol to Mazoë Valley, 122, 123, 270, 278, 279, 283.

K

Kaheia's Kraal, 136.
Keith, Mr., 189-192.
"Kimberley," steam-tug, conveying Mounted Infantry up Pungwe River, 26, 27, 29, 41, 42, 46, 49, 50, 57, 58.

King-Harman, Lieut. W. A., of Irish Company, 58, 171, 181, 228, 254, 266.

King's Own Yorkshire Light Infantry, 69, 238.

King's Royal Rifles, 95, 209, 266, 268-270.

Kunzi, Rebel Chief, 130, 245, 249, 294.

L

Lancers, 9th, at Pietermaritzburg, 260.

Law's Store, 141, 250, 272, 275, 283, 287.

Ledsham, Capt., in charge of Ordnance Stores at Durban, 19.

Leicester Regt., 1st Battalion, at Wynberg, 8, 9.

Leigh-Lye, Lieut. Fredk., of Umtali Rifles, wounded, 192, 193, 270.

INDEX

Leslie's Store, 64.
Lister, Mr. H. C., 246.
Lock, Private H., of King's Royal Rifles, wounded, 95, 270.
Lomagundi, Chief, 129, 190, 209, 220, 223, 235, 271-277, 292.
Lone Kop, 100.
Lovell, Dr., Acting Medical Officer to Mashonaland Field Force, 69, 96.
Ludlow, Capt., of Army Service Corps, 238, 255, 257.

M

M'Kay, Private J., of Royal Irish Regt., wounded, 201, 270.
McMahon, Capt. Sir H., commanding Irish Coy. Mounted Infantry—Granite Range in Mazoë Valley cleared by, 6, 10, 15, 19, 20, 60, 62, 73, 104, 109, 111, 136, 164, 165, 168, 170-187, 196, 200, 201, 266, 270, 286, 289, 291.
M'Slopa's followers, Capt. Turner's revenge for murders by, 11, 124, 154, 274, 275, 278.
Machado, Col., Governor of the Territory of the Mozambique Company, 24, 25, 28, 29, 34, 35, 67, 121, 259.
Machecci River, 106.
Mackey, Private W., of Royal Irish Regt., wounded, 95.
Makabussi River, 119.
Makoni, Rebel Chief, Capture and death of, 31, 33, 76, 78, 80-99, 107, 109, 111, 121, 131-135, 137, 165, 249, 268-270, 286, 290.
Mangwendi's Kraal taken, 108, 112-114, 249, 286.
Maninie River, 222, 231, 236.
Manyerbeera's Kraal, 192, 268, 270, 291.
Mapondera's Kraal taken, 209, 217, 241, 249, 293.
Marandellas, 30, 100, 101, 104, 108, 114, 116, 128, 130, 132, 140, 144, 147, 148, 192, 193, 234, 237, 239, 249, 250, 268-271, 276, 277, 283, 287, 294.
Mashangombi, Rebel Chief, 126, 129, 145, 154, 155, 190-192, 197, 199, 226, 234, 249, 269, 274, 275, 289, 292.
Mashonaland Mounted Police, 102, 107, 122, 161, 163, 174, 176, 243, 255, 262, 278, 280, 283, 288.
Massikessi or Macequeece, Portuguese town of, 63, 128, 258.
Matabeleland, 12, 33, 101, 102, 121, 129, 156, 166, 167, 191, 198, 243, 251, 252.
Matabeleland Relief Force, commanded by Lieut.-Col. Plumer, 100, 102, 128, 132, 133, 238, 269, 282, 291, 293, 294.
Matibo's Kraal, 212, 214.
Maxham, Surg.-Col., of Army Medical Staff, Chief Medical Officer in S. Africa, 20, 32, 43, 50, 53.
Maynhardt, Native Commissioner, Murder of, 230, 274.

Mazoë :—Fort, 126, 128, 162, 163, 170-173, 176, 179, 186, 241, 283, 284. Valley, 122, 123, 126, 130, 137, 163-165, 167, 168, 170-187, 217, 220, 235, 241, 249, 250, 268-276, 278, 279, 281, 283, 284, 290, 291, 293.

Mazwe, Ex-Native Policeman, 163, 174-180.

Medical Staff Corps forming part of Mashonaland Field Force, 17, 20, 27, 30, 31, 44, 45, 59, 60, 69, 81, 96, 128, 169, 183, 212, 220, 265, 277, 285, 287, 292, 293.

Meziti's Kraal, 80.

Middleton, Lieut. M., of York and Lancaster Regt., joining Mashonaland Field Force at Beira, 31, 69.

Milton, Mr., 244-246.

Moberly, Capt., of Rhodesia Horse, 126, 183, 187, 221, 231, 281, 282, 284.

Moleyns, Capt. Hon. F. W. Eveleigh de, Commander of Mashonaland Police, 243, 255.

Montague, Mr., Commander of the Burghers at Umtali, 32, 36, 64.

Montgomery, Capt. F. K., of Rhodesia Horse, wounded, 137, 270.

Moore, Mr., Manager of Beira Railway, 35, 41, 50, 57.

Morris, Lieut., of Umtali Rifles, mortally wounded, 192, 193, 239, 268.

Morumba's Kraal taken, 198.

Mother Patrick at Salisbury Hospital, 186, 256.

Mounted Infantry :—Duties and Characteristics of, 5, 6. English, Highland, Irish, and Rifle Cos. (see those titles). Organization of Companies, Sections and Subsections— Conditions for selection of officers and men, 2, 3, 4.

Mounted Troop, Rhodesia Horse, commanded by Capt. Daly, 142, 156, 203, 204, 220, 221, 225, 226, 276, 289, 291, 295.

Mzimilima's Kraal, 152.

N

Natal, 239, 258, 262, 278, 290.

"Natal Troop," 124, 128, 143, 144, 147, 148, 152, 203, 212, 217, 219, 222, 234, 269, 270, 277-283, 288, 289, 292, 294, 295.

Native Contingent forming part of Mashonaland Field Force, 81, 91, 109, 110, 113, 124, 128, 159, 171, 182-184, 198, 201, 206-209, 214, 220, 221, 225, 226, 230, 233, 234, 250, 280-286, 288-295.

Nedwidji's Kraal, 104.

Nesbitt's, V.C., Capt. R., patrol to Alice Mine, 107, 122, 123, 136, 142, 278-280, 283, 288.

Nesbit, Cr.-Sergt. H. F., 6.

Newman, Capt., commanding Dismounted Troop, Rhodesia Horse, 142, 288.

Newnham, Medical Officer, 177.

INDEX

Nicholls, Mr. J. E., Lieut. in Rhodesia Horse, joining Mashonaland Field Force as Galloper, 21, 45, 106, 116, 120, 156, 159, 186, 194, 219, 253.
Norfolk Regiment, 205, 209, 265, 268.
Norton's Farm, Murders at, 11, 162, 183, 197, 250, 271, 273, 274, 278, 291, 295.
Nyamatswitswi River, 78, 81, 85, 94.
Nyanda, Witch-doctress, 130, 184, 185.
Nyarota, 80.

O

O'Reilly's Road, 78.
Odzi River, 73, 76, 78.
Orton, Mr. and Mrs., escaping from Balleyhooley, 118, 119.

P

Paget, Col., 143.
Pease, Capt. W. L., joining Mashonaland Field Force, 59, 69, 70, 192, 238, 250, 291, 293-295.
Penalonga Range, 64.
Perry, Capt. H. W., in charge of Ordnance Store at Cape Town, 15.
Pietermaritzburg, 21, 168, 260, 262.
Pilson, Lieut. A. F., of Irish Company, 58, 159, 160, 162, 183, 184, 187, 221, 223, 266, 291.
Plumer, Lieut.-Col., commanding Matabeleland Relief Force, 100, 133.

Pungwe River, 22, 26, 27, 29, 34, 40-42, 47-50, 57, 61.

Q

Quata's Kraal taken, 198.
Queen's Birthday at Cape Town, 9, 10.

R

Revue River, 63.
Rhodes, Mr., 202, 242, 247.
Rhodesia Horse, 21, 45, 126, 128, 137, 142, 156, 157, 171, 173, 180-183, 198, 203, 204, 216, 220, 221, 224-226, 240, 253, 269, 270, 276-278, 281-283, 285, 288-295.
Rifle Company of Mounted Infantry, commanded by Capt. Jenner, 2, 6, 7, 15, 17, 44, 57, 72, 73, 81, 82, 84, 85, 88, 92, 93, 95, 98, 105, 106, 108, 109, 128, 130, 140, 141, 144, 147, 155, 199, 203-209, 213, 215, 216, 241, 252, 259-263, 266, 268-270, 286, 287, 289, 293, 294.
Roach, Capt. J., joining Mounted Infantry as Intelligence Officer, 17, 45, 116-118, 120, 157, 158, 177, 182, 194, 219, 255.
Rosenthal, Mr., Landlord of Commercial Hotel in Salisbury, 245, 255.
Ross :—Carnegie-Ross, Mr., British Consul at Beira, 25, 57, 66, 67, 259. Lieut., 171, 289, 290. Native Commissioner, 78, 79, 81, 83, 84, 87, 89, 90, 133, 134.

INDEX

Royal Artillery forming part of Mashonaland Field Force, 17, 27, 31, 44, 60, 72, 81, 89-91, 128, 147, 183, 249, 252, 285-287, 289, 291-294.
Royal Dublin Fusiliers, 6, 183, 184, 198, 201, 265, 266, 269, 270.
Royal Engineers joining Mashonaland Field Force at Beira, 27, 30, 31, 41, 42, 44, 56, 58, 60, 72, 73, 81, 82, 84, 85, 88, 91, 93, 95-97, 106, 108, 127, 128, 268, 285-287.
Royal Irish Fusiliers, 183, 266.
Royal Irish Regt., 171, 182, 201, 266, 268-270.
Royal Irish Rifles, 171, 266.
Royal Welsh Fusiliers, 6, 201, 266, 270.
Rusapi River, 78.
Ruya River, 130, 156, 158, 159, 249.

S

St. Aubyn, Lieut., commanding Section of Rifle Company, 56, 116-118, 120, 135, 136, 140, 266, 288.
Salisbury, 11-14, 17, 19, 21, 26, 27, 29-31, 33, 52, 61, 70, 71, 81, 94, 98, 100, 102, 105-108, 114, 116-132, 135-145, 147, 148, 152, 153, 156, 275, 277, 282, 285, 287.
Salisbury Rifles, 128, 136, 142, 156, 159-161, 170, 183-185, 198, 201, 216, 217, 220, 221, 224, 268, 289-294.
Sange River, 223.
Saw, Surg.-Capt. F. A., 17, 45, 212, 265.
Sawerthal, Mr., Chartered Company's Representative, 40, 41, 62, 63.
Scanlan, Sir Thos., 131, 163, 175.
Seaforth Highlanders, 6, 262, 266.
Seigert, Trooper C., of Matabeleland Relief Force, wounded, 238, 270.
Shangaans forming detachment of Native Contingent, 171, 181, 234.
Simbanoota's Kraal taken, 156-162, 202, 249, 268, 269, 290.
Singala's Kraal taken, 242, 294.
Sinoia, 215, 217, 220, 224-229, 236, 243, 249, 293.
Sirua River, 197.
Sixty-two Mile Station of Beira-Fontesvilla Railway, 54, 56.
Sladen, Lieut. C. St. B., of Royal Engineers, joining Mashonaland Field Force at Beira, 31, 56.
Soswie's Kraal, 238.
Southey, Lieut. C. E., of Irish Company, 183, 223, 228, 266.
Stephens, Lieut. R. B., commanding Section of Rifle Company, 57, 63, 266.
Stevens, Mr. J. A., Secretary of British South Africa Company at Cape Town, 16.
Stockley, Lieut. M. M. P., 225.
Suter, Messrs., 25, 39.
Swanson, Capt. F. H. A., of West Riding Regt., joining Mashonaland Field Force, 59, 260.
Swart, Trooper, killed, 242, 270.

INDEX

T

Taberer, Chief Native Commissioner in Mashonaland, 80, 81, 103, 104, 112.
Table Bay, 8, 17.
Tandi, Rebel Chief, 250, 295.
Taylor :—Capt., commanding Natal Troop, 143, 152, 270, 279-281, 289, 295. Native Commissioner, 149, 150.
Tennant, Major, commanding Artillery Troop of Rhodesia Horse, 141, 142, 156, 158, 159, 161, 290.
Thaba Insimbi Hill, 211, 226.
Thompson, Lieut. C. B., of Royal Engineers, joining Mashonaland Field Force at Beira, 31.
Tod, Capt., commanding Highland Company of Mounted Infantry, 6, 262, 266.
Tora's Kraal taken, 198.
Townshend, Lieut. S. C., of Royal Artillery, embarking with Mounted Infantry at Cape Town, 17, 71, 89, 91.
Tully, Corporal, of Rhodesia Horse, wounded, 182, 270.
Turk's Farm, 116.
Turner, Capt. P. A., Assistant Staff Officer to Mashonaland Field Force, patrol to M'Slopa's Kraal, 121, 124, 129, 255, 257, 278.

U

Umfuli River, 154, 192, 200, 203, 278.
Umfusi River, 79.
Umtali, 26, 28-33, 36-38, 40, 52, 59, 60, 62, 64-71, 75, 81, 85, 97, 98, 100, 102-105, 114, 117, 126, 128, 132, 134, 169, 237, 239, 243, 249, 250, 252-254, 257, 258, 272, 274, 276, 277, 285, 288.
Umtali Artillery, commanded by Lieut. Fichardt, 69, 128, 291, 293, 294.
Umtali Rifles, commanded by Major Browne, 65, 66, 69, 72, 81, 82, 84, 85, 88, 95, 99, 102, 128, 132, 192, 238, 268, 270, 276, 285-287, 290, 291, 293.
Umtassa, Chief, 29, 32, 80, 134, 249.
Umtegeza, Rebel Chief, 129, 130, 137, 143, 144, 146, 147, 149-152, 249, 270.
Umvukwe Mountains, 213, 214, 233, 249, 272, 276, 280.
Ushewekunsi's Kraal, 141.

V

Vernon, Lieut. H. E., of Rifle Company, 10, 266.
Vickers, Private S., of Rifle Company, killed, 93, 95, 98, 268.
Victoria, 127, 128, 143, 147, 250, 294.
Vintcent, Judge, Commandant General at Salisbury, 13, 19, 33, 38, 39, 108, 116-118, 120, 121, 123, 124, 131, 138, 141, 163, 164, 170, 174-177, 243, 244, 247.
Vulliamy, Lieut.-Col. C. W., commanding Leicester Regiment at Wynberg, 8.

Vyvyan, Brigade-Major to Sir Fredk. Carrington, 246.

W

Watts, Major, commanding Column of Matabeleland Relief Force, 100-102, 104, 105, 107, 132-134, 137, 140, 219, 290.

West Riding Regt. reinforcing Mashonaland Field Force at Fontesvilla, 59, 67, 69, 70, 72, 82, 99, 121, 124, 128, 132, 157, 210, 212, 234, 238, 259, 260, 269, 270, 278, 285, 290, 293.

Wickham, Private W., of Royal Irish Regiment, killed, 95, 98, 268.

"Widgeon," H.M.S., commanded by Capt. Hunt at Beira, 22, 27, 34, 41, 54.

White, Capt. Hon. C., commanding detachment of Buluwayo Field Force, Patrol to Hartley of, 120, 122, 126-129, 135, 282, 285.

White's Farm, 116, 140, 268, 271, 274.

Wood, Capt. W. W., of West Riding Regt., joining Mashonaland Field Force at Fontesvilla, 59.

Wynberg, 8-10, 59.

Y

York and Lancaster Regt. reinforcing Mounted Infantry at Beira, 27, 30, 31, 44, 58, 59, 66, 67, 69, 127, 128.

Young, Trooper D., of Umtali Rifles, wounded, 95, 270.

Z

Zabi, 152.
Zambesi, 12, 226, 233.
Zimba's Kraal, 216, 226, 292.
Zimbo River, 197, 212, 215.

A CATALOGUE OF BOOKS AND ANNOUNCEMENTS OF METHUEN AND COMPANY PUBLISHERS : LONDON 36 ESSEX STREET W.C.

CONTENTS

	PAGE
FORTHCOMING BOOKS,	2
POETRY,	8
BELLES LETTRES,	9
ILLUSTRATED BOOKS,	11
HISTORY,	12
BIOGRAPHY,	14
TRAVEL, ADVENTURE AND TOPOGRAPHY,	15
NAVAL AND MILITARY,	17
GENERAL LITERATURE,	18
SCIENCE,	19
TECHNOLOGY,	20
PHILOSOPHY,	20
THEOLOGY,	21
FICTION,	23
BOOKS FOR BOYS AND GIRLS,	34
THE PEACOCK LIBRARY,	34
UNIVERSITY EXTENSION SERIES,	35
SOCIAL QUESTIONS OF TO-DAY	36
CLASSICAL TRANSLATIONS	37
EDUCATIONAL BOOKS,	37

FEBRUARY 1898

FEBRUARY 1898.

MESSRS. METHUEN'S ANNOUNCEMENTS

Poetry

THE POEMS OF WILLIAM SHAKESPEARE. Edited with an Introduction and Notes by GEORGE WYNDHAM, M.P. *Demy 8vo. Buckram, gilt top.* 10s. 6d.

This edition contains the 'Venus,' 'Lucrece' and Sonnets, and is prefaced with an elaborate introduction of over 140 pp. The text is founded on the first quartos, with an endeavour to retain the original reading. A set of notes deals with the problems of Date, The Rival Poets, Typography, and Punctuation; and the editor has commented on obscure passages in the light of contemporary works. The publishers believe that no such complete edition has ever been published.

Travel and Adventure

THREE YEARS IN SAVAGE AFRICA. By LIONEL DECLE. With an Introduction by H. M. STANLEY, M.P. With 100 Illustrations and 5 Maps. *Demy 8vo.* 21s.

Few Europeans have had the same opportunity of studying the barbarous parts of Africa as Mr. Decle. Starting from the Cape, he visited in succession Bechuanaland, the Zambesi, Matabeleland and Mashonaland, the Portuguese settlement on the Zambesi, Nyasaland, Ujiji, the headquarters of the Arabs, German East Africa, Uganda (where he saw fighting in company with the late Major 'Roddy' Owen), and British East Africa. In his book he relates his experiences, his minute observations of native habits and customs, and his views as to the work done in Africa by the various European Governments, whose operations he was able to study. The whole journey extended over 7000 miles, and occupied exactly three years.

EXPLORATION AND HUNTING IN CENTRAL AFRICA. By Major A. ST. H. GIBBONS, F.R.G.S. With 8 full-page Illustrations by C. WHYMPER, photographs and Map. *Demy 8vo.* 15s.

This is an account of travel and adventure among the Marotse and contiguous tribes, with a description of their customs, characteristics, and history, together with the author's experiences in hunting big game. The illustrations are by Mr. Charles Whymper, and from photographs. There is a map by the author of the hitherto unexplored regions lying between the Zambezi and Kafukwi rivers and from 18° to 15° S. lat.

WITH THE MASHONALAND FIELD FORCE, 1896. By Lieut.-Colonel ALDERSON. With numerous Illustrations and Plans. *Demy 8vo.* 12s. 6d.

This is an account of the military operations in Mashonaland by the officer who commanded the troops in that district during the late rebellion. Besides its interest as a story of warfare, it will have a peculiar value as an account of the services of mounted infantry by one of the chief authorities on the subject.

MESSRS. METHUEN'S ANNOUNCEMENTS 3

CAMPAIGNING ON THE UPPER NILE AND NIGER.
By Lieut. SEYMOUR VANDELEUR. With an Introduction by Sir G.
GOLDIE. With two Maps, Illustrations and Plans. *Large Cr. 8vo.*
10s. 6d.

A narrative of service (1) in the Equatorial Lakes and on the Upper Nile in 1895 and 1896; and (2) under Sir George Goldie in the Niger campaign of January 1897, describing the capture of Bida and Ilorin, and the French occupation of Boussa. The book thus deals with the two districts of Africa where now the French and English stand face to face.

THE NIGER SOURCES. By Colonel J. TROTTER, R.A.
With a Map and Illustrations. *Crown 8vo.* 5s.

A book which at the present time should be of considerable interest, being an account of a Commission appointed for frontier delimitation.

LIFE AND PROGRESS IN AUSTRALASIA. By MICHAEL
DAVITT, M.P. With two Maps. *Crown 8vo.* 6s. 500 pp.

This book, the outcome of a recent journey through the seven Australasian colonies, is an attempt to give to English readers a more intimate knowledge of a continent colonised by their own race. The author sketches the general life, resources, politics, parties, progress, prospects, and scenery of each colony. He made a careful examination of the West Australian goldfields, and he has paid special attention to the development of practical politics in the colonies. The book is full of anecdotes and picturesque description.

History and Biography

A HISTORY OF THE ART OF WAR. By C. W. OMAN,
M.A., Fellow of All Souls', Oxford. Vol. II. MEDIÆVAL WARFARE. *Demy 8vo Illustrated.* 21s.

Mr. Oman is engaged on a History of the Art of War, of which the above, though covering the middle period from the fall of the Roman Empire to the general use of gunpowder in Western Europe, is the first instalment. The first battle dealt with will be Adrianople (378) and the last Navarette (1367). There will appear later a volume dealing with the Art of War among the Ancients, and another covering the 15th, 16th, and 17th centuries.
The book will deal mainly with tactics and strategy, fortifications and siegecraft, but subsidiary chapters will give some account of the development of arms and armour, and of the various forms of military organization known to the Middle Ages.

RELIGION AND CONSCIENCE IN ANCIENT EGYPT.
By W. M. FLINDERS PETRIE, D.C.L., LL.D. *Fully Illustrated.
Crown 8vo.* 2s. 6d.

This volume deals mainly with the historical growth of the Egyptian religion, and the arrangement of all the moral sayings into something like a handbook. But far larger interests are also discussed as the origin of intolerance, the fusion of religions, the nature of conscience, and the experimental illustration of British conscience.

SYRIA AND EGYPT FROM THE TELL EL AMARNA
TABLETS. By W. M. FLINDERS PETRIE, D.C.L., LL.D. *Crown 8vo.* 2s. 6d.

This book describes the results of recent researches and discoveries and the light thereby thrown on Egyptian history.

MESSRS. METHUEN'S ANNOUNCEMENTS

THE DECLINE AND FALL OF THE ROMAN EMPIRE. By EDWARD GIBBON. A New Edition, edited with Notes, Appendices, and Maps by J. B. BURY, M.A., Fellow of Trinity College, Dublin. *In Seven Volumes. Demy 8vo, gilt top.* 8s. 6d. *each. Crown 8vo.* 6s. *each. Vol. V.*

THE EASTERN QUESTION IN THE EIGHTEENTH CENTURY. By ALBERT SOREL of the French Academy. Translated by F. C. BRAMWELL, M.A., with an Introduction by R. C. L. FLETCHER, Fellow of Magdalen College, Oxford. With a Map. *Crown 8vo.* 4s. 6d.

This book is a study of the political conditions which led up to and governed the first partition of Poland, and the Russo-Turkish war of 1768-1774. It is probably the best existing examination of Eastern European politics in the eighteenth century, and is an early work of one of the ablest of living historians.

THE LETTERS OF VICTOR HUGO. Translated from the French by F. CLARKE, M.A. *In Two Volumes. Demy 8vo.* 10s. 6d. *each. Vol. II.* 1815-35.

A HISTORY OF THE GREAT NORTHERN RAILWAY, 1845-95. By C. H. GRINLING. With Maps and many Illustrations. *Demy 8vo.* 10s. 6d.

A record of Railway enterprise and development in Northern England, containing much matter hitherto unpublished. It appeals both to the general reader and to those specially interested in railway construction and management.

ANARCHISM. By E. V. ZENKER. *Demy 8vo.* 7s. 6d.

A critical study and history, as well as trenchant criticism of the Anarchist movement in Europe. The book has aroused considerable attention on the Continent.

THOMAS CRANMER. By A. J. MASON, D.D., Canon of Canterbury. With a Portrait. *Crown 8vo.* 3s. 6d.

[*Leaders of Religion.*

Theology

THE MINISTRY OF DEACONESSES. By CECILIA ROBINSON, Deaconess. With an Introduction by the LORD BISHOP OF WINCHESTER, and an Appendix by Professor ARMITAGE ROBINSON. *Crown 8vo.* 3s. 6d.

This book is a review of the history and theory of the office and work of a Deaconess and it may be regarded as authoritative.

DISCIPLINE AND LAW. By H. HENSLEY HENSON, B.D., Fellow of All Soul's, Oxford; Incumbent of St. Mary's Hospital, Ilford; Chaplain to the Bishop of St. Albans. *Fcap. 8vo.* 2s. 6d.

This volume of devotional addresses, suitable for Lent, is concerned with the value, method, and reward of Discipline; and with Law—family, social and individual.

REASONABLE CHRISTIANITY. By HASTINGS RASHDALL, M.A., Fellow and Tutor of New College, Oxford. *Crown 8vo.* 6s

This volume consists of twenty sermons, preached chiefly before the University of Oxford. They are an attempt to translate into the language of modern thought some of the leading ideas of Christian theology and ethics.

MESSRS. METHUEN'S ANNOUNCEMENTS

THE HOLY SACRIFICE. By F. WESTON, M.A., Curate of St. Matthew's, Westminster. *Pott 8vo.* 1s.

A small volume of devotions at the Holy Communion, especially adapted to the needs of servers and of those who do not communicate.

The Churchman's Library.

Edited by J. H. BURN, B.D.

A series of books by competent scholars on Church History, Institutions, and Doctrine, for the use of clerical and lay readers.

THE BEGINNINGS OF ENGLISH CHRISTIANITY. By W. E. COLLINS, M.A., Professor of Ecclesiastical History at King's College, London. With Map. *Crown 8vo.* 3s. 6d.

An investigation in detail, based upon original authorities, of the beginnings of the English Church, with a careful account of earlier Celtic Christianity. The larger aspects of the continental movement are described, and some very full appendices treat of a number of special subjects.

SOME NEW TESTAMENT PROBLEMS. By ARTHUR WRIGHT, Fellow and Tutor of Queen's College, Cambridge. *Crown 8vo.* 6s.

This book deals with a number of important problems from the standpoint of the 'Higher Criticism,' and is written in the hope of advancing the historico-critical study of the Synoptic Gospels and of the Acts.

The Library of Devotion.

Messrs. METHUEN have arranged to publish under the above title a number of the older masterpieces of devotional literature. It is their intention to entrust each volume of the series to an editor who will not only attempt to bring out the spiritual importance of the book, but who will lavish such scholarly care upon it as is generally expended only on editions of the ancient classics.

The books will be furnished with such Introductions and Notes as may be necessary to explain the standpoint of the author, and to comment on such difficulties as the ordinary reader may find, without unnecessary intrusion between the author and reader.

Mr. Laurence Housman has designed a title-page and a cover design. *Pott 8vo.* 2s.; *leather* 3s.

THE CONFESSIONS OF ST. AUGUSTINE. Newly Translated, with an Introduction and Notes, by C. BIGG, D.D., late Student of Christ Church.

This volume contains the nine books of the 'Confessions' which are suitable for devotional purposes.

THE CHRISTIAN YEAR. By JOHN KEBLE. With Introduction and Notes, by WALTER LOCK, D.D., Warden of Keble College, Ireland Professor at Oxford.

MESSRS. METHUEN'S ANNOUNCEMENTS

THE IMITATION OF CHRIST. A Revised Translation with an Introduction, by C. BIGG, D.D., late Student of Christ Church.

Dr. Bigg has made a practically new translation of this book, which the reader will have, almost for the first time, exactly in the shape in which it left the hands of the author.

A BOOK OF DEVOTIONS. By J. W. STANBRIDGE, M.A., Rector of Bainton, Canon of York, and sometime Fellow of St. John's College, Oxford. *Pott 8vo.*

This book contains devotions, Eucharistic, daily and occasional, for the use of members of the English Church, sufficiently diversified for those who possess other works of the kind. It is intended to be a companion in private and public worship, and is in harmony with the thoughts of the best Devotional writers.

General Literature

THE GOLFING PILGRIM. By HORACE G. HUTCHINSON. *Crown 8vo. 6s.*

This book, by a famous golfer, contains the following sketches lightly and humorously written :—The Prologue—The Pilgrim at the Shrine—Mecca out of Season—The Pilgrim at Home—The Pilgrim Abroad—The Life of the Links—A Tragedy by the Way—Scraps from the Scrip—The Golfer in Art—Early Pilgrims in the West —An Interesting Relic.

WORKHOUSES AND PAUPERISM. By LOUISA TWINING. *Crown 8vo. 2s. 6d.* [*Social Questions Series.*

Educational

THE ODES AND EPODES OF HORACE. Translated by A. D. GODLEY, M.A., Fellow of Magdalen College, Oxford. *Crown 8vo. 2s.* [*Classical Translations.*

PASSAGES FOR UNSEEN TRANSLATION. By E. C. MARCHANT, M.A., Fellow of Peterhouse, Cambridge; and A. M. COOK, M.A., late Scholar of Wadham College, Oxford: Assistant Masters at St. Paul's School. *Crown 8vo. 3s. 6d.*

This book contains Two Hundred Latin and Two Hundred Greek Passages, and has been very carefully compiled to meet the wants of V. and VI. Form Boys at Public Schools. It is also well adapted for the use of Honour men at the Universities.

EASY LATIN EXERCISES ON THE SYNTAX OF THE SHORTER AND REVISED LATIN PRIMER. By A. M. M. STEDMAN, M.A. With Vocabulary. *Seventh and Cheaper Edition. Crown 8vo. 1s. 6d.* Issued with the consent of Dr. Kennedy.

A new and cheaper edition, thoroughly revised by Mr. C. G. Botting, of St. Paul's School.

TEST CARDS IN EUCLID AND ALGEBRA. By D. S. CALDERWOOD, Headmaster of the Normal School, Edinburgh. In a Packet of 40, with Answers. 1s.

A set of cards for advanced pupils in elementary schools.

MESSRS. METHUEN'S ANNOUNCEMENTS

Byzantine Texts

Edited by J. B. BURY, M.A., Professor of Modern History at Trinity College, Dublin.

EVAGRIUS. Edited by PROFESSOR LÉON PARMENTIER of Liége and M. BIDEZ of Gand. *Demy 8vo.*

PSELLUS (HISTORIA). Edited by C. SATHAS. *Demy 8vo.*

Fiction

SIMON DALE. By ANTHONY HOPE. Illustrated by W. ST. J. HARPER. *Crown 8vo.* 6s.
A romance of the reign of Charles II., and Mr. Anthony Hope's first historical novel.

TRAITS AND CONFIDENCES. By The Hon. EMILY LAWLESS, Author of 'Hurrish,' 'Maelcho,' etc. *Crown 8vo.* 6s.

THE VINTAGE. By E. F. BENSON, Author of 'Dodo.' Illustrated by G. P. JACOMB-HOOD. *Crown 8vo.* 6s.
A romance of the Greek War of Independence.

A VOYAGE OF CONSOLATION. By SARA JEANETTE DUNCAN. Author of 'An American Girl in London.' *Crown 8vo.* 6s.
The adventures of an American girl in Europe.

A NEW NOVEL. By B. M. CROKER, Author of 'Proper Pride.' *Crown 8vo.* 6s.

ACROSS THE SALT SEAS. By J. BLOUNDELLE-BURTON. *Crown 8vo.* 6s.

MISS ERIN. By M. E. FRANCIS, Author of 'In a Northern Village.' *Crown 8vo.* 6s.

WILLOWBRAKE. By R. MURRAY GILCHRIST. *Crown 8vo.* 6s.

THE KLOOF BRIDE. By ERNEST GLANVILLE, Author of 'The Fossicker.' Illustrated. *Crown 8vo.* 3s. 6d.
A story of South African Adventure.

BIJLI, THE DANCER. By JAMES BLYTHE PATTON. Illustrated. *Crown 8vo.* 6s.
A Romance of India.

JOSIAH'S WIFE. By NORMA LORIMER. *Crown 8vo.* 6s.

BETWEEN SUN AND SAND. By W. C. SCULLY, Author of 'The White Hecatomb.' *Crown 8vo.* 6s.

CROSS TRAILS. By VICTOR WAITE. Illustrated. *Crown 8vo.* 6s.
A romance of adventure in America and Australia.

THE PHILANTHROPIST. By LUCY MAYNARD. *Crown 8vo.* 6s.

VAUSSORE. By FRANCIS BRUNE. *Crown 8vo.* 6s.

A LIST OF
MESSRS. METHUEN'S
PUBLICATIONS

◆

Poetry

RUDYARD KIPLING'S NEW POEMS

Rudyard Kipling. THE SEVEN SEAS. By RUDYARD KIPLING. *Third Edition. Crown 8vo. Buckram, gilt top.* 6s.

'The new poems of Mr. Rudyard Kipling have all the spirit and swing of their predecessors. Patriotism is the solid concrete foundation on which Mr. Kipling has built the whole of his work.'—*Times.*

'The Empire has found a singer; it is no depreciation of the songs to say that statesmen may have, one way or other, to take account of them.'—*Manchester Guardian.*

'Animated through and through with indubitable genius.'—*Daily Telegraph.*

'Packed with inspiration, with humour, with pathos.'—*Daily Chronicle.*

'All the pride of empire, all the intoxication of power, all the ardour, the energy, the masterful strength and the wonderful endurance and death-scorning pluck which are the very bone and fibre and marrow of the British character are here.'—*Daily Mail.*

Rudyard Kipling. BARRACK-ROOM BALLADS. By RUDYARD KIPLING. *Twelfth Edition. Crown 8vo.* 6s.

'Mr. Kipling's verse is strong, vivid, full of character. . . . Unmistakable genius rings in every line.'—*Times.*

'The ballads teem with imagination, they palpitate with emotion. We read them with laughter and tears; the metres throb in our pulses, the cunningly ordered words tingle with life; and if this be not poetry, what is?'—*Pall Mall Gazette.*

"Q." POEMS AND BALLADS. By "Q." *Crown 8vo.* 3s. 6d.

'This work has just the faint, ineffable touch and glow that make poetry.'—*Speaker.*

"Q." GREEN BAYS: Verses and Parodies. By "Q.," Author of 'Dead Man's Rock,' etc. *Second Edition. Crown 8vo.* 3s. 6d.

E. Mackay. A SONG OF THE SEA. By ERIC MACKAY. *Second Edition. Fcap. 8vo.* 5s.

'Everywhere Mr. Mackay displays himself the master of a style marked by all the characteristics of the best rhetoric.'—*Globe.*

Ibsen. BRAND. A Drama by HENRIK IBSEN. Translated by WILLIAM WILSON. *Second Edition. Crown 8vo.* 3s. 6d.

'The greatest world-poem of the nineteenth century next to "Faust." It is in the same set with "Agamemnon," with "Lear," with the literature that we now instinctively regard as high and holy.'—*Daily Chronicle.*

MESSRS. METHUEN'S LIST 9

"A. G." VERSES TO ORDER. By "A. G." *Cr. 8vo. 2s. 6d. net.*

'A capital specimen of light academic poetry. These verses are very bright and engaging, easy and sufficiently witty.'—*St. James's Gazette.*

Cordery. THE ODYSSEY OF HOMER. A Translation by J. G. CORDERY. *Crown 8vo. 7s. 6d.*

'This new version of the Odyssey fairly deserves a place of honour among its many rivals. Perhaps there is none from which a more accurate knowledge of the original can be gathered with greater pleasure, at least of those that are in metre.'—*Manchester Guardian.*

Belles Lettres, Anthologies, etc.

R. L. Stevenson. VAILIMA LETTERS. By ROBERT LOUIS STEVENSON. With an Etched Portrait by WILLIAM STRANG, and other Illustrations. *Second Edition. Crown 8vo. Buckram. 7s. 6d.*

'Few publications have in our time been more eagerly awaited than these "Vailima Letters," giving the first fruits of the correspondence of Robert Louis Stevenson. But, high as the tide of expectation has run, no reader can possibly be disappointed in the result.'—*St. James's Gazette.*

Henley. ENGLISH LYRICS. Selected and Edited by W. E. HENLEY. *Crown 8vo. Buckram gilt top. 6s.*

'It is a body of choice and lovely poetry.'—*Birmingham Gazette.*
'Mr. Henley's notes, in their brevity and their fulness, their information and their suggestiveness, seem to us a model of what notes should be.'—*Manchester Guardian.*

Henley and Whibley. A BOOK OF ENGLISH PROSE. Collected by W. E. HENLEY and CHARLES WHIBLEY. *Crown 8vo. Buckram gilt top. 6s.*

'A unique volume of extracts—an art gallery of early prose.'—*Birmingham Post.*
'An admirable companion to Mr. Henley's "Lyra Heroica."'—*Saturday Review.*
'Quite delightful. A greater treat for those not well acquainted with pre-Restoration prose could not be imagined.'—*Athenæum.*

H. C. Beeching. LYRA SACRA: An Anthology of Sacred Verse. Edited by H. C. BEECHING, M.A. *Crown 8vo. Buckram. 6s.*

'A charming selection, which maintains a lofty standard of excellence.'—*Times.*

"Q." THE GOLDEN POMP: A Procession of English Lyrics from Surrey to Shirley, arranged by A. T. QUILLER COUCH. *Crown 8vo. Buckram. 6s.*

'A delightful volume: a really golden "Pomp."'—*Spectator.*

W. B. Yeats. AN ANTHOLOGY OF IRISH VERSE. Edited by W. B. YEATS. *Crown 8vo. 3s. 6d.*

'An attractive and catholic selection.'—*Times.*

Messrs. Methuen's List

G. W. Steevens. MONOLOGUES OF THE DEAD. By G. W. STEEVENS. *Foolscap 8vo.* 3s. 6d.

A series of Soliloquies in which famous men of antiquity—Julius Cæsar, Nero, Alcibiades, etc., attempt to express themselves in the modes of thought and language of to-day.

'The effect is sometimes splendid, sometimes bizarre, but always amazingly clever.' —*Pall Mall Gazette.*

Victor Hugo. THE LETTERS OF VICTOR HUGO. Translated from the French by F. CLARKE, M.A. *In Two Volumes. Demy 8vo.* 10s. 6d. each. *Vol. I.* 1815-35.

C. H. Pearson. ESSAYS AND CRITICAL REVIEWS. By C. H. PEARSON, M.A., Author of 'National Life and Character.' With a Portrait. *Demy 8vo.* 10s. 6d.

W. M. Dixon. A PRIMER OF TENNYSON. By W. M. DIXON, M.A., Professor of English Literature at Mason College. *Crown 8vo.* 2s. 6d.

'Much sound and well-expressed criticism and acute literary judgments. The bibliography is a boon.'—*Speaker.*

W. A. Craigie. A PRIMER OF BURNS. By W. A. CRAIGIE. *Crown 8vo.* 2s. 6d.

'A valuable addition to the literature of the poet.'—*Times.*
'An admirable introduction.'—*Globe.*

Magnus. A PRIMER OF WORDSWORTH. By LAURIE MAGNUS. *Crown 8vo.* 2s. 6d.

'A valuable contribution to Wordsworthian literature.'—*Literature.*
'A well-made primer, thoughtful and informing.'—*Manchester Guardian.*

Sterne. THE LIFE AND OPINIONS OF TRISTRAM SHANDY. By LAWRENCE STERNE. With an Introduction by CHARLES WHIBLEY, and a Portrait. *2 vols.* 7s.

'Very dainty volumes are these; the paper, type, and light-green binding are all very agreeable to the eye. *Simplex munditiis* is the phrase that might be applied to them.'—*Globe.*

Congreve. THE COMEDIES OF WILLIAM CONGREVE. With an Introduction by G. S. STREET, and a Portrait. *2 vols.* 7s.

Morier. THE ADVENTURES OF HAJJI BABA OF ISPAHAN. By JAMES MORIER. With an Introduction by E. G. BROWNE, M.A., and a Portrait. *2 vols.* 7s.

Walton. THE LIVES OF DONNE, WOTTON, HOOKER, HERBERT, AND SANDERSON. By IZAAK WALTON. With an Introduction by VERNON BLACKBURN, and a Portrait. 3s. 6d.

Johnson. THE LIVES OF THE ENGLISH POETS. By SAMUEL JOHNSON, LL.D. With an Introduction by J. H. MILLAR, and a Portrait. *3 vols.* 10s. 6d.

MESSRS. METHUEN'S LIST

Burns. THE POEMS OF ROBERT BURNS. Edited by ANDREW LANG and W. A. CRAIGIE. With Portrait. *Demy 8vo, gilt top.* 6s.

This edition contains a carefully collated Text, numerous Notes, critical and textual, a critical and biographical Introduction, and a Glossary.

'Among the editions in one volume, Mr. Andrew Lang's will take the place of authority.'—*Times.*

F. Langbridge. BALLADS OF THE BRAVE: Poems of Chivalry, Enterprise, Courage, and Constancy. Edited by Rev. F. LANGBRIDGE. *Crown 8vo.* 3s. 6d. *School Edition.* 2s. 6d.

'A very happy conception happily carried out. These "Ballads of the Brave" are intended to suit the real tastes of boys, and will suit the taste of the great majority.' —*Spectator.* 'The book is full of splendid things.'—*World.*

Illustrated Books

Bedford. NURSERY RHYMES. With many Coloured Pictures. By F. D. BEDFORD. *Super Royal 8vo.* 5s.

'An excellent selection of the best known rhymes, with beautifully coloured pictures exquisitely printed.'—*Pall Mall Gazette.*
'The art is of the newest, with well harmonised colouring.'—*Spectator.*

S. Baring Gould. A BOOK OF FAIRY TALES retold by S. BARING GOULD. With numerous illustrations and initial letters by ARTHUR J. GASKIN. *Second Edition. Crown 8vo. Buckram.* 6s.

'Mr. Baring Gould is deserving of gratitude, in re-writing in honest, simple style the old stories that delighted the childhood of "our fathers and grandfathers."'— *Saturday Review.*

S. Baring Gould. OLD ENGLISH FAIRY TALES. Collected and edited by S. BARING GOULD. With Numerous Illustrations by F. D. BEDFORD. *Second Edition. Crown 8vo. Buckram.* 6s.

'A charming volume. The stories have been selected with great ingenuity from various old ballads and folk-tales, and now stand forth, clothed in Mr. Baring Gould's delightful English, to enchant youthful readers.'—*Guardian.*

S. Baring Gould. A BOOK OF NURSERY SONGS AND RHYMES. Edited by S. BARING GOULD, and Illustrated by the Birmingham Art School. *Buckram, gilt top. Crown 8vo.* 6s.

'The volume is very complete in its way, as it contains nursery songs to the number of 77, game-rhymes, and jingles. To the student we commend the sensible introduction, and the explanatory notes.'—*Birmingham Gazette.*

H. C. Beeching. A BOOK OF CHRISTMAS VERSE. Edited by H. C. BEECHING, M.A., and Illustrated by WALTER CRANE. *Crown 8vo, gilt top.* 5s.

A collection of the best verse inspired by the birth of Christ from the Middle Ages to the present day.
An anthology which, from its unity of aim and high poetic excellence, has a better right to exist than most of its fellows.'—*Guardian.*

History

Gibbon. THE DECLINE AND FALL OF THE ROMAN EMPIRE. By EDWARD GIBBON. A New Edition, Edited with Notes, Appendices, and Maps, by J. B. BURY, M.A., Fellow of Trinity College, Dublin. *In Seven Volumes. Demy 8vo. Gilt top. 8s. 6d. each. Also crown 8vo. 6s. each. Vols. I., II., III., and IV.*

'The time has certainly arrived for a new edition of Gibbon's great work.... Professor Bury is the right man to undertake this task. His learning is amazing, both in extent and accuracy. The book is issued in a handy form, and at a moderate price, and it is admirably printed.'—*Times.*

'This edition, so far as one may judge from the first instalment, is a marvel of erudition and critical skill, and it is the very minimum of praise to predict that the seven volumes of it will supersede Dean Milman's as the standard edition of our great historical classic.'—*Glasgow Herald.*

'The beau-ideal Gibbon has arrived at last.'—*Sketch.*

'At last there is an adequate modern edition of Gibbon. . . . The best edition the nineteenth century could produce.'—*Manchester Guardian.*

Flinders Petrie. A HISTORY OF EGYPT, FROM THE EARLIEST TIMES TO THE PRESENT DAY. Edited by W. M. FLINDERS PETRIE, D.C.L., LL.D., Professor of Egyptology at University College. *Fully Illustrated. In Six Volumes. Crown 8vo. 6s. each.*

Vol. I. PREHISTORIC TIMES TO XVITH. DYNASTY. W. F. M. Petrie. *Third Edition.*

Vol. II. THE XVIITH AND XVIIITH DYNASTIES. W. M. F. Petrie. *Second Edition.*

'A history written in the spirit of scientific precision so worthily represented by Dr. Petrie and his school cannot but promote sound and accurate study, and supply a vacant place in the English literature of Egyptology.'—*Times.*

Flinders Petrie. EGYPTIAN TALES. Edited by W. M. FLINDERS PETRIE. Illustrated by TRISTRAM ELLIS. *In Two Volumes. Crown 8vo. 3s. 6d. each.*

'A valuable addition to the literature of comparative folk-lore. The drawings are really illustrations in the literal sense of the word.'—*Globe.*

'It has a scientific value to the student of history and archæology.'—*Scotsman.*

'Invaluable as a picture of life in Palestine and Egypt.'—*Daily News.*

Flinders Petrie. EGYPTIAN DECORATIVE ART. By W. M. FLINDERS PETRIE. With 120 Illustrations. *Cr. 8vo. 3s. 6d.*

'Professor Flinders Petrie is not only a profound Egyptologist, but an accomplished student of comparative archæology. In these lectures he displays both qualifications with rare skill in elucidating the development of decorative art in Egypt, and in tracing its influence on the art of other countries.'—*Times.*

S. Baring Gould. THE TRAGEDY OF THE CÆSARS. With numerous Illustrations from Busts, Gems, Cameos, etc. By S. BARING GOULD. *Fourth Edition. Royal 8vo. 15s.*

'A most splendid and fascinating book on a subject of undying interest. The great feature of the book is the use the author has made of the existing portraits of the Caesars, and the admirable critical subtlety he has exhibited in dealing with this line of research. It is brilliantly written, and the illustrations are supplied on a scale of profuse magnificence.'—*Daily Chronicle.*

H. de B. Gibbins. INDUSTRY IN ENGLAND: HISTORICAL OUTLINES. By H. DE B. GIBBINS, M.A., D.Litt. With 5 Maps. *Second Edition. Demy 8vo.* 10s. 6d.

This book is written with the view of affording a clear view of the main facts of English Social and Industrial History placed in due perspective.

H. E. Egerton. A HISTORY OF BRITISH COLONIAL POLICY. By H. E. EGERTON, M.A. *Demy 8vo.* 12s. 6d.

This book deals with British Colonial policy historically from the beginnings of English colonisation down to the present day. The subject has been treated by itself, and it has thus been possible within a reasonable compass to deal with a mass of authority which must otherwise be sought in the State papers. The volume is divided into five parts:—(1) The Period of Beginnings, 1497-1650; (2) Trade Ascendancy, 1651-1830; (3) The Granting of Responsible Government, 1831-1860; (4) *Laissez Aller*, 1861-1885; (5) Greater Britain.

'The whole story of the growth and administration of our colonial empire is comprehensive and well arranged, and is set forth with marked ability.'—*Daily Mail.*
'It is a good book, distinguished by accuracy in detail, clear arrangement of facts, and a broad grasp of principles.'—*Manchester Guardian.*
'Able, impartial, clear. . . . A most valuable volume.'—*Athenæum.*

A. Clark. THE COLLEGES OF OXFORD: Their History and their Traditions. By Members of the University. Edited by A. CLARK, M.A., Fellow and Tutor of Lincoln College. *8vo.* 12s. 6d.

'A work which will certainly be appealed to for many years as the standard book on the Colleges of Oxford.'—*Athenæum.*

Perrens. THE HISTORY OF FLORENCE FROM 1434 TO 1492. By F. T. PERRENS. *8vo.* 12s. 6d.

A history of Florence under the domination of Cosimo, Piero, and Lorenzo de Medicis.

J. Wells. A SHORT HISTORY OF ROME. By J. WELLS, M.A., Fellow and Tutor of Wadham Coll., Oxford. With 4 Maps. *Crown 8vo.* 3s. 6d.

This book is intended for the Middle and Upper Forms of Public Schools and for Pass Students at the Universities. It contains copious Tables, etc.

'An original work written on an original plan, and with uncommon freshness and vigour.'—*Speaker.*

O. Browning. A SHORT HISTORY OF MEDIÆVAL ITALY, A.D. 1250-1530. By OSCAR BROWNING, Fellow and Tutor of King's College, Cambridge. *Second Edition. In Two Volumes. Crown 8vo.* 5s. each.

VOL. I. 1250-1409.—Guelphs and Ghibellines.
VOL. II. 1409-1530.—The Age of the Condottieri.

'Mr. Browning is to be congratulated on the production of a work of immense labour and learning.'—*Westminster Gazette.*

O'Grady. THE STORY OF IRELAND. By STANDISH O'GRADY, Author of 'Finn and his Companions.' *Cr. 8vo.* 2s. 6d.

'Most delightful, most stimulating. Its racy humour, its original imaginings, make it one of the freshest, breeziest volumes.'—*Methodist Times.*

Biography

S. Baring Gould. THE LIFE OF NAPOLEON BONAPARTE. By S. BARING GOULD. With over 450 Illustrations in the Text and 12 Photogravure Plates. *Large quarto. Gilt top.* 36s.

'The best biography of Napole in our tongue, nor have the French as good a biographer of their hero. A book very nearly as good as Southey's "Life of Nelson."'—*Manchester Guardian.*

'The main feature of this gorgeous volume is its great wealth of beautiful photogravures and finely-executed wood engravings, constituting a complete pictorial chronicle of Napoleon I.'s personal history from the days of his early childhood at Ajaccio to the date of his second interment under the dome of the Invalides in Paris.'—*Daily Telegraph.*

'Particular notice is due to the vast collection of contemporary illustrations.'—*Guardian.*

'Nearly all the illustrations are real contributions to history.'—*Westminster Gazette.*

Morris Fuller. THE LIFE AND WRITINGS OF JOHN DAVENANT, D.D. (1571-1641), Bishop of Salisbury. By MORRIS FULLER, B.D. *Demy 8vo.* 10s. 6d.

'A valuable contribution to ecclesiastical history.'—*Birmingham Gazette.*

J. M. Rigg. ST. ANSELM OF CANTERBURY: A CHAPTER IN THE HISTORY OF RELIGION. By J. M. RIGG. *Demy 8vo.* 7s. 6d.

'Mr. Rigg has told the story of the great Primate's life with scholarly ability, and has thereby contributed an interesting chapter to the history of the Norman period.'—*Daily Chronicle.*

F. W. Joyce. THE LIFE OF SIR FREDERICK GORE OUSELEY. By F. W. JOYCE, M.A. With Portraits and Illustrations. *Crown 8vo.* 7s. 6d.

'This book has been undertaken in quite the right spirit, and written with sympathy, insight, and considerable literary skill.'—*Times.*

W. G. Collingwood. THE LIFE OF JOHN RUSKIN. By W. G. COLLINGWOOD, M.A. With Portraits, and 13 Drawings by Mr. Ruskin. *Second Edition.* 2 vols. 8vo. 32s.

'No more magnificent volumes have been published for a long time.'—*Times.*

'It is long since we had a biography with such delights of substance and of form. Such a book is a pleasure for the day, and a joy for ever.'—*Daily Chronicle.*

C. Waldstein. JOHN RUSKIN: a Study. By CHARLES WALDSTEIN, M.A., Fellow of King's College, Cambridge. With a Photogravure Portrait after Professor HERKOMER. *Post 8vo.* 5s.

'A thoughtful, impartial, well-written criticism of Ruskin's teaching, intended to separate what the author regards as valuable and permanent from what is transient and erroneous in the great master's writing.'—*Daily Chronicle.*

Darmesteter. THE LIFE OF ERNEST RENAN. By MADAME DARMESTETER. With Portrait. *Second Edition. Cr. 8vo. 6s.*
A biography of Renan by one of his most intimate friends.
'A polished gem of biography, superior in its kind to any attempt that has been made of recent years in England. Madame Darmesteter has indeed written for English readers "*The Life of Ernest Renan.*"'—*Athenæum.*
'It is a fascinating and biographical and critical study, and an admirably finished work of literary art.'—*Scotsman.*
'It is interpenetrated with the dignity and charm, the mild, bright, classical grace of form and treatment that Renan himself so loved; and it fulfils to the uttermost the delicate and difficult achievement it sets out to accomplish.'—*Academy.*

W. H. Hutton. THE LIFE OF SIR THOMAS MORE. By W. H. HUTTON, M.A. *With Portraits. Crown 8vo. 5s.*
'The book lays good claim to high rank among our biographies. It is excellently, even lovingly, written.'—*Scotsman.*   'An excellent monograph.'—*Times.*

Travel, Adventure and Topography

Johnston. BRITISH CENTRAL AFRICA. By Sir H. H. JOHNSTON, K.C.B. With nearly Two Hundred Illustrations, and Six Maps. *Second Edition. Crown 4to. 30s. net.*
'A fascinating book, written with equal skill and charm—the work at once of a literary artist and of a man of action who is singularly wise, brave, and experienced. It abounds in admirable sketches from pencil.'—*Westminster Gazette.*
'A delightful book . . . collecting within the covers of a single volume all that is known of this part of our African domains. The voluminous appendices are of extreme value.'—*Manchester Guardian.*
'The book takes front rank as a standard work by the one man competent to write it.'—*Daily Chronicle.*
'The book is crowded with important information, and written in a most attractive style; it is worthy, in short, of the author's established reputation.'—*Standard.*

Prince Henri of Orleans. FROM TONKIN TO INDIA. By PRINCE HENRI OF ORLEANS. Translated by HAMLEY BENT, M.A. With 100 Illustrations and a Map. *Second Edition. Crown 4to, gilt top. 25s.*
The travels of Prince Henri in 1895 from China to the valley of the Bramaputra covered a distance of 2100 miles, of which 1600 was through absolutely unexplored country. No fewer than seventeen ranges of mountains were crossed at altitudes of from 11,000 to 13,000 feet. The journey was made memorable by the discovery of the sources of the Irrawaddy.
'A welcome contribution to our knowledge. The narrative is full and interesting, and the appendices give the work a substantial value.'—*Times.*
'The Prince's travels are of real importance . . . his services to geography have been considerable. The volume is beautifully illustrated.'—*Athenæum.*
'The story is instructive and fascinating, and will certainly make one of the books of 1898. The book attracts by its delightful print and fine illustrations. A nearly model book of travel.'—*Pall Mall Gazette.*
'An entertaining record of pluck and travel in important regions.'—*Daily Chronicle.*
'The illustrations are admirable and quite beyond praise.'—*Glasgow Herald.*
'The Prince's story is charmingly told, and presented with an attractiveness which will make it, in more than one sense, an outstanding book of the season.'—*Birmingham Post.*
'An attractive book which will prove of considerable interest and no little value. A narrative of a remarkable journey.'—*Literature.*
'China is the country of the hour. All eyes are turned towards her, and Messrs. Methuen have opportunely selected the moment to launch Prince Henri's work.'—*Liverpool Daily Post.*

Messrs. Methuens List

R. S. S. Baden-Powell. THE DOWNFALL OF PREMPEH. A Diary of Life in Ashanti, 1895. By Colonel BADEN-POWELL. With 21 Illustrations and a Map. *Demy 8vo.* 10s. 6d.

'A compact, faithful, most readable record of the campaign.'—*Daily News.*

R. S. S. Baden-Powell. THE MATEBELE CAMPAIGN 1896. By Colonel BADEN-POWELL. With nearly 100 Illustrations. *Second Edition. Demy 8vo.* 15s.

'As a straightforward account of a great deal of plucky work unpretentiously done, this book is well worth reading. The simplicity of the narrative is all in its favour, and accords in a peculiarly English fashion with the nature of the subject.' *Times.*

Captain Hinde. THE FALL OF THE CONGO ARABS. By L. HINDE. With Plans, etc. *Demy 8vo.* 12s. 6d.

'The book is full of good things, and of sustained interest.'—*St. James's Gazette.*
'A graphic sketch of one of the most exciting and important episodes in the struggle for supremacy in Central Africa between the Arabs and their European rivals. Apart from the story of the campaign, Captain Hinde's book is mainly remarkable for the fulness with which he discusses the question of cannibalism. It is, indeed, the only connected narrative—in English, at any rate—which has been published of this particular episode in African history.'—*Times.*

W. Crooke. THE NORTH-WESTERN PROVINCES OF INDIA: THEIR ETHNOLOGY AND ADMINISTRATION. By W. CROOKE. With Maps and Illustrations. *Demy 8vo.* 10s. 6d.

'A carefully and well-written account of one of the most important provinces of the Empire. In seven chapters Mr. Crooke deals successively with the land in its physical aspect, the province under Hindoo and Mussulman rule, the province under British rule, the ethnology and sociology of the province, the religious and social life of the people, the land and its settlement, and the native peasant in his relation to the land. The illustrations are good and well selected, and the map is excellent.'—*Manchester Guardian.*

A. Boisragon. THE BENIN MASSACRE. By CAPTAIN BOISRAGON. With Portrait and Map. *Second Edition. Crown 8vo.* 3s. 6d.

'If the story had been written four hundred years ago it would be read to-day as an English classic.'—*Scotsman.*
'If anything could enhance the horror and the pathos of this remarkable book it is the simple style of the author, who writes as he would talk, unconscious of his own heroism, with an artlessness which is the highest art.'—*Pall Mall Gazette.*

H. S. Cowper. THE HILL OF THE GRACES: OR, THE GREAT STONE TEMPLES OF TRIPOLI. By H. S. COWPER, F.S.A. With Maps, Plans, and 75 Illustrations. *Demy 8vo.* 10s. 6d.

'The book has the interest of all first-hand work, directed by an intelligent man towards a worthy object, and it forms a valuable chapter of what has now become quite a large and important branch of antiquarian research.'—*Times.*

Kinnaird Rose. WITH THE GREEKS IN THESSALY. By W. KINNAIRD ROSE, Reuter's Correspondent. With Plans and 23 Illustrations. *Crown 8vo.* 6s.

W. B. Worsfold. SOUTH AFRICA. By W. B. WORSFOLD, M.A. *With a Map. Second Edition. Crown 8vo.* 6s.

'A monumental work compressed into a very moderate compass.'—*World.*

Naval and Military

G. W. Steevens. NAVAL POLICY: By. G. W. STEEVENS. *Demy 8vo.* 6s.

This book is a description of the British and other more important navies of the world, with a sketch of the lines on which our naval policy might possibly be developed.
'An extremely able and interesting work.'—*Daily Chronicle.*

D. Hannay. A SHORT HISTORY OF THE ROYAL NAVY, FROM EARLY TIMES TO THE PRESENT DAY. By DAVID HANNAY. Illustrated. 2 *Vols. Demy 8vo.* 7s. 6d. *each.* Vol. I., 1200-1688.

' We read it from cover to cover at a sitting, and those who go to it for a lively and brisk picture of the past, with all its faults and its grandeur, will not be disappointed. The historian is competent, and he is endowed with literary skill and style.'—*Standard.*
'We can warmly recommend Mr. Hannay's volume to any intelligent student of naval history. Great as is the merit of Mr. Hannay's historical narrative, the merit of his strategic exposition is even greater.'—*Times.*
'His book is brisk and pleasant reading, for he is gifted with a most agreeable style. His reflections are philosophical, and he has seized and emphasised just those points which are of interest.'—*Graphic.*

Cooper King. THE STORY OF THE BRITISH ARMY. By Lieut.-Colonel COOPER KING, of the Staff College, Camberley. Illustrated. *Demy 8vo.* 7s. 6d.

'An authoritative and accurate story of England's military progress.'—*Daily Mail.*
'This handy volume contains, in a compendious form, a brief but adequate sketch of the story of the British army.'—*Daily News.*

R. Southey. ENGLISH SEAMEN (Howard, Clifford, Hawkins, Drake, Cavendish). By ROBERT SOUTHEY. Edited, with an Introduction, by DAVID HANNAY. *Second Edition. Crown 8vo.* 6s.

'Admirable and well-told stories of our naval history.'—*Army and Navy Gazette.*
'A brave, inspiring book.'—*Black and White.*

W. Clark Russell. THE LIFE OF ADMIRAL LORD COLLINGWOOD. By W. CLARK RUSSELL, With Illustrations by F. BRANGWYN. *Third Edition. Crown 8vo.* 6s.

'A book which we should like to see in the hands of every boy in the country.'—*St. James's Gazette.* 'A really good book.'—*Saturday Review.*

E. L. S. Horsburgh. THE CAMPAIGN OF WATERLOO. By E. L. S. HORSBURGH, B.A. *With Plans. Crown 8vo.* 5s.

'A brilliant essay—simple, sound, and thorough.'—*Daily Chronicle.*

H. B. George. BATTLES OF ENGLISH HISTORY. By H. B. GEORGE, M.A., Fellow of New College, Oxford. *With numerous Plans. Third Edition. Crown 8vo.* 6s.

'Mr. George has undertaken a very useful task—that of making military affairs intelligible and instructive to non-military readers—and has executed it with laudable intelligence and industry, and with a large measure of success.'—*Times.*

General Literature

S. Baring Gould. OLD COUNTRY LIFE. By S. BARING GOULD. With Sixty-seven Illustrations. *Large Crown 8vo. Fifth Edition.* 6s.

'"Old Country Life," as healthy wholesome reading, full of breezy life and movement, full of quaint stories vigorously told, will not be excelled by any book to be published throughout the year. Sound, hearty, and English to the core.'—*World.*

S. Baring Gould. HISTORIC ODDITIES AND STRANGE EVENTS. By S. BARING GOULD. *Fourth Edition. Crown 8vo.* 6s.

'A collection of exciting and entertaining chapters. The whole volume is delightful reading.'—*Times.*

S. Baring Gould. FREAKS OF FANATICISM. By S. BARING GOULD. *Third Edition. Crown 8vo.* 6s.

'Mr. Baring Gould has a keen eye for colour and effect, and the subjects he has chosen give ample scope to his descriptive and analytic faculties. A perfectly fascinating book.'—*Scottish Leader.*

S. Baring Gould. A GARLAND OF COUNTRY SONG: English Folk Songs with their Traditional Melodies. Collected and arranged by S. BARING GOULD and H. F. SHEPPARD. *Demy 4to.* 6s.

S. Baring Gould. SONGS OF THE WEST: Traditional Ballads and Songs of the West of England, with their Traditional Melodies. Collected by S. BARING GOULD, M.A., and H. F. SHEPPARD, M.A. Arranged for Voice and Piano. In 4 Parts. *Parts I., II., III.,* 3s. *each. Part IV.,* 5s. *In one Vol., French morocco,* 15s.

'A rich collection of humour, pathos, grace, and poetic fancy.'—*Saturday Review.*

S. Baring Gould. YORKSHIRE ODDITIES AND STRANGE EVENTS. *Fourth Edition. Crown 8vo.* 6s.

S. Baring Gould. STRANGE SURVIVALS AND SUPERSTITIONS. With Illustrations. By S. BARING GOULD. *Crown 8vo. Second Edition.* 6s.

S. Baring Gould. THE DESERTS OF SOUTHERN FRANCE. By S. BARING GOULD. 2 *vols. Demy 8vo.* 32s.

Cotton Minchin. OLD HARROW DAYS. By J. G. COTTON MINCHIN. *Crown 8vo. Second Edition.* 5s.

'This book is an admirable record.'—*Daily Chronicle.*

'Mr. Cotton Minchin's bright and breezy reminiscences of 'Old Harrow Days' will delight all Harrovians, old and young, and may go far to explain the abiding enthusiasm of old Harrovians for their school to readers who have not been privileged to be their schoolfellows.'—*Times.*

W. E. Gladstone. THE SPEECHES OF THE RT. HON. W. E. GLADSTONE, M.P. Edited by A. W. HUTTON, M.A., and H. J. COHEN, M.A. With Portraits. 8vo. *Vols. IX. and X.* 12s. 6d. *each.*

MESSRS. METHUEN'S LIST

J. Wells. OXFORD AND OXFORD LIFE. By Members of the University. Edited by J. WELLS, M.A., Fellow and Tutor of Wadham College. *Crown 8vo.* 3s. 6d.
'We congratulate Mr. Wells on the production of a readable and intelligent account of Oxford as it is at the present time, written by persons who are possessed of a close acquaintance with the system and life of the University.'—*Athenæum.*

J. Wells. OXFORD AND ITS COLLEGES. By J. WELLS, M.A., Fellow and Tutor of Wadham College. Illustrated by E. H. NEW. *Second Edition. Fcap. 8vo.* 3s. *Leather.* 4s.
This is a guide—chiefly historical—to the Colleges of Oxford. It contains numerous illustrations.
'An admirable and accurate little treatise, attractively illustrated.'—*World.*
'A luminous and tasteful little volume.'—*Daily Chronicle.*
'Exactly what the intelligent visitor wants.'—*Glasgow Herald.*

C. G. Robertson. VOCES ACADEMICÆ. By C. GRANT ROBERTSON, M.A., Fellow of All Souls', Oxford. *With a Frontispiece. Pott. 8vo.* 3s. 6d.
'Decidedly clever and amusing.'—*Athenæum.*
'The dialogues are abundantly smart and amusing.'—*Glasgow Herald.*
'A clever and entertaining little book.'—*Pall Mall Gazette.*

L. Whibley. GREEK OLIGARCHIES : THEIR ORGANISATION AND CHARACTER. By L. WHIBLEY, M.A., Fellow of Pembroke College, Cambridge. *Crown 8vo.* 6s.
'An exceedingly useful handbook : a careful and well-arranged study.'—*Times.*

L. L. Price. ECONOMIC SCIENCE AND PRACTICE. By L. L. PRICE, M.A., Fellow of Oriel College, Oxford. *Crown 8vo.* 6s.
'The book is well written, giving evidence of considerable literary ability, and clear mental grasp of the subject under consideration.'—*Western Morning News.*

J. S. Shedlock. THE PIANOFORTE SONATA : Its Origin and Development. By J. S. SHEDLOCK. *Crown 8vo.* 5s.
'This work should be in the possession of every musician and amateur. A concise and lucid history of the origin of one of the most important forms of musical composition. A very valuable work for reference.'—*Athenæum.*

E. M. Bowden. THE EXAMPLE OF BUDDHA : Being Quotations from Buddhist Literature for each Day in the Year. Compiled by E. M. BOWDEN. *Third Edition.* 16mo. 2s. 6d.

Morgan-Browne. SPORTING AND ATHLETIC RECORDS. By H. MORGAN-BROWNE. *Crown 8vo.* 1s. *paper*; 1s. 6d. *cloth.*
'Should meet a very wide demand.'—*Daily Mail.*
'A very careful collection, and the first one of its kind.'—*Manchester Guardian.*
'Certainly the most valuable of all books of its kind.'—*Birmingham Gazette.*

Science

Freudenreich. DAIRY BACTERIOLOGY. A Short Manual for the Use of Students. By Dr. ED. VON FREUDENREICH. Translated by J. R. AINSWORTH DAVIS, B.A. *Crown 8vo.* 2s. 6d.

Chalmers Mitchell. OUTLINES OF BIOLOGY. By P.
CHALMERS MITCHELL, M.A., *Illustrated. Crown 8vo.* 6s.
A text-book designed to cover the new Schedule issued by the Royal College of Physicians and Surgeons.

G. Massee. A MONOGRAPH OF THE MYXOGASTRES. By
GEORGE MASSEE. With 12 Coloured Plates. *Royal 8vo.* 18s. net.
'A work much in advance of any book in the language treating of this group of organisms. Indispensable to every student of the Myxogastres.'—*Nature.*

Technology

Stephenson and Suddards. ORNAMENTAL DESIGN FOR WOVEN FABRICS. By C. STEPHENSON, of The Technical College, Bradford, and F. SUDDARDS, of The Yorkshire College, Leeds. With 65 full-page plates, and numerous designs and diagrams in the text. *Demy 8vo.* 7s. 6d.
'The book is very ably done, displaying an intimate knowledge of principles, good taste, and the faculty of clear exposition.'—*Yorkshire Post.*

HANDBOOKS OF TECHNOLOGY.
Edited by PROFESSORS GARNETT and WERTHEIMER.

HOW TO MAKE A DRESS. By J. A. E. WOOD.
Illustrated. Crown 8vo. 1s. 6d.
A text-book for students preparing for the City and Guilds examination, based on the syllabus. The diagrams are numerous.
'Though primarily intended for students, Miss Wood's dainty little manual may be consulted with advantage by any girls who want to make their own frocks. The directions are simple and clear, and the diagrams very helpful.'—*Literature.*
'A splendid little book.'—*Evening News.*

Philosophy

L. T. Hobhouse. THE THEORY OF KNOWLEDGE. By
L. T. HOBHOUSE, Fellow of C.C.C, Oxford. *Demy 8vo.* 21s.
'The most important contribution to English philosophy since the publication of Mr. Bradley's "Appearance and Reality." Full of brilliant criticism and of positive theories which are models of lucid statement.'—*Glasgow Herald.*
'A brilliantly written volume.'—*Times.*

W. H. Fairbrother. THE PHILOSOPHY OF T. H. GREEN.
By W. H. FAIRBROTHER, M.A. *Crown 8vo.* 3s. 6d.
'In every way an admirable book.'—*Glasgow Herald.*

F. W. Bussell. THE SCHOOL OF PLATO: its Origin and its Revival under the Roman Empire. By F. W. BUSSELL, D.D., Fellow and Tutor of Brasenose College, Oxford. *Demy 8vo.* 10s. 6d.
'A highly valuable contribution to the history of ancient thought.'—*Glasgow Herald.*
'A clever and stimulating book, provocative of thought and deserving careful reading.'
—*Manchester Guardian.*

F. S. Granger. THE WORSHIP OF THE ROMANS. By F. S. GRANGER, M.A., Litt.D., Professor of Philosophy at University College, Nottingham. *Crown 8vo.* 6s.

'A scholarly analysis of the religious ceremonies, beliefs, and superstitions of ancient Rome, conducted in the new light of comparative anthropology.'—*Times.*

Theology

HANDBOOKS OF THEOLOGY.

General Editor, A. ROBERTSON, D.D., Principal of King's College, London.

THE XXXIX. ARTICLES OF THE CHURCH OF ENGLAND. Edited with an Introduction by E. C. S. GIBSON, D.D., Vicar of Leeds, late Principal of Wells Theological College. *Second and Cheaper Edition in One Volume. Demy 8vo.* 12s. 6d.

' Dr. Gibson is a master of clear and orderly exposition, and he has enlisted in his service all the mechanism of variety of type which so greatly helps to elucidate a complicated subject. And he has in a high degree a quality very necessary, but rarely found, in commentators on this topic, that of absolute fairness. His book is pre-eminently honest.'—*Times.*

'After a survey of the whole book, we can bear witness to the transparent honesty of purpose, evident industry, and clearness of style which mark its contents. They maintain throughout a very high level of doctrine and tone.'—*Guardian.*

'An elaborate and learned book, excellently adapted to its purpose.'—*Speaker.*

'The most convenient and most acceptable commentary.'—*Expository Times.*

AN INTRODUCTION TO THE HISTORY OF RELIGION. By F. B. JEVONS, M.A., Litt.D., Principal of Bishop Hatfield's Hall. *Demy 8vo.* 10s. 6d.

' Dr. Jevons has written a notable work, which we can strongly recommend to the serious attention of theologians and anthropologists.'—*Manchester Guardian.*

' The merit of this book lies in the penetration, the singular acuteness and force of the author's judgment. He is at once critical and luminous, at once just and suggestive. A comprehensive and thorough book.'—*Birmingham Post.*

THE DOCTRINE OF THE INCARNATION. By R. L. OTTLEY, M.A., late fellow of Magdalen College, Oxon., and Principal of Pusey House. *In Two Volumes. Demy 8vo.* 15s.

'Learned and reverent: lucid and well arranged.'—*Record.*

'Accurate, well ordered, and judicious.'—*National Observer.*

'A clear and remarkably full account of the main currents of speculation. Scholarly precision . . . genuine tolerance . . . intense interest in his subject—are Mr. Ottley's merits.'—*Guardian.*

C. F. Andrews. CHRISTIANITY AND THE LABOUR QUESTION. By C. F. ANDREWS, B.A. *Crown 8vo.* 2s. 6d.

S. R. Driver. SERMONS ON SUBJECTS CONNECTED WITH THE OLD TESTAMENT. By S. R. DRIVER, D.D., Canon of Christ Church, Regius Professor of Hebrew in the University of Oxford. *Crown 8vo.* 6s.

'A welcome companion to the author's famous 'Introduction.' No man can read these discourses without feeling that Dr. Driver is fully alive to the deeper teaching of the Old Testament.'—*Guardian.*

T. K. Cheyne. FOUNDERS OF OLD TESTAMENT CRITICISM. By T. K. CHEYNE, D.D., Oriel Professor at Oxford. *Large crown 8vo. 7s. 6d.*

This book is a historical sketch of O. T. Criticism in the form of biographical studies from the days of Eichhorn to those of Driver and Robertson Smith.

'A very learned and instructive work.'—*Times.*

H. H. Henson. LIGHT AND LEAVEN : HISTORICAL AND SOCIAL SERMONS. By the Rev. H. HENSLEY HENSON, M.A., Fellow of All Souls', Incumbent of St. Mary's Hospital, Ilford. *Crown 8vo. 6s.*

'They are always reasonable as well as vigorous, and they are none the less impressive because they regard the needs of a life on this side of a hereafter.'—*Scotsman.*

W. H. Bennett. A PRIMER OF THE BIBLE. By Prof. W. H. BENNETT. *Second Edition. Crown 8vo. 2s. 6d.*

'The work of an honest, fearless, and sound critic, and an excellent guide in a small compass to the books of the Bible.'—*Manchester Guardian.*

'A unique primer. Mr. Bennett has collected and condensed a very extensive and diversified amount of material, and no one can consult his pages and fail to acknowledge indebtedness to his undertaking.'—*English Churchman.*

C. H. Prior. CAMBRIDGE SERMONS. Edited by C. H. PRIOR, M.A., Fellow and Tutor of Pembroke College. *Crown 8vo. 6s.*

A volume of sermons preached before the University of Cambridge by various preachers, including the late Archbishop of Canterbury and Bishop Westcott.

E. B. Layard. RELIGION IN BOYHOOD. Notes on the Religious Training of Boys. By E. B. LAYARD, M.A. *18mo. 1s.*

W. Yorke Faussett. THE *DE CATECHIZANDIS RUDIBUS* OF ST. AUGUSTINE. Edited, with Introduction, Notes, etc., by W. YORKE FAUSSETT, M.A., late Scholar of Balliol Coll. *Crown 8vo. 3s. 6d.*

An edition of a Treatise on the Essentials of Christian Doctrine, and the best methods of impressing them on candidates for baptism.

A Kempis. THE IMITATION OF CHRIST. By THOMAS À KEMPIS. With an Introduction by DEAN FARRAR. Illustrated by C. M. GERE, and printed in black and red. *Second Edition. Fcap. 8vo. Buckram. 3s. 6d. Padded morocco, 5s.*

'Amongst all the innumerable English editions of the "Imitation," there can have been few which were prettier than this one, printed in strong and handsome type, with all the glory of red initials.'—*Glasgow Herald.*

J. Keble. THE CHRISTIAN YEAR. By JOHN KEBLE. With an Introduction and Notes by W. LOCK, D.D., Warden of Keble College, Ireland Professor at Oxford. Illustrated by R. ANNING BELL. *Second Edition. Fcap. 8vo. Buckram. 3s. 6d. Padded morocco, 5s.*

'The present edition is annotated with all the care and insight to be expected from Mr. Lock. The progress and circumstances of its composition are detailed in the Introduction. There is an interesting Appendix on the MSS. of the "Christian Year," and another giving the order in which the poems were written. A "Short Analysis of the Thought" is prefixed to each, and any difficulty in the text is explained in a note.'—*Guardian.*

Leaders of Religion

Edited by H. C. BEECHING, M.A. *With Portraits, crown 8vo.*

A series of short biographies of the most prominent leaders of religious life and thought of all ages and countries.

The following are ready—

CARDINAL NEWMAN. By R. H. HUTTON.
JOHN WESLEY. By J. H. OVERTON, M.A.
BISHOP WILBERFORCE. By G. W. DANIEL, M.A.
CARDINAL MANNING. By A. W. HUTTON, M.A.
CHARLES SIMEON. By H. C. G. MOULE, M.A.
JOHN KEBLE. By WALTER LOCK, D.D.
THOMAS CHALMERS. By Mrs. OLIPHANT.
LANCELOT ANDREWES. By R. L. OTTLEY, M.A.
AUGUSTINE OF CANTERBURY. By E. L. CUTTS, D.D.
WILLIAM LAUD. By W. H. HUTTON, B.D.
JOHN KNOX. By F. M'CUNN.
JOHN HOWE. By R. F. HORTON, D.D.
BISHOP KEN. By F. A. CLARKE, M.A.
GEORGE FOX, THE QUAKER. By T. HODGKIN, D.C.L.
JOHN DONNE. By AUGUSTUS JESSOPP, D.D.

Other volumes will be announced in due course.

Fiction

SIX SHILLING NOVELS

Marie Corelli's Novels

Crown 8vo. 6s. each.

A ROMANCE OF TWO WORLDS. *Seventeenth Edition.*
VENDETTA. *Thirteenth Edition.*
THELMA. *Seventeenth Edition.*
ARDATH. *Eleventh Edition.*
THE SOUL OF LILITH. *Ninth Edition.*
WORMWOOD. *Eighth Edition.*
BARABBAS: A DREAM OF THE WORLD'S TRAGEDY. *Thirty-first Edition.*

'The tender reverence of the treatment and the imaginative beauty of the writing have reconciled us to the daring of the conception, and the conviction is forced on us that even so exalted a subject cannot be made too familiar to us, provided it be presented in the true spirit of Christian faith. The amplifications of the Scripture narrative are often conceived with high poetic insight, and this "Dream of the World's Tragedy" is, despite some trifling incongruities, a lofty and not inadequate paraphrase of the supreme climax of the inspired narrative.'—*Dublin Review.*

MESSRS. METHUEN'S LIST

THE SORROWS OF SATAN. *Thirty-sixth Edition.*

'A very powerful piece of work. . . . The conception is magnificent, and is likely to win an abiding place within the memory of man. . . . The author has immense command of language, and a limitless audacity. . . . This interesting and remarkable romance will live long after much of the ephemeral literature of the day is forgotten. . . . A literary phenomenon . . . novel, and even sublime.'—W. T. STEAD in the *Review of Reviews.*

Anthony Hope's Novels
Crown 8vo. 6s. each.

THE GOD IN THE CAR. *Seventh Edition.*

'A very remarkable book, deserving of critical analysis impossible within our limit; brilliant, but not superficial; well considered, but not elaborated; constructed with the proverbial art that conceals, but yet allows itself to be enjoyed by readers to whom fine literary method is a keen pleasure.'—*The World.*

A CHANGE OF AIR. *Fourth Edition.*

'A graceful, vivacious comedy, true to human nature. The characters are traced with a masterly hand.'—*Times.*

A MAN OF MARK. *Fourth Edition.*

'Of all Mr. Hope's books, "A Man of Mark" is the one which best compares with "The Prisoner of Zenda."'—*National Observer.*

THE CHRONICLES OF COUNT ANTONIO. *Third Edition.*

'It is a perfectly enchanting story of love and chivalry, and pure romance. The Count is the most constant, desperate, and modest and tender of lovers, a peerless gentleman, an intrepid fighter, a faithful friend, and a magnanimous foe.'—*Guardian.*

PHROSO. Illustrated by H. R. MILLAR. *Third Edition.*

'The tale is thoroughly fresh, quick with vitality, stirring the blood, and humorously, dashingly told.'—*St. James's Gazette.*
'A story of adventure, every page of which is palpitating with action.'—*Speaker.*
'From cover to cover "Phroso" not only engages the attention, but carries the reader in little whirls of delight from adventure to adventure.'—*Academy.*

S. Baring Gould's Novels
Crown 8vo. 6s. each.

'To say that a book is by the author of "Mehalah" is to imply that it contains a story cast on strong lines, containing dramatic possibilities, vivid and sympathetic descriptions of Nature, and a wealth of ingenious imagery.'—*Speaker.*
'That whatever Mr. Baring Gould writes is well worth reading, is a conclusion that may be very generally accepted. His views of life are fresh and vigorous, his language pointed and characteristic, the incidents of which he makes use are striking and original, his characters are life-like, and though somewhat exceptional people, are drawn and coloured with artistic force. Add to this that his descriptions of scenes and scenery are painted with the loving eyes and skilled hands of a master of his art, that he is always fresh and never dull, and under such conditions it is no wonder that readers have gained confidence both in his power of amusing and satisfying them, and that year by year his popularity widens.'—*Court Circular.*

ARMINELL: A Social Romance. *Fourth Edition.*

URITH: A Story of Dartmoor. *Fifth Edition.*

'The author is at his best.'—*Times.*

MESSRS. METHUEN'S LIST

IN THE ROAR OF THE SEA. *Sixth Edition.*
'One of the best imagined and most enthralling stories the author has produced.'
—*Saturday Review.*

MRS. CURGENVEN OF CURGENVEN. *Fourth Edition.*
'The swing of the narrative is splendid.'—*Sussex Daily News.*

CHEAP JACK ZITA. *Fourth Edition.*
'A powerful drama of human passion.'—*Westminster Gazette.*
'A story worthy the author.'—*National Observer.*

THE QUEEN OF LOVE. *Fourth Edition.*
'Can be heartily recommended to all who care for cleanly, energetic, and interesting fiction.'—*Sussex Daily News.*

KITTY ALONE. *Fourth Edition.*
'A strong and original story, teeming with graphic description, stirring incident, and, above all, with vivid and enthralling human interest.'—*Daily Telegraph.*

NOÉMI: A Romance of the Cave-Dwellers. Illustrated by R. CATON WOODVILLE. *Third Edition.*
'A powerful story, full of strong lights and shadows.'—*Standard.*

THE BROOM-SQUIRE. Illustrated by FRANK DADD. *Fourth Edition.*
'A strain of tenderness is woven through the web of his tragic tale, and its atmosphere is sweetened by the nobility and sweetness of the heroine's character.'—*Daily News.*

THE PENNYCOMEQUICKS. *Third Edition.*

DARTMOOR IDYLLS.
'A book to read, and keep and read again; for the genuine fun and pathos of it will not early lose their effect.'—*Vanity Fair.*

GUAVAS THE TINNER. Illustrated by FRANK DADD. *Second Edition.*
'There is a kind of flavour about this book which alone elevates it above the ordinary novel. The story itself has a grandeur in harmony with the wild and rugged scenery which is its setting.'—*Athenæum.*

BLADYS. *Second Edition.*
'A story of thrilling interest.'—*Scotsman.*
'A sombre but powerful story.'—*Daily Mail.*

Gilbert Parker's Novels

Crown 8vo. 6s. each.

PIERRE AND HIS PEOPLE. *Fourth Edition.*
'Stories happily conceived and finely executed. There is strength and genius in Mr. Parker's style.'—*Daily Telegraph.*

MRS. FALCHION. *Fourth Edition.*
'A splendid study of character.'—*Athenæum.*
'But little behind anything that has been done by any writer of our time.'—*Pall Mall Gazette.* 'A very striking and admirable novel.'—*St. James's Gazette.*

THE TRANSLATION OF A SAVAGE.
'The plot is original and one difficult to work out; but Mr. Parker has done it with great skill and delicacy. The reader who is not interested in this original, fresh, and well-told tale must be a dull person indeed.'—*Daily Chronicle.*

THE TRAIL OF THE SWORD. *Fifth Edition.*

'A rousing and dramatic tale. A book like this, in which swords flash, great surprises are undertaken, and daring deeds done, in which men and women live and love in the old passionate way, is a joy inexpressible.'—*Daily Chronicle.*

WHEN VALMOND CAME TO PONTIAC: The Story of a Lost Napoleon. *Fourth Edition.*

'Here we find romance—real, breathing, living romance. The character of Valmond is drawn unerringly. The book must be read, we may say re-read, for any one thoroughly to appreciate Mr. Parker's delicate touch and innate sympathy with humanity.'—*Pall Mall Gazette.*

AN ADVENTURER OF THE NORTH: The Last Adventures of 'Pretty Pierre.' *Second Edition.*

'The present book is full of fine and moving stories of the great North, and it will add to Mr. Parker's already high reputation.'—*Glasgow Herald.*

THE SEATS OF THE MIGHTY. *Illustrated. Ninth Edition.*

'The best thing he has done; one of the best things that any one has done lately.'—*St. James's Gazette.*

'Mr. Parker seems to become stronger and easier with every serious novel that he attempts. He shows the matured power which his former novels have led us to expect, and has produced a really fine historical novel. The finest novel he has yet written.'—*Athenæum.*

'A great book.'—*Black and White.*

'One of the strongest stories of historical interest and adventure that we have read for many a day. . . . A notable and successful book.'—*Speaker.*

THE POMP OF THE LAVILETTES. *Second Edition.* 3s. 6d.

'Living, breathing romance, genuine and unforced pathos, and a deeper and more subtle knowledge of human nature than Mr. Parker has ever displayed before. It is, in a word, the work of a true artist.'—*Pall Mall Gazette.*

Conan Doyle. ROUND THE RED LAMP. By A. CONAN DOYLE, Author of 'The White Company,' 'The Adventures of Sherlock Holmes,' etc. *Fifth Edition. Crown 8vo.* 6s.

'The book is, indeed, composed of leaves from life, and is far and away the best view that has been vouchsafed us behind the scenes of the consulting-room. It is very superior to "The Diary of a late Physician."'—*Illustrated London News.*

Stanley Weyman. UNDER THE RED ROBE. By STANLEY WEYMAN, Author of 'A Gentleman of France.' With Twelve Illustrations by R. Caton Woodville. *Twelfth Edition. Crown 8vo.* 6s.

'A book of which we have read every word for the sheer pleasure of reading, and which we put down with a pang that we cannot forget it all and start again.'—*Westminster Gazette.*

'Every one who reads books at all must read this thrilling romance, from the first page of which to the last the breathless reader is haled along. An inspiration of manliness and courage.'—*Daily Chronicle.*

Lucas Malet. THE WAGES OF SIN. By LUCAS MALET. *Thirteenth Edition. Crown 8vo.* 6s.

Lucas Malet. THE CARISSIMA. By LUCAS MALET, Author of 'The Wages of Sin,' etc. *Third Edition. Crown 8vo.* 6s.

Messrs. Methuen's List

S. R. Crockett. LOCHINVAR. By S. R. CROCKETT, Author of 'The Raiders,' etc. Illustrated. *Second Edition. Crown 8vo. 6s.*

'Full of gallantry and pathos, of the clash of arms, and brightened by episodes of humour and love. . . . Mr. Crockett has never written a stronger or better book. An engrossing and fascinating story. The love story alone is enough to make the book delightful.'—*Westminster Gazette.*

Arthur Morrison. TALES OF MEAN STREETS. By ARTHUR MORRISON. *Fourth Edition. Crown 8vo. 6s.*

'Told with consummate art and extraordinary detail. In the true humanity of the book lies its justification, the permanence of its interest, and its indubitable triumph.'—*Athenæum.*
'A great book. The author's method is amazingly effective, and produces a thrilling sense of reality. The writer lays upon us a master hand. The book is simply appalling and irresistible in its interest. It is humorous also; without humour it would not make the mark it is certain to make.'—*World.*

Arthur Morrison. A CHILD OF THE JAGO. By ARTHUR MORRISON. *Third Edition. Crown 8vo. 6s.*

'The book is a masterpiece.'—*Pall Mall Gazette.*
'Told with great vigour and powerful simplicity.'—*Athenæum.*

Mrs. Clifford. A FLASH OF SUMMER. By Mrs. W. K. CLIFFORD, Author of 'Aunt Anne,' etc. *Second Edition. Crown 8vo. 6s.*

'The story is a very sad and a very beautiful one, exquisitely told, and enriched with many subtle touches of wise and tender insight.'—*Speaker.*

Emily Lawless. HURRISH. By the Honble. EMILY LAWLESS, Author of 'Maelcho,' etc. *Fifth Edition. Crown 8vo. 6s.*

A reissue of Miss Lawless' most popular novel, uniform with 'Maelcho.'

Emily Lawless. MAELCHO: a Sixteenth Century Romance. By the Honble. EMILY LAWLESS. *Second Edition. Crown 8vo. 6s.*

'A really great book.'—*Spectator.*
'There is no keener pleasure in life than the recognition of genius. A piece of work of the first order, which we do not hesitate to describe as one of the most remarkable literary achievements of this generation.'—*Manchester Guardian.*

Jane Barlow. A CREEL OF IRISH STORIES. By JANE BARLOW, Author of 'Irish Idylls.' *Second Edition. Crown 8vo. 6s.*

'Vivid and singularly real.'—*Scotsman.*
'Genuinely and naturally Irish.'—*Scotsman.*
'The sincerity of her sentiments, the distinction of her style, and the freshness of her themes, combine to lift her work far above the average level of contemporary fiction.'—*Manchester Guardian.*

J. H. Findlater. THE GREEN GRAVES OF BALGOWRIE. By JANE H. FINDLATER. *Fourth Edition. Crown 8vo. 6s.*

'A powerful and vivid story.'—*Standard.*
'A beautiful story, sad and strange as truth itself.'—*Vanity Fair.*
'A work of remarkable interest and originality.'—*National Observer.*
'A very charming and pathetic tale.'—*Pall Mall Gazette.*
'A singularly original, clever, and beautiful story.'—*Guardian.*
'Reveals to us a new writer of undoubted faculty and reserve force.'—*Spectator.*
'An exquisite idyll, delicate, affecting, and beautiful.'—*Black and White.*

J. H. Findlater. A DAUGHTER OF STRIFE. By JANE HELEN FINDLATER, Author of 'The Green Graves of Balgowrie.' *Crown 8vo.* 6s.

'A story of strong human interest.'—*Scotsman.*
'It has a sweet flavour of olden days delicately conveyed.'—*Manchester Guardian.*
'Her thought has solidity and maturity.'—*Daily Mail.*

Mary Findlater. OVER THE HILLS. By MARY FINDLATER. *Crown 8vo.* 6s.

'A strong and fascinating piece of work.'—*Scotsman.*
'A charming romance, and full of incident. The book is fresh and strong.'—*Speaker.*
'There is quiet force and beautiful simplicity in this book which will make the author's name loved in many a household.'—*Literary World.*
'Admirably fresh and broad in treatment. The novel is markedly original and excellently written.'—*Daily Chronicle.*
'A strong and wise book of deep insight and unflinching truth.'—*Birmingham Post.*
'Miss Mary Findlater combines originality with strength.'—*Daily Mail.*

H. G. Wells. THE STOLEN BACILLUS, and other Stories. By H. G. WELLS. *Second Edition. Crown 8vo.* 6s.

'The ordinary reader of fiction may be glad to know that these stories are eminently readable from one cover to the other, but they are more than that; they are the impressions of a very striking imagination, which, it would seem, has a great deal within its reach.'—*Saturday Review.*

H. G. Wells. THE PLATTNER STORY AND OTHERS. By H. G. WELLS. *Second Edition. Crown 8vo.* 6s.

'Weird and mysterious, they seem to hold the reader as by a magic spell.'—*Scotsman.*
'No volume has appeared for a long time so likely to give equal pleasure to the simplest reader and to the most fastidious critic.'—*Academy.*

E. F. Benson. DODO: A DETAIL OF THE DAY. By E. F. BENSON. *Sixteenth Edition. Crown 8vo.* 6s.

'A delightfully witty sketch of society.'—*Spectator.*
'A perpetual feast of epigram and paradox.'—*Speaker.*

E. F. Benson. THE RUBICON. By E. F. BENSON, Author of 'Dodo.' *Fifth Edition. Crown 8vo.* 6s.

Mrs. Oliphant. SIR ROBERT'S FORTUNE. By MRS. OLIPHANT. *Crown 8vo.* 6s.

'Full of her own peculiar charm of style and simple, subtle character-painting comes her new gift, the delightful story.'—*Pall Mall Gazette.*

Mrs. Oliphant. THE TWO MARYS. By MRS. OLIPHANT. *Second Edition. Crown 8vo.* 6s.

Mrs. Oliphant. THE LADY'S WALK. By Mrs. OLIPHANT. *Second Edition. Crown 8vo.* 6s.

'A story of exquisite tenderness, of most delicate fancy.'—*Pall Mall Gazette.*
'It contains many of the finer characteristics of her best work.'—*Scotsman.*
'It is little short of sacrilege on the part of a reviewer to attempt to sketch its outlines or analyse its peculiar charm.'—*Spectator.*

MESSRS. METHUEN'S LIST

W. E. Norris. MATTHEW AUSTIN. By W. E. NORRIS, Author of 'Mademoiselle de Mersac,' etc. *Fourth Edition. Crown 8vo.* 6s.

"An intellectually satisfactory and morally bracing novel."—*Daily Telegraph.*

W. E. Norris. HIS GRACE. By W. E. NORRIS. *Third Edition. Crown 8vo.* 6s.

'Mr. Norris has drawn a really fine character in the Duke of Hurstbourne, at once unconventional and very true to the conventionalities of life.'—*Athenæum.*

W. E. Norris. THE DESPOTIC LADY AND OTHERS. By W. E. NORRIS. *Crown 8vo.* 6s.

'A budget of good fiction of which no one will tire.'—*Scotsman.*

W. E. Norris. CLARISSA FURIOSA. By W. E. NORRIS, *Crown 8vo.* 6s.

'As a story it is admirable, as a *jeu d'esprit* it is capital, as a lay sermon studded with gems of wit and wisdom it is a model.'—*The World.*

W. Clark Russell. MY DANISH SWEETHEART. By W. CLARK RUSSELL, Author of 'The Wreck of the Grosvenor,' etc. *Illustrated. Fourth Edition. Crown 8vo.* 6s.

Robert Barr. THE MUTABLE MANY. By ROBERT BARR, Author of 'In the Midst of Alarms,' 'A Woman Intervenes,' etc. *Second Edition. Crown 8vo.* 6s.

'Very much the best novel that Mr. Barr has yet given us. There is much insight in it, much acute and delicate appreciation of the finer shades of character and much excellent humour.'—*Daily Chronicle.*
'An excellent story. It contains several excellently studied characters, and is filled with lifelike pictures of modern life.'—*Glasgow Herald.*

Robert Barr. IN THE MIDST OF ALARMS. By ROBERT BARR. *Third Edition. Crown 8vo.* 6s.

'A book which has abundantly satisfied us by its capital humour.'—*Daily Chronicle.*
'Mr. Barr has achieved a triumph whereof he has every reason to be proud.'—*Pall Mall Gazette.*

J. Maclaren Cobban. THE KING OF ANDAMAN: A Saviour of Society. By J. MACLAREN COBBAN. *Crown 8vo.* 6s.

'An unquestionably interesting book. It contains one character, at least, who has in him the root of immortality, and the book itself is ever exhaling the sweet savour of the unexpected.'—*Pall Mall Gazette.*

J. Maclaren Cobban. WILT THOU HAVE THIS WOMAN? By J. M. COBBAN, Author of 'The King of Andaman.' *Crown 8vo.* 6s.

Robert Hichens. BYEWAYS. By ROBERT HICHENS. Author of 'Flames,' etc. *Crown 8vo.* 6s.

'A very high artistic instinct and striking command of language raise Mr. Hichens' work far above the ruck.'—*Pall Mall Gazette.*
'The work is undeniably that of a man of striking imagination and no less striking powers of expression.'—*Daily News.*

Percy White. A PASSIONATE PILGRIM. By PERCY WHITE, Author of 'Mr. Bailey-Martin.' *Crown 8vo.* 6s.

'A work which it is not hyperbole to describe as of rare excellence.'—*Pall Mall Gazette.*
'The clever book of a shrewd and clever author.'—*Athenæum.*
'Mr. Percy White's strong point is analysis, and he has shown himself, before now, capable of building up a good book upon that foundation.'—*Standard.*

W. Pett Ridge. SECRETARY TO BAYNE, M.P. By W. PETT RIDGE. *Crown 8vo.* 6s.

'Sparkling, vivacious, adventurous.—*St. James's Gazette.*
'Ingenious, amusing, and especially smart.'—*World.*
'The dialogue is invariably alert and highly diverting.'—*Spectator.*

J. S. Fletcher. THE BUILDERS. By J. S. FLETCHER, Author of 'When Charles I. was King.' *Second Edition. Crown 8vo.* 6s.

'Replete with delightful descriptions.'—*Vanity Fair.*
'The background of country life has never, perhaps, been sketched more realistically.'—*World.*

Andrew Balfour. BY STROKE OF SWORD. By ANDREW BALFOUR. Illustrated by W. CUBITT COOKE. *Fourth Edition. Crown 8vo.* 6s.

'A banquet of good things.'—*Academy.*
'A recital of thrilling interest, told with unflagging vigour.'—*Globe*
'An unusually excellent example of a semi-historic romance.'—*World.*
'Manly, healthy, and patriotic.'—*Glasgow Herald.*

I. Hooper. THE SINGER OF MARLY. By I. HOOPER. Illustrated by W. CUBITT COOKE. *Crown 8vo.* 6s.

'Its scenes are drawn in vivid colours, and the characters are all picturesque.'—*Scotsman.*
'A novel as vigorous as it is charming.'—*Literary World.*

M. C. Balfour. THE FALL OF THE SPARROW. By M. C. BALFOUR. *Crown 8vo.* 6s.

'A powerful novel.'—*Daily Telegraph.*
'It is unusually powerful, and the characterization is uncommonly good.'—*World.*
'It is a well-knit, carefully-wrought story.'—*Academy.*

H. Morrah. A SERIOUS COMEDY. By HERBERT MORRAH. *Crown 8vo.* 6s.

H. Morrah. THE FAITHFUL CITY. By HERBERT MORRAH, Author of 'A Serious Comedy.' *Crown 8vo.* 6s.

L. B. Walford. SUCCESSORS TO THE TITLE. By Mrs. WALFORD, Author of 'Mr. Smith,' etc. *Second Edition. Crown 8vo.* 6s.

Mary Gaunt. KIRKHAM'S FIND. By Mary Gaunt, Author of 'The Moving Finger.' *Crown 8vo.* 6s.

'A really charming novel.'—*Standard.*
'A capital book, in which will be found lively humour, penetrating insight, and the sweet savour of a thoroughly healthy moral.'—*Speaker.*

M. M. Dowie. GALLIA. By Ménie Muriel Dowie, Author of 'A Girl in the Carpathians.' *Third Edition. Crown 8vo.* 6s.

'The style is generally admirable, the dialogue not seldom brilliant, the situations surprising in their freshness and originality, while the characters live and move, and the story itself is readable from title-page to colophon.'—*Saturday Review.*

J. A. Barry. IN THE GREAT DEEP. By J. A. Barry, Author of 'Steve Brown's Bunyip.' *Crown 8vo.* 6s.

'A collection of really admirable short stories of the sea, very simply told, and placed before the reader in pithy and telling English.'—*Westminster Gazette.*

J. B. Burton. IN THE DAY OF ADVERSITY. By J. Bloundelle-Burton.' *Second Edition. Crown 8vo.* 6s.

'Unusually interesting and full of highly dramatic situations.—*Guardian.*

J. B. Burton. DENOUNCED. By J. Bloundelle-Burton. *Second Edition. Crown 8vo.* 6s.

'The plot is an original one, and the local colouring is laid on with a delicacy and an accuracy of detail which denote the true artist.'—*Broad Arrow.*

J. B. Burton. THE CLASH OF ARMS. By J. Bloundelle-Burton, Author of 'In the Day of Adversity.' *Second Edition. Crown 8vo.* 6s.

'A brave story—brave in deed, brave in word, brave in thought.'—*St. James's Gazette.*
'A fine, manly, spirited piece of work.'—*World.*

W. C. Scully. THE WHITE HECATOMB. By W. C. Scully, Author of 'Kafir Stories.' *Crown 8vo.* 6s.

'It reveals a marvellously intimate understanding of the Kaffir mind, allied with literary gifts of no mean order.'—*African Critic.*

Julian Corbett. A BUSINESS IN GREAT WATERS. By Julian Corbett. *Second Edition. Crown 8vo.* 6s.

'Mr. Corbett writes with immense spirit. The salt of the ocean is in it, and the right heroic ring resounds through its gallant adventures.'—*Speaker.*

L. Cope Cornford. CAPTAIN JACOBUS: A ROMANCE OF THE ROAD. By L. Cope Cornford. Illustrated. *Crown 8vo.* 6s.

'An exceptionally good story of adventure and character.'—*World.*

L. Daintrey. THE KING OF ALBERIA. A Romance of the Balkans. By Laura Daintrey. *Crown 8vo.* 6s.

M. A. Owen. THE DAUGHTER OF ALOUETTE. By Mary A. Owen. *Crown 8vo.* 6s.

Mrs. Pinsent. CHILDREN OF THIS WORLD. By ELLEN F. PINSENT, Author of 'Jenny's Case.' *Crown 8vo.* 6s.

G. Manville Fenn. AN ELECTRIC SPARK. By G. MANVILLE FENN, Author of 'The Vicar's Wife,' 'A Double Knot,' etc. *Second Edition. Crown 8vo.* 6s.

L. S. McChesney. UNDER SHADOW OF THE MISSION. By L. S. MCCHESNEY. *Crown 8vo.* 6s.

'Those whose minds are open to the finer issues of life, who can appreciate graceful thought and refined expression of it, from them this volume will receive a welcome as enthusiastic as it will be based on critical knowledge.'—*Church Times.*

J. F. Brewer. THE SPECULATORS. By J. F. BREWER. *Second Edition. Crown 8vo.* 6s.

Ronald Ross. THE SPIRIT OF STORM. By RONALD ROSS, Author of 'The Child of Ocean.' *Crown 8vo.* 6s.

C. P. Wolley. THE QUEENSBERRY CUP. A Tale of Adventure. By CLIVE P. WOLLEY. *Illustrated. Crown 8vo.* 6s.

T. L. Paton. A HOME IN INVERESK. By T. L. PATON. *Crown 8vo.* 6s.

John Davidson. MISS ARMSTRONG'S AND OTHER CIRCUMSTANCES. By JOHN DAVIDSON. *Crown 8vo.* 6s.

H. Johnston. DR. CONGALTON'S LEGACY. By HENRY JOHNSTON. *Crown 8vo.* 6s.

R. Pryce. TIME AND THE WOMAN. By RICHARD PRYCE. *Second Edition. Crown 8vo.* 6s.

Mrs. Watson. THIS MAN'S DOMINION. By the Author of 'A High Little World.' *Second Edition. Crown 8vo.* 6s.

Marriott Watson. DIOGENES OF LONDON. By H. B. MARRIOTT WATSON. *Crown 8vo. Buckram.* 6s.

M. Gilchrist. THE STONE DRAGON. By MURRAY GILCHRIST. *Crown 8vo. Buckram.* 6s.

E. Dickinson. A VICAR'S WIFE. By EVELYN DICKINSON. *Crown 8vo.* 6s.

E. M. Gray. ELSA. By E. M'QUEEN GRAY. *Crown 8vo.* 6s.

THREE-AND-SIXPENNY NOVELS
Crown 8vo.

DERRICK VAUGHAN, NOVELIST. By EDNA LYALL.
MARGERY OF QUETHER. By S. BARING GOULD.
JACQUETTA. By S. BARING GOULD.
SUBJECT TO VANITY. By MARGARET BENSON.
THE SIGN OF THE SPIDER. By BERTRAM MITFORD.
THE MOVING FINGER. By MARY GAUNT.
JACO TRELOAR. By J. H. PEARCE.
THE DANCE OF THE HOURS. By 'VERA.'
A WOMAN OF FORTY. By ESMÉ STUART.
A CUMBERER OF THE GROUND. By CONSTANCE SMITH.
THE SIN OF ANGELS. By EVELYN DICKINSON.
AUT DIABOLUS AUT NIHIL. By X. L.
THE COMING OF CUCULAIN. By STANDISH O'GRADY.
THE GODS GIVE MY DONKEY WINGS. By ANGUS EVAN ABBOTT.
THE STAR GAZERS. By G. MANVILLE FENN.
THE POISON OF ASPS. By R. ORTON PROWSE.
THE QUIET MRS. FLEMING. By R. PRYCE.
DISENCHANTMENT. By F. MABEL ROBINSON.
THE SQUIRE OF WANDALES. By A. SHIELD.
A REVEREND GENTLEMAN. By J. M. COBBAN.
A DEPLORABLE AFFAIR. By W. E. NORRIS.
A CAVALIER'S LADYE. By Mrs. DICKER.
THE PRODIGALS. By Mrs. OLIPHANT.
THE SUPPLANTER. By P. NEUMANN.
A MAN WITH BLACK EYELASHES. By H. A. KENNEDY.
A HANDFUL OF EXOTICS. By S. GORDON.
AN ODD EXPERIMENT. By HANNAH LYNCH.
SCOTTISH BORDER LIFE. By JAMES C. DIBDIN.

HALF-CROWN NOVELS
A Series of Novels by popular Authors.

HOVENDEN, V.C. By F. MABEL ROBINSON.
THE PLAN OF CAMPAIGN. By F. MABEL ROBINSON.
MR. BUTLER'S WARD. By F. MABEL ROBINSON.
ELI'S CHILDREN. By G. MANVILLE FENN.
A DOUBLE KNOT. By G. MANVILLE FENN.
DISARMED. By M. BETHAM EDWARDS.
A MARRIAGE AT SEA. By W. CLARK RUSSELL.
IN TENT AND BUNGALOW. By the Author of 'Indian Idylls.'

MY STEWARDSHIP. By E. M'QUEEN GRAY.
JACK'S FATHER. By W. E. NORRIS.
JIM B.
A LOST ILLUSION. By LESLIE KEITH.

Lynn Linton. THE TRUE HISTORY OF JOSHUA DAVIDSON, Christian and Communist. By E. LYNN LINTON. *Eleventh Edition. Post 8vo.* 1s.

Books for Boys and Girls

A Series of Books by well-known Authors, well illustrated.

THREE-AND-SIXPENCE EACH

THE ICELANDER'S SWORD. By S. BARING GOULD.
TWO LITTLE CHILDREN AND CHING. By EDITH E. CUTHELL.
TODDLEBEN'S HERO. By M. M. BLAKE.
ONLY A GUARD-ROOM DOG. By EDITH E. CUTHELL.
THE DOCTOR OF THE JULIET. By HARRY COLLINGWOOD.
MASTER ROCKAFELLAR'S VOYAGE. By W. CLARK RUSSELL.
SYD BELTON: Or, The Boy who would not go to Sea. By G. MANVILLE FENN.
THE WALLYPUG IN LONDON. By G. E. FARROW.

The Peacock Library

A Series of Books for Girls by well-known Authors, handsomely bound in blue and silver, and well illustrated.

THREE-AND-SIXPENCE EACH

A PINCH OF EXPERIENCE. By L. B. WALFORD.
THE RED GRANGE. By Mrs. MOLESWORTH.
THE SECRET OF MADAME DE MONLUC. By the Author of 'Mdle Mori.'
DUMPS. By Mrs. PARR, Author of 'Adam and Eve.'
OUT OF THE FASHION. By L. T. MEADE.
A GIRL OF THE PEOPLE. By L. T. MEADE.
HEPSY GIPSY. By L. T. MEADE. 2s. 6d.
THE HONOURABLE MISS. By L. T. MEADE.
MY LAND OF BEULAH. By Mrs. LEITH ADAMS.

University Extension Series

A series of books on historical, literary, and scientific subjects, suitable for extension students and home-reading circles. Each volume is complete in itself, and the subjects are treated by competent writers in a broad and philosophic spirit.

Edited by J. E. SYMES, M.A.,
Principal of University College, Nottingham.

Crown 8vo. Price (with some exceptions) 2s. 6d.

The following volumes are ready:—

THE INDUSTRIAL HISTORY OF ENGLAND. By H. DE B. GIBBINS, D.Litt., M.A., late Scholar of Wadham College, Oxon., Cobden Prizeman. *Fifth Edition, Revised. With Maps and Plans.* 3s.

'A compact and clear story of our industrial development. A study of this concise but luminous book cannot fail to give the reader a clear insight into the principal phenomena of our industrial history. The editor and publishers are to be congratulated on this first volume of their venture, and we shall look with expectant interest for the succeeding volumes of the series.'—*University Extension Journal.*

A HISTORY OF ENGLISH POLITICAL ECONOMY. By L. L. PRICE, M.A., Fellow of Oriel College, Oxon. *Second Edition.*

PROBLEMS OF POVERTY: An Inquiry into the Industrial Conditions of the Poor. By J. A. HOBSON, M.A. *Third Edition.*

VICTORIAN POETS. By A. SHARP.

THE FRENCH REVOLUTION. By J. E. SYMES, M.A.

PSYCHOLOGY. By F. S. GRANGER, M.A. *Second Edition.*

THE EVOLUTION OF PLANT LIFE: Lower Forms. By G. MASSEE. *With Illustrations.*

AIR AND WATER. By V. B. LEWES, M.A. *Illustrated.*

THE CHEMISTRY OF LIFE AND HEALTH. By C. W. KIMMINS, M.A. *Illustrated.*

THE MECHANICS OF DAILY LIFE. By V. P. SELLS, M.A. *Illustrated.*

ENGLISH SOCIAL REFORMERS. By H. DE B. GIBBINS, D.Litt., M.A.

ENGLISH TRADE AND FINANCE IN THE SEVENTEENTH CENTURY. By W. A. S. HEWINS, B.A.

THE CHEMISTRY OF FIRE. The Elementary Principles of Chemistry. By M. M. PATTISON MUIR, M.A. *Illustrated.*

A TEXT-BOOK OF AGRICULTURAL BOTANY. By M. C. POTTER, M.A., F.L.S. *Illustrated.* 3s. 6d.

THE VAULT OF HEAVEN. A Popular Introduction to Astronomy. By R. A. GREGORY. *With numerous Illustrations.*

METEOROLOGY. The Elements of Weather and Climate. By H. N. DICKSON, F.R.S.E., F.R. Met. Soc. *Illustrated.*

A MANUAL OF ELECTRICAL SCIENCE. By GEORGE J. BURCH, M.A. *With numerous Illustrations.* 3s.

MESSRS. METHUEN'S LIST

THE EARTH. An Introduction to Physiography. By EVAN SMALL, M.A. *Illustrated.*

INSECT LIFE. By F. W. THEOBALD, M.A. *Illustrated.*

ENGLISH POETRY FROM BLAKE TO BROWNING. By W. M. DIXON, M.A.

ENGLISH LOCAL GOVERNMENT. By E. JENKS, M.A., Professor of Law at University College, Liverpool.

THE GREEK VIEW OF LIFE. By G. L. DICKINSON, Fellow of King's College, Cambridge. *Second Edition.*

Social Questions of To-day

Edited by H. DE B. GIBBINS, D.Litt., M.A.

Crown 8vo. 2s. 6d.

A series of volumes upon those topics of social, economic, and industrial interest that are at the present moment foremost in the public mind. Each volume of the series is written by an author who is an acknowledged authority upon the subject with which he deals.

The following Volumes of the Series are ready :—

TRADE UNIONISM—NEW AND OLD. By G. HOWELL. *Second Edition.*

THE CO-OPERATIVE MOVEMENT TO-DAY. By G. J. HOLYOAKE. *Second Edition.*

MUTUAL THRIFT. By Rev. J. FROME WILKINSON, M.A.

PROBLEMS OF POVERTY. By J. A. HOBSON, M.A. *Third Edition.*

THE COMMERCE OF NATIONS. By C. F. BASTABLE, M.A., Professor of Economics at Trinity College, Dublin.

THE ALIEN INVASION. By W. H. WILKINS, B.A.

THE RURAL EXODUS. By P. ANDERSON GRAHAM.

LAND NATIONALIZATION. By HAROLD COX, B.A.

A SHORTER WORKING DAY. By H. DE B. GIBBINS, D.Litt., M.A., and R. A. HADFIELD, of the Hecla Works, Sheffield.

BACK TO THE LAND: An Inquiry into the Cure for Rural Depopulation By H. E. MOORE.

TRUSTS, POOLS AND CORNERS. By J. STEPHEN JEANS.

THE FACTORY SYSTEM. By R. W. COOKE-TAYLOR.

THE STATE AND ITS CHILDREN. By GERTRUDE TUCKWELL.

MESSRS. METHUEN'S LIST

WOMEN'S WORK. By LADY DILKE, Miss BULLEY, and Miss WHITLEY.

MUNICIPALITIES AT WORK. The Municipal Policy of Six Great Towns, and its Influence on their Social Welfare. By FREDERICK DOLMAN.

SOCIALISM AND MODERN THOUGHT. By M. KAUFMANN.

THE HOUSING OF THE WORKING CLASSES. By E. BOWMAKER.

MODERN CIVILIZATION IN SOME OF ITS ECONOMIC ASPECTS. By W. CUNNINGHAM, D.D., Fellow of Trinity College, Cambridge.

THE PROBLEM OF THE UNEMPLOYED. By J. A. HOBSON, B.A.,

LIFE IN WEST LONDON. By ARTHUR SHERWELL, M.A. *Second Edition.*

RAILWAY NATIONALIZATION. By CLEMENT EDWARDS.

Classical Translations

Edited by H. F. FOX, M.A., Fellow and Tutor of Brasenose College, Oxford.

ÆSCHYLUS—Agamemnon, Chöephoroe, Eumenides. Translated by LEWIS CAMPBELL, LL.D., late Professor of Greek at St. Andrews. 5*s.*

CICERO—De Oratore I. Translated by E. N. P. MOOR, M.A. 3*s.* 6*d.*

CICERO — Select Orations (Pro Milone, Pro Murena, Philippic II., In Catilinam). Translated by H. E. D. BLAKISTON, M.A., Fellow and Tutor of Trinity College, Oxford. 5*s.*

CICERO—De Natura Deorum. Translated by F. BROOKS, M.A., late Scholar of Balliol College, Oxford. 3*s.* 6*d.*

LUCIAN—Six Dialogues (Nigrinus, Icaro-Menippus, The Cock, The Ship, The Parasite, The Lover of Falsehood). Translated by S. T. IRWIN, M.A., Assistant Master at Clifton; late Scholar of Exeter College, Oxford. 3*s.* 6*d.*

SOPHOCLES—Electra and Ajax. Translated by E. D. A. MORSHEAD, M.A., Assistant Master at Winchester. 2*s.* 6*d.*

TACITUS—Agricola and Germania. Translated by R. B. TOWNSHEND, late Scholar of Trinity College, Cambridge. 2*s.* 6*d.*

Educational Books

CLASSICAL

PLAUTI BACCHIDES. Edited with Introduction, Commentary, and Critical Notes by J. M'COSH, M.A. *Fcap.* 4*to.* 12*s.* 6*d.*

'The notes are copious, and contain a great deal of information that is good and useful.'—*Classical Review.*

TACITI AGRICOLI. With Introduction, Notes, Map, etc. By R. F. DAVIS, M.A., Assistant Master at Weymouth College. *Crown 8vo.* 2*s.*

TACITI GERMANIA. By the same Editor. *Crown 8vo.* 2*s.*

HERODOTUS: EASY SELECTIONS. With Vocabulary. By A. C. LIDDELL, M.A. *Fcap. 8vo.* 1*s.* 6*d.*

SELECTIONS FROM THE ODYSSEY. By E. D. STONE, M.A., late Assistant Master at Eton. *Fcap. 8vo.* 1s. 6d.

PLAUTUS: THE CAPTIVI. Adapted for Lower Forms by J. H. FRESSE, M.A., late Fellow of St. John's, Cambridge. 1s. 6d.

DEMOSTHENES AGAINST CONON AND CALLICLES. Edited with Notes and Vocabulary, by F. DARWIN SWIFT, M.A., formerly Scholar of Queen's College, Oxford. *Fcap. 8vo.* 2s.

EXERCISES ON LATIN ACCIDENCE. By S. E. WINBOLT, Assistant Master at Christ's Hospital. *Crown 8vo.* 1s. 6d.

An elementary book adapted for Lower Forms to accompany the shorter Latin primer.
'Skilfully arranged.'—*Glasgow Herald*.
'Accurate and well arranged.'—*Athenæum*.

NOTES ON GREEK AND LATIN SYNTAX. By G. BUCKLAND GREEN, M.A., Assistant Master at Edinburgh Academy, late Fellow of St. John's College, Oxon. *Crown 8vo.* 2s. 6d.

Notes and explanations on the chief difficulties of Greek and Latin Syntax, with numerous passages for exercise.
'Supplies a gap in educational literature.'—*Glasgow Herald*.

GERMAN

A COMPANION GERMAN GRAMMAR. By H. DE B. GIBBINS, D.Litt., M.A., Assistant Master at Nottingham High School. *Crown 8vo.* 1s. 6d.

GERMAN PASSAGES FOR UNSEEN TRANSLATION. By E. M'QUEEN GRAY. *Crown 8vo.* 2s. 6d.

SCIENCE

THE WORLD OF SCIENCE. Including Chemistry, Heat, Light, Sound, Magnetism, Electricity, Botany, Zoology, Physiology, Astronomy, and Geology. By R. ELLIOTT STEEL, M.A., F.C.S. 147 Illustrations. *Second Edition. Crown 8vo.* 2s. 6d.

ELEMENTARY LIGHT. By R. E. STEEL. With numerous Illustrations. *Crown 8vo.* 4s. 6d.

ENGLISH

ENGLISH RECORDS. A Companion to the History of England. By H. E. MALDEN, M.A. *Crown 8vo.* 3s. 6d.

A book which aims at concentrating information upon dates, genealogy, officials, constitutional documents, etc., which is usually found scattered in different volumes.

THE ENGLISH CITIZEN: HIS RIGHTS AND DUTIES. By H. E. MALDEN, M.A. 1s. 6d.

A DIGEST OF DEDUCTIVE LOGIC. By JOHNSON BARKER, B.A. *Crown 8vo.* 2s. 6d.

MESSRS. METHUEN'S LIST

METHUEN'S COMMERCIAL SERIES

Edited by H. DE B. GIBBINS, D.Litt., M.A.

BRITISH COMMERCE AND COLONIES FROM ELIZABETH TO VICTORIA. By H. DE B. GIBBINS, D.Litt., M.A. 2s. *Second Edition.*

COMMERCIAL EXAMINATION PAPERS. By H. DE B. GIBBINS, D.Litt., M.A., 1s. 6d.

THE ECONOMICS OF COMMERCE. By H. DE B. GIBBINS, D.Litt., M.A. 1s. 6d.

FRENCH COMMERCIAL CORRESPONDENCE. By S. E. BALLY, Modern Language Master at the Manchester Grammar School. 2s. *Second Edition.*

GERMAN COMMERCIAL CORRESPONDENCE. By S. E. BALLY, 2s. 6d.

A FRENCH COMMERCIAL READER. By S. E. BALLY. 2s.

COMMERCIAL GEOGRAPHY, with special reference to Trade Routes, New Markets, and Manufacturing Districts. By L. W. LYDE, M.A., of the Academy, Glasgow. 2s. *Second Edition.*

A PRIMER OF BUSINESS. By S. JACKSON, M.A. 1s. 6d.

COMMERCIAL ARITHMETIC. By F. G. TAYLOR, M.A. 1s. 6d.

PRÉCIS WRITING AND OFFICE CORRESPONDENCE. By E. E. WHITFIELD, M.A. 2s.

WORKS BY A. M. M. STEDMAN, M.A.

INITIA LATINA: Easy Lessons on Elementary Accidence. *Second Edition.* Fcap. 8vo. 1s.

FIRST LATIN LESSONS. *Fourth Edition.* Crown 8vo. 2s.

FIRST LATIN READER. With Notes adapted to the Shorter Latin Primer and Vocabulary. *Fourth Edition revised.* 18mo. 1s. 6d.

EASY SELECTIONS FROM CAESAR. Part I. The Helvetian War. 18mo. 1s.

EASY SELECTIONS FROM LIVY. Part I. The Kings of Rome. 18mo. 1s. 6d.

EASY LATIN PASSAGES FOR UNSEEN TRANSLATION. *Fifth Edition.* Fcap. 8vo. 1s. 6d.

EXEMPLA LATINA. First Lessons in Latin Accidence. With Vocabulary. Crown 8vo. 1s.

EASY LATIN EXERCISES ON THE SYNTAX OF THE SHORTER AND REVISED LATIN PRIMER. With Vocabulary. *Seventh and cheaper Edition re-written.* Crown 8vo. 1s. 6d. Issued with the consent of Dr. Kennedy.

THE LATIN COMPOUND SENTENCE: Rules and Exercises. Crown 8vo. 1s. 6d. With Vocabulary. 2s.

NOTANDA QUAEDAM: Miscellaneous Latin Exercises on Common Rules and Idioms. *Third Edition.* Fcap. 8vo. 1s. 6d. With Vocabulary. 2s.

LATIN VOCABULARIES FOR REPETITION: Arranged according to Subjects. *Sixth Edition.* Fcap. 8vo. 1s. 6d.

A VOCABULARY OF LATIN IDIOMS AND PHRASES. 18mo. *Second Edition.* 1s.
STEPS TO GREEK. 18mo. 1s.
EASY GREEK PASSAGES FOR UNSEEN TRANSLATION. *Third Edition revised.* Fcap. 8vo. 1s. 6d.
GREEK VOCABULARIES FOR REPETITION. Arranged according to Subjects. *Second Edition.* Fcap. 8vo. 1s. 6d.
GREEK TESTAMENT SELECTIONS. For the use of Schools. *Third Edition.* With Introduction, Notes, and Vocabulary. Fcap. 8vo. 2s. 6d.
STEPS TO FRENCH. *Second Edition.* 18mo. 8d.
FIRST FRENCH LESSONS. *Second Edition.* Crown 8vo. 1s.
EASY FRENCH PASSAGES FOR UNSEEN TRANSLATION. *Third Edition revised.* Fcap. 8vo. 1s. 6d.
EASY FRENCH EXERCISES ON ELEMENTARY SYNTAX. With Vocabulary. Crown 8vo. 2s. 6d.
FRENCH VOCABULARIES FOR REPETITION: Arranged according to Subjects. *Fifth Edition.* Fcap. 8vo. 1s.

SCHOOL EXAMINATION SERIES

EDITED BY A. M. M. STEDMAN, M.A. *Crown 8vo.* 2s. 6d.

FRENCH EXAMINATION PAPERS IN MISCELLANEOUS GRAMMAR AND IDIOMS. By A. M. M. STEDMAN, M.A. *Ninth Edition.*
A KEY, issued to Tutors and Private Students only, to be had on application to the Publishers. *Fourth Edition. Crown 8vo.* 6s. *net.*
LATIN EXAMINATION PAPERS IN MISCELLANEOUS GRAMMAR AND IDIOMS. By A. M. M. STEDMAN, M.A. *Eighth Edition.*
KEY (*Third Edition*) issued as above. 6s. *net.*
GREEK EXAMINATION PAPERS IN MISCELLANEOUS GRAMMAR AND IDIOMS. By A. M. M. STEDMAN, M.A. *Fifth Edition.*
KEY (*Second Edition*) issued as above. 6s. *net.*
GERMAN EXAMINATION PAPERS IN MISCELLANEOUS GRAMMAR AND IDIOMS. By R. J. MORICH, Manchester. *Fifth Edition.*
KEY (*Second Edition*) issued as above. 6s. *net.*
HISTORY AND GEOGRAPHY EXAMINATION PAPERS. By C. H. SPENCE, M.A., Clifton College.
SCIENCE EXAMINATION PAPERS. By R. E. STEEL, M.A., F.C.S., Chief Natural Science Master, Bradford Grammar School. *In two vols.* Part I. Chemistry; Part II. Physics.
GENERAL KNOWLEDGE EXAMINATION PAPERS. By A. M. M. STEDMAN, M.A. *Third Edition.*
KEY (*Second Edition*) issued as above. 7s. *net.*

Printed by T. and A. CONSTABLE, Printers to Her Majesty
at the Edinburgh University Press

www.ingramcontent.com/pod-product-compliance
Lightning Source LLC
Chambersburg PA
CBHW030403230426
43664CB00007BB/720